CONTENT AMERICAN LITERATURE
REVISED EDITION

PUBLISHED BY THE UNITED STATES
DEPARTMENT OF STATE

STAFF
WRITTEN BY: KATHRYN VANSPANCKEREN
EXECUTIVE EDITOR: GEORGE CLACK
MANAGING EDITOR: PAUL MALAMUD
CONTRIBUTING EDITOR: KATHLEEN HUG
ART DIRECTOR / DESIGNER:
THADDEUS A. MIKSINSKI, JR.
PICTURE EDITOR: JOANN STERN

Front Cover: © 1994 Christopher Little

ABOUT THE AUTHOR
Kathryn VanSpanckeren
is Professor of English at the
University of Tampa, has
lectured in American literature
widely abroad, and is former
director of the Fulbright-spon-
sored Summer Institute in
American Literature for
international scholars. Her
publications include poetry and
scholarship. She received
her Bachelors degree from the
University of California,
Berkeley, and her Ph.D. from
Harvard University.

CHAPTER 1

EARLY AMERICAN AND COLONIAL PERIOD TO 1776

American literature begins with the orally transmitted myths, legends, tales, and lyrics (always songs) of Indian cultures. There was no written literature among the more than 500 different Indian languages and tribal cultures that existed in North America before the first Europeans arrived. As a result, Native American oral literature is quite diverse. Narratives from quasi-nomadic hunting cultures like the Navaho are different from stories of settled agricultural tribes such as the pueblo-dwelling Acoma; the stories of northern lakeside dwellers such as the Ojibwa often differ radically from stories of desert tribes like the Hopi.

Tribes maintained their own religions — worshipping gods, animals, plants, or sacred persons. Systems of government ranged from democracies to councils of elders to theocracies. These tribal variations enter into the oral literature as well.

Still, it is possible to make a few generalizations. Indian stories, for example, glow with reverence for nature as a spiritual as well as physical mother. Nature is alive and endowed with spiritual forces; main characters may be animals or plants, often totems associated with a tribe, group, or individual. The closest to the Indian sense of holiness in later American literature is Ralph Waldo Emerson's transcendental "Over-Soul," which pervades all of life.

The Mexican tribes revered the divine Quetzalcoatl, a god of the Toltecs and Aztecs, and some tales of a high god or culture were told elsewhere. However, there are no long, standardized religious cycles about one supreme divinity. The closest equivalents to Old World spiritual narratives are often accounts of shamans' initiations and voyages. Apart from these, there are stories about culture heroes such as the Ojibwa tribe's Manabozho or the Navajo tribe's Coyote. These tricksters are treated with varying degrees of respect. In one tale they may act like heroes, while in another they may seem selfish or foolish. Although past authorities, such as the Swiss psychologist Carl Jung, have deprecated trickster tales as expressing the inferior, amoral side of the psyche, contemporary scholars — some of them Native Americans — point out that Odysseus and Prometheus, the revered Greek heroes, are essentially tricksters as well.

Examples of almost every oral genre can be found in American Indian literature: lyrics, chants, myths, fairy tales, humorous anecdotes, incantations, riddles, proverbs, epics, and legendary histories. Accounts of migrations and ancestors abound, as do vision or healing songs and tricksters' tales. Certain creation stories are particularly popular. In one well-known creation story, told with variations among many tribes, a turtle holds up the world. In a Cheyenne version, the creator, Maheo, has four chances to fashion the world from a watery universe. He sends four water birds diving to try to bring up earth from the bottom. The snow goose, loon, and mallard soar high into the sky and sweep down in a dive, but cannot reach bottom; but the little coot, who cannot fly, succeeds in bringing up some mud in his bill. Only one creature, humble Grandmother Turtle, is the right shape to support the mud world Maheo shapes on her shell — hence the Indian name for America, "Turtle Island."

The songs or poetry, like the narratives, range from the sacred to the light and humorous: There are lullabies, war chants, love songs, and special songs for children's games, gambling, various chores, magic, or dance ceremonials. Generally the songs are repetitive. Short poem-songs given in dreams sometimes have the clear imagery and subtle mood associated with Japanese haiku or Eastern-influenced imagistic poetry. A Chippewa song runs:

A loon I thought it was
But it was
My love's
splashing oar.

Vision songs, often very short, are another distinctive form. Appearing in dreams or visions, sometimes with no warning, they may be healing, hunting, or love songs. Often they are personal, as in this Modoc song:

I
the song
I walk here.

Indian oral tradition and its relation to American literature as a whole is one of the richest and least explored topics in American studies. The Indian contribution to America is greater than is often believed. The hundreds of Indian words in everyday American English include "canoe," "tobacco," "potato," "moccasin," "moose," "persimmon," "raccoon," "tomahawk," and "totem." Contemporary Native American writing, discussed in chapter 8, also contains works of great beauty.

THE LITERATURE OF EXPLORATION

Had history taken a different turn, the United States easily could have been a part of the great Spanish or French overseas empires. Its present inhabitants might speak Spanish and form one nation with Mexico, or speak French and be joined with Canadian Francophone Quebec and Montreal.

Yet the earliest explorers of America were not English, Spanish, or French. The first European record of exploration in America is in a Scandinavian language. The Old Norse *Vinland Saga* recounts how the adventurous Leif Ericson and a band of wandering Norsemen settled briefly somewhere on the northeast coast of America — probably Nova Scotia, in Canada — in the first decade of the 11th century, almost 400 years before the next recorded European discovery of the New World.

The first known and sustained contact between the Americas and the rest of the world, however, began with the famous voyage of an Italian explorer, Christopher Columbus, funded by the Spanish rulers Ferdinand and Isabella. Columbus's journal in his "Epistola," printed in 1493, recounts the trip's drama — the terror of the men, who feared monsters and thought they might fall off the edge of the world; the near-mutiny; how Columbus faked the ships' logs so the men would not know how much farther they had travelled than anyone had gone before; and the first sighting of land as they neared America.

Bartolomé de las Casas is the richest source of information about the early contact between American Indians and Europeans. As a young priest he helped conquer Cuba. He transcribed Columbus's journal, and late in life wrote a long, vivid *History of the Indians* criticizing their enslavement by the Spanish.

Initial English attempts at colonization were disasters. The first colony was set up in 1585 at Roanoke, off the coast of North Carolina; all its colonists disappeared, and to this day legends are told about blue-eyed Croatan Indians of the area. The second colony was more permanent: Jamestown, established in 1607. It endured starvation, brutality, and misrule. However, the literature of the period paints America in glowing colors as the land of riches and opportunity. Accounts of the colonizations became world-renowned. The exploration of Roanoke was carefully recorded by Thomas Hariot in *A Brief and*

True Report of the New-Found Land of Virginia (1588). Hariot's book was quickly translated into Latin, French, and German; the text and pictures were made into engravings and widely republished for over 200 years.

The Jamestown colony's main record, the writings of Captain John Smith, one of its leaders, is the exact opposite of Hariot's accurate, scientific account. Smith was an incurable romantic, and he seems to have embroidered his adventures. To him we owe the famous story of the Indian maiden, Pocahontas. Whether fact or fiction, the tale is ingrained in the American historical imagination. The story recounts how Pocahontas, favorite daughter of Chief Powhatan, saved Captain Smith's life when he was a prisoner of the chief. Later, when the English persuaded Powhatan to give Pocahontas to them as a hostage, her gentleness, intelligence, and beauty impressed the English, and, in 1614, she married John Rolfe, an English gentleman. The marriage initiated an eight-year peace between the colonists and the Indians, ensuring the survival of the struggling new colony.

In the 17th century, pirates, adventurers, and explorers opened the way to a second wave of permanent colonists, bringing their wives, children, farm implements, and craftsmen's tools. The early literature of exploration, made up of diaries, letters, travel journals, ships' logs, and reports to the explorers' financial backers — European rulers or, in mercantile England and Holland, joint stock companies — gradually was supplanted by records of the settled colonies. Because England eventually took possession of the North American colonies, the best-known and most-anthologized colonial literature is English. As American minority literature continues to flower in the 20th century and American life becomes increasingly multicultural, scholars are rediscovering the importance of the continent's mixed ethnic heritage. Although the story of literature now turns to the English accounts, it is important to recognize its richly cosmopolitan beginnings.

THE COLONIAL PERIOD IN NEW ENGLAND

It is likely that no other colonists in the history of the world were as intellectual as the Puritans. Between 1630 and 1690, there were as many university graduates in the northeastern section of the United States, known as New England, as in the mother country — an astounding fact when one considers that most educated people of the time were aristocrats who were unwilling to risk their lives in wilderness conditions. The self-made and often self-educated Puritans were notable exceptions. They wanted education to understand and execute God's will as they established their colonies throughout New England.

The Puritan definition of good writing was that which brought home a full awareness of the importance of worshipping God and of the spiritual dangers that the soul faced on Earth. Puritan style varied enormously — from complex metaphysical poetry to homely journals and crushingly pedantic religious history. Whatever the style or genre, certain themes remained constant. Life was seen as a test; failure led to eternal damnation and hellfire, and success to heavenly bliss. This world was an arena of constant battle between the forces of God and the forces of Satan, a formidable enemy with many disguises. Many Puritans excitedly awaited the "millennium," when Jesus would return to Earth, end human misery, and inaugurate 1,000 years of peace and prosperity.

Scholars have long pointed out the link between Puritanism and capitalism: Both rest on ambition, hard work, and an intense striving for success. Although individual Puritans could not know, in strict theological terms, whether they were "saved" and among the elect who would go to heaven, Puritans tended to feel that earthly

"The First Thanksgiving," a painting by J.L.G. Ferris, depicts America's early settlers and Native Americans celebrating a bountiful harvest.

success was a sign of election. Wealth and status were sought not only for themselves, but as welcome reassurances of spiritual health and promises of eternal life.

Moreover, the concept of stewardship encouraged success. The Puritans interpreted all things and events as symbols with deeper spiritual meanings, and felt that in advancing their own profit and their community's well-being, they were also furthering God's plans. They did not draw lines of distinction between the secular and religious spheres: All of life was an expression of the divine will — a belief that later resurfaces in Transcendentalism.

In recording ordinary events to reveal their spiritual meaning, Puritan authors commonly cited the Bible, chapter and verse. History was a symbolic religious panorama leading to the Puritan triumph over the New World and to God's kingdom on Earth.

The first Puritan colonists who settled New England exemplified the seriousness of Reformation Christianity. Known as the "Pilgrims," they were a small group of believers who had migrated from England to Holland — even then known for its religious tolerance — in 1608, during a time of persecutions.

Like most Puritans, they interpreted the Bible literally. They read and acted on the text of the Second Book of Corinthians — "Come out from among them and be ye separate, saith the Lord." Despairing of purifying the Church of England from within, "Separatists" formed underground "covenanted" churches that swore loyalty to the group instead of the king. Seen as traitors to the king as well as heretics damned to hell, they were often persecuted. Their separation took them ultimately to the New World.

William Bradford (1590-1657)

William Bradford was elected governor of Plymouth in the Massachusetts Bay Colony shortly after the Separatists landed. He was a deeply pious, self-educated man who had learned several languages, including Hebrew, in order to "see with his own eyes the ancient oracles of God in their native beauty." His participation in the migration to Holland and the *Mayflower* voyage to Plymouth, and his duties as governor, made him ideally suited to be the first historian of his colony. His history, *Of Plymouth Plantation* (1651), is a clear and compelling account of the colony's beginning. His description of the first view of America is justly famous:

Being thus passed the vast ocean, and a sea of troubles...they had now no friends to welcome them nor inns to entertain or refresh their weatherbeaten bodies; no houses or much less towns to repair to, to seek for succor...savage barbarians...were readier to fill their sides with arrows than otherwise. And for the reason it was winter, and they that know the winters of that country, know them to be sharp and violent, and subject to cruel and fierce storms...all stand upon them with a weatherbeaten face, and the whole country, full of woods and thickets, represented a wild and savage hue.

Bradford also recorded the first document of colonial self-governance in the English New World, the "Mayflower Compact," drawn up while the Pilgrims were still on board ship. The compact was a harbinger of the Declaration of Independence to come a century and a half later.

Puritans disapproved of such secular amusements as dancing and card-playing, which were associated with ungodly aristocrats and immoral living. Reading or writing "light" books also fell into this category. Puritan minds poured their tremendous energies into nonfiction and pious genres: poetry, sermons, theological tracts, and histories. Their intimate diaries and meditations record the rich inner lives of this introspective and intense people.

Anne Bradstreet (c. 1612-1672)

The first published book of poems by an American was also the first American book to be published by a woman — Anne Bradstreet. It is not surprising that the book was published in England, given the lack of printing presses in the early years of the first American colonies. Born and educated in England, Anne Bradstreet was the daughter of an earl's estate manager. She emigrated with her family when she was 18. Her husband eventually became governor of the Massachusetts Bay Colony, which later grew into the great city of Boston. She preferred her long, religious poems on conventional subjects such as the seasons, but contemporary readers most enjoy the witty poems on subjects from daily life and her warm and loving poems to her husband and children. She was inspired by English metaphysical poetry, and her book *The Tenth Muse Lately Sprung Up in America* (1650) shows the influence of Edmund Spenser, Philip Sidney, and other English poets as well. She often uses elaborate conceits or extended metaphors. "To My Dear and Loving Husband" (1678) uses the oriental imagery, love theme, and idea of comparison popular in Europe at the time, but gives these a pious meaning at the poem's conclusion:

If ever two were one, then surely we.
If ever man were loved by wife, then thee;
If ever wife was happy in a man,
Compare with me, ye women, if you can.
I prize thy love more than whole mines of gold
Or all the riches that the East doth hold.
My love is such that rivers cannot quench,
Nor ought but love from thee, give recompense.
Thy love is such I can no way repay,
The heavens reward thee manifold, I pray.
Then while we live, in love let's so persevere
That when we live no more, we may live ever.

Edward Taylor (c. 1644-1729)

Like Anne Bradstreet, and, in fact, all of New England's first writers, the intense, brilliant poet and minister Edward Taylor was born in England. The son of a yeoman farmer — an independent farmer who owned his own land — Taylor was a teacher who sailed to New England in 1668 rather than take an oath of loyalty to the Church of England. He studied at Harvard College, and, like most Harvard-trained ministers, he knew Greek, Latin, and Hebrew. A selfless and pious man, Taylor acted as a missionary to the settlers when he accepted his lifelong job as a minister in the frontier town of Westfield, Massachusetts, 160 kilometers into the thickly forested, wild interior. Taylor was the best-educated man in the area, and he put his knowledge to use, working as the town minister, doctor, and civic leader.

Modest, pious, and hard-working, Taylor never published his poetry, which was discovered only in the 1930s. He would, no doubt, have seen his work's discovery as divine providence; today's readers should be grateful to have his poems — the finest examples of 17th-century poetry in North America.

Taylor wrote a variety of verse: funeral elegies, lyrics, a medieval "debate," and a 500-page *Metrical History of Christianity* (mainly a history of martyrs). His best works, according to modern critics, are the series of short preparatory meditations.

Michael Wigglesworth (1631-1705)

Michael Wigglesworth, like Taylor an English-born, Harvard-educated Puritan minister who practiced medicine, is the third New England colonial poet of note. He continues the Puritan themes in his best-known work, *The Day of Doom* (1662). A long narrative that often falls into doggerel, this terrifying popularization of Calvinistic doctrine was the most popular poem of the colonial period. This first American best-seller is an appalling portrait of damnation to hell in ballad meter.

It is terrible poetry — but everybody loved it. It fused the fascination of a horror story with the authority of John Calvin. For more than two centuries, people memorized this long, dreadful monument to religious terror; children proudly recited it, and elders quoted it in everyday speech. It is not such a leap from the terrible punishments of this poem to the ghastly self-inflicted wound of Nathaniel Hawthorne's guilty Puritan minister, Arthur Dimmesdale, in *The Scarlet Letter* (1850) or Herman Melville's crip-pled Captain Ahab, a New England Faust whose quest for forbidden knowledge sinks the ship of American humanity in *Moby-Dick* (1851). (*Moby-Dick* was the favorite novel of 20th-century American novelist William Faulkner, whose profound and disturbing works suggest that the dark, metaphysical vision of Protestant America has not yet been exhausted.)

Like most colonial literature, the poems of early New England imitate the form and technique of the mother country, though the religious passion and frequent biblical references, as well as the new setting, give New England writing a special identity. Isolated New World writers also lived before the advent of rapid transportation and electronic communications. As a result, colonial writers were imitating writing that was already out of date in England. Thus, Edward Taylor, the best American poet of his day, wrote metaphysical poetry after it had become unfashionable in England. At times, as in Taylor's poetry, rich works of striking originality grew out of colonial isolation.

Colonial writers often seemed ignorant of such great English authors as Ben Jonson. Some colonial writers rejected English poets who belonged to a different sect as well, thereby cutting themselves off from the finest lyric and dramatic models the English language had produced. In addition, many colonials remained ignorant due to the lack of books.

The great model of writing, belief, and conduct was the Bible, in an authorized English translation that was already outdated when it came out. The age of the Bible, so much older than the Roman church, made it authoritative to Puritan eyes.

New England Puritans clung to the tales of the Jews in the Old Testament, believing that they, like the Jews, were persecuted for their faith, that they knew the one true God, and that they were the chosen elect who would establish the New Jerusalem — a heaven on Earth. The

Puritans were aware of the parallels between the ancient Jews of the Old Testament and themselves. Moses led the Israelites out of captivity from Egypt, parted the Red Sea through God's miraculous assistance so that his people could escape, and received the divine law in the form of the Ten Commandments. Like Moses, Puritan leaders felt they were rescuing their people from spiritual corruption in England, passing miraculously over a wild sea with God's aid, and fashioning new laws and new forms of government after God's wishes.

Colonial worlds tend to be archaic, and New England certainly was no exception. New England Puritans were archaic by choice, conviction, and circumstance.

Samuel Sewall (1652-1730)

Easier to read than the highly religious poetry full of Biblical references are the historical and secular accounts that recount real events using lively details. Governor John Winthrop's *Journal* (1790) provides the best information on the early Massachusetts Bay Colony and Puritan political theory.

Samuel Sewall's *Diary*, which records the years 1674 to 1729, is lively and engaging. Sewall fits the pattern of early New England writers we have seen in Bradford and Taylor. Born in England, Sewall was brought to the colonies at an early age. He made his home in the Boston area, where he graduated from Harvard, and made a career of legal, administrative, and religious work.

COTTON MATHER

Engraving © The Bettmann Archive

Sewall was born late enough to see the change from the early, strict religious life of the Puritans to the later, more worldly Yankee period of mercantile wealth in the New England colonies; his *Diary*, which is often compared to Samuel Pepys's English diary of the same period, inadvertently records the transition.

Like Pepys's diary, Sewall's is a minute record of his daily life, reflecting his interest in living piously and well. He notes little purchases of sweets for a woman he was courting, and their disagreements over whether he should affect aristocratic and expensive ways such as wearing a wig and using a coach.

Mary Rowlandson (c. 1635-c.1678)

The earliest woman prose writer of note is Mary Rowlandson, a minister's wife who gives a clear, moving account of her 11-week captivity by Indians during an Indian massacre in 1676. The book undoubtedly fanned the flame of anti-Indian sentiment, as did John Williams's *The Redeemed Captive* (1707), describing his two years in captivity by French and Indians after a massacre. Such writings as women produced are usually domestic accounts requiring no special education. It may be argued that women's literature benefits from its homey realism and common-sense wit; certainly works like Sarah Kemble Knight's lively *Journal* (1825) of a daring solo trip in 1704 from Boston to New York and back escapes the baroque complexity of much Puritan writing.

Cotton Mather (1663-1728)

No account of New England colonial literature would be complete without mentioning Cotton Mather, the master pedant. The third in the four-generation Mather dynasty of Massachusetts Bay, he wrote at length of New England in over 500 books and pamphlets. Mather's 1702 *Magnalia Christi Americana* (*Ecclesiastical History of New England*), his most ambitious work, exhaustively chronicles the settlement of New England through a series of biographies. The huge book presents the holy Puritan errand into the wilderness to establish God's kingdom; its structure is a narrative progression of representative American "Saint's Lives." His zeal somewhat redeems his pompousness: "I write the wonders of the Christian religion, flying from the deprivations of Europe to the American strand."

Roger Williams (c. 1603-1683)

As the 1600s wore on into the 1700s, religious dogmatism gradually dwindled, despite sporadic, harsh Puritan efforts to stem the tide of tolerance. The minister Roger Williams suffered for his own views on religion. An English-born son of a tailor, he was banished from Massachusetts in the middle of New England's ferocious winter in 1635. Secretly warned by Governor John Winthrop of Massachusetts, he survived only by living with Indians; in 1636, he established a new colony at Rhode Island that would welcome persons of different religions.

A graduate of Cambridge University (England), he retained sympathy for working people and diverse views. His ideas were ahead of his time. He was an early critic of imperialism, insisting that European kings had no right to grant land charters because American land belonged to the Indians. Williams also believe in the separation between church and state — still a fundamental principle in America today. He held that the law courts should not have the power to punish people for religious reasons — a stand that undermined the strict New England theocracies. A believer in equality and democracy, he was a lifelong friend of the Indians. Williams's numerous books include one of the first phrase books of Indian languages, *A Key Into the Languages of America* (1643). The book also is an embryonic ethnography, giving bold descriptions of Indian life based on the time he had lived among the tribes. Each chapter is devoted to one topic — for example, eating and mealtime. Indian words and phrases pertaining to this topic are mixed with comments, anecdotes, and a concluding poem. The end of the first chapter reads:

> If nature's sons, both wild and tame,
> Humane and courteous be,
> How ill becomes it sons of God
> To want humanity.

In the chapter on words about entertainment, he comments that "it is a strange truth that a man shall generally find more free entertainment and refreshing among these barbarians, than amongst thousands that call themselves Christians."

Williams's life is uniquely inspiring. On a visit to England during the bloody Civil War there, he drew upon his survival in frigid New England to organize firewood deliveries to the poor of London during the winter, after their supply of coal had been cut off. He wrote lively defenses of religious toleration not only for different Christian sects, but also for non-Christians. "It is the will and command of God, that...a permission of the most Paganish, Jewish, Turkish, or Antichristian consciences and worships, be granted to all men, in all nations...," he wrote in *The Bloudy Tenent of Persecution for Cause of Conscience* (1644). The intercultural experience of living among gracious and humane Indians undoubtedly accounts for much of his wisdom.

Influence was two-way in the colonies. For example, John Eliot translated the Bible into Narragansett. Some Indians converted to Christianity. Even today, the Native American church is a mixture of Christianity and Indian traditional belief.

The spirit of toleration and religious freedom that gradually grew in the American colonies was first established in Rhode Island and Pennsylvania, home of the Quakers. The humane and tolerant Quakers, or "Friends," as they were known, believed in the sacredness of the individual conscience as the fountainhead of social order and morality. The fundamental Quaker belief in universal love and brotherhood made them deeply democratic and opposed to dogmatic religious authority. Driven out of strict Massachusetts, which feared their influence, they established a very successful colony, Pennsylvania, under William Penn in 1681.

John Woolman (1720-1772)

The best-known Quaker work is the long *Journal* (1774) of John Woolman, documenting his inner life in a pure, heartfelt style of great sweetness that has drawn praise from many American and English writers. This remarkable man left his comfortable home in town to sojourn with the Indians in the wild interior because he thought he might learn from them and share

JONATHAN EDWARDS

their ideas. He writes simply of his desire to "feel and understand their life, and the Spirit they live in." Woolman's justice-loving spirit naturally turns to social criticism: "I perceived that many white People do often sell Rum to the Indians, which, I believe, is a great Evil."

Woolman was also one of the first antislavery writers, publishing two essays, "Some Considerations on the Keeping of Negroes," in 1754 and 1762. An ardent humanitarian, he followed a path of "passive obedience" to authorities and laws he found unjust, prefiguring Henry David Thoreau's celebrated essay, "Civil Disobedience" (1849), by generations.

Jonathan Edwards (1703-1758)

The antithesis of John Woolman is Jonathan Edwards, who was born only 17 years before the Quaker notable. Woolman had little formal schooling; Edwards was highly educated. Woolman followed his inner light; Edwards was devoted to the law and authority. Both men were fine writers, but they revealed opposite poles of the colonial religious experience.

Edwards was molded by his extreme sense of duty and by the rigid Puritan environment, which conspired to make him defend strict and gloomy Calvinism from the forces of liberalism springing up around him. He is best known for his frightening, powerful sermon, "Sinners in the Hands of an Angry God" (1741):

> [I]f God should let you go, you would immediately sink, and sinfully descend, and plunge into the bottomless gulf...The God that holds you over the pit of hell, much as one holds a spider or some loathsome insect over the fire, abhors you, and is dreadfully provoked....he looks upon you as worthy of nothing else but to be cast into the bottomless gulf.

Edwards's sermons had enormous impact, sending whole congregations into hysterical fits of weeping. In the long run, though, their grotesque harshness alienated people from the Calvinism that Edwards valiantly defended. Edwards's dogmatic, medieval sermons no longer fit the experiences of relatively peaceful, prosperous 18th-century colonists. After Edwards, fresh, liberal currents of tolerance gathered force.

LITERATURE IN THE SOUTHERN AND MIDDLE COLONIES

Pre-revolutionary southern literature was aristocratic and secular, reflecting the dominant social and economic systems of the southern plantations. Early English immigrants were drawn to the southern colonies because of economic opportunity rather than religious freedom.

Although many southerners were poor farmers or tradespeople living not much better than slaves, the southern literate upper class was shaped by the classical, Old World ideal of a noble landed gentry made possible by slavery. The institution released wealthy southern whites from manual labor, afforded them leisure, and made the dream of an aristocratic life in the American wilderness possible. The Puritan emphasis on hard work, education, and earnest-

ness was rare — instead we hear of such pleasures as horseback riding and hunting. The church was the focus of a genteel social life, not a forum for minute examinations of conscience.

William Byrd (1674-1744)

Southern culture naturally revolved around the ideal of the gentleman. A Renaissance man equally good at managing a farm and reading classical Greek, he had the power of a feudal lord.

William Byrd describes the gracious way of life at his plantation, Westover, in his famous letter of 1726 to his English friend Charles Boyle, Earl of Orrery:

> Besides the advantages of pure air, we abound in all kinds of provisions without expense (I mean we who have plantations). I have a large family of my own, and my doors are open to everybody, yet I have no bills to pay, and half-a-crown will rest undisturbed in my pockets for many moons altogether.
>
> Like one of the patriarchs, I have my flock and herds, my bondmen and bondwomen, and every sort of trade amongst my own servants, so that I live in a kind of independence on everyone but Providence.

William Byrd epitomizes the spirit of the southern colonial gentry. The heir to 1,040 hectares, which he enlarged to 7,160 hectares, he was a merchant, trader, and planter. His library of 3,600 books was the largest in the South. He was born with a lively intelligence that his father augmented by sending him to excellent schools in England and Holland. He visited the French Court, became a Fellow of the Royal Society, and was friendly with some of the leading English writers of his day, particularly William Wycherley and William Congreve. His London diaries are the opposite of those of the New England Puritans, full of fancy dinners, glittering parties, and womanizing, with little introspective soul-searching.

Byrd is best known today for his lively *History of the Dividing Line*, a diary of a 1729 trip of some weeks and 960 kilometers into the interior to survey the line dividing the neighboring colonies of Virginia and North Carolina. The quick impressions that vast wilderness, Indians, half-savage whites, wild beasts, and every sort of difficulty made on this civilized gentleman form a uniquely American and very southern book. He ridicules the first Virginia colonists, "about a hundred men, most of them reprobates of good families," and jokes that at Jamestown, "like true Englishmen, they built a church that cost no more than fifty pounds, and a tavern that cost five hundred." Byrd's writings are fine examples of the keen interest southerners took in the material world: the land, Indians, plants, animals, and settlers.

Robert Beverley (c. 1673-1722)

Robert Beverley, another wealthy planter and author of *The History and Present State of Virginia* (1705, 1722) records the history of the Virginia colony in a humane and vigorous style. Like Byrd, he admired the Indians and remarked on the strange European superstitions about Virginia — for example, the belief "that the country turns all people black who go there." He noted the great hospitality of southerners, a trait maintained today.

Humorous satire — a literary work in which human vice or folly is attacked through irony, derision, or wit — appears frequently in the colonial South. A group of irritated settlers lampooned Georgia's philanthropic founder, General James Oglethorpe, in a tract entitled *A True and Historical Narrative of the Colony of Georgia* (1741). They pretended to praise him for keeping them so poor and overworked that they had to develop "the valuable virtue of humility" and shun "the anxieties of any further ambition."

The rowdy, satirical poem "The Sotweed Factor" satirizes the colony of Maryland, where the author, an Englishman named Ebenezer Cook, had unsuccessfully tried his hand as a tobacco merchant. Cook exposed the crude ways of the colony with high-spirited humor, and accused the colonists of cheating him. The poem concludes with an exaggerated curse: "May wrath divine then lay those regions waste / Where no man's faithful nor a woman chaste."

In general, the colonial South may fairly be linked with a light, worldly, informative, and realistic literary tradition. Imitative of English literary fashions, the southerners attained imaginative heights in witty, precise observations of distinctive New World conditions.

Olaudah Equiano (Gustavus Vassa) (c. 1745-c. 1797)

Important black writers like Olaudah Equiano and Jupiter Hammon emerged during the colonial period. Equiano, an Ibo from Niger (West Africa), was the first black in America to write an autobiography, *The Interesting Narrative of the Life of Olaudah Equiano, or Gustavus Vassa, the African* (1789). In the book — an early example of the slave narrative genre — Equiano gives an account of his native land and the horrors and cruelties of his captivity and enslavement in the West Indies. Equiano, who converted to Christianity, movingly laments his cruel "un-Christian" treatment by Christians — a sentiment many African-Americans would voice in centuries to come.

Jupiter Hammon (c. 1720-c. 1800)

The black American poet Jupiter Hammon, a slave on Long Island, New York, is remembered for his religious poems as well as for *An Address to the Negroes of the State of New York* (1787), in which he advocated freeing children of slaves instead of condemning them to hereditary slavery. His poem "An Evening Thought" was the first poem published by a black male in America.

CHAPTER 2

DEMOCRATIC ORIGINS AND REVOLUTIONARY WRITERS, 1776-1820

The hard-fought American Revolution against Britain (1775-1783) was the first modern war of liberation against a colonial power. The triumph of American independence seemed to many at the time a divine sign that America and her people were destined for greatness. Military victory fanned nationalistic hopes for a great new literature. Yet with the exception of outstanding political writing, few works of note appeared during or soon after the Revolution.

American books were harshly reviewed in England. Americans were painfully aware of their excessive dependence on English literary models. The search for a native literature became a national obsession. As one American magazine editor wrote, around 1816, "Dependence is a state of degradation fraught with disgrace, and to be dependent on a foreign mind for what we can ourselves produce is to add to the crime of indolence the weakness of stupidity."

Cultural revolutions, unlike military revolutions, cannot be successfully imposed but must grow from the soil of shared experience. Revolutions are expressions of the heart of the people; they grow gradually out of new sensibilities and wealth of experience. It would take 50 years of accumulated history for America to earn its cultural independence and to produce the first great generation of American writers: Washington Irving, James Fenimore Cooper, Ralph Waldo Emerson, Henry David Thoreau, Herman Melville, Nathaniel Hawthorne, Edgar Allan Poe, Walt Whitman, and Emily Dickinson. America's literary independence was slowed by a lingering identification with England, an excessive imitation of English or classical literary models, and difficult economic and political conditions that hampered publishing.

Revolutionary writers, despite their genuine patriotism, were of necessity self-conscious, and they could never find roots in their American sensibilities. Colonial writers of the revolutionary generation had been born English, had grown to maturity as English citizens, and had cultivated English modes of thought and English fashions in dress and behavior. Their parents and grandparents were English (or European), as were all their friends. Added to this, American awareness of literary fashion still lagged behind the English, and this time lag intensified American imitation. Fifty years after their fame in England, English neoclassic writers such as Joseph Addison, Richard Steele, Jonathan Swift, Alexander Pope, Oliver Goldsmith, and Samuel Johnson were still eagerly imitated in America.

Moreover, the heady challenges of building a new nation attracted talented and educated people to politics, law, and diplomacy. These pursuits brought honor, glory, and financial security. Writing, on the other hand, did not pay. Early American writers, now separated from England, effectively had no modern publishers, no audience, and no adequate legal protection. Editorial assistance, distribution, and publicity were rudimentary.

Until 1825, most American authors paid printers to publish their work. Obviously only the leisured and independently wealthy, like Washington Irving and the New York Knickerbocker group, or the group of Connecticut poets knows as the Hartford Wits, could afford to indulge their interest in writing. The exception, Benjamin Franklin, though from a poor family, was a printer by trade and could publish his own work.

Charles Brockden Brown was more typical. The author of several interesting Gothic romances, Brown was the first American author to attempt to live from his writing. But his short life ended in poverty.

The lack of an audience was another problem. The small cultivated audience in America wanted well-known European authors, partly out of the exaggerated respect with which former colonies regarded their previous rulers. This preference for English works was not entirely unreasonable, considering the inferiority of American output, but it worsened the situation by depriving American authors of an audience. Only journalism offered financial remuneration, but the mass audience wanted light, undemanding verse and short topical essays — not long or experimental work.

The absence of adequate copyright laws was perhaps the clearest cause of literary stagnation. American printers pirating English best-sellers understandably were unwilling to pay an American author for unknown material. The unauthorized reprinting of foreign books was originally seen as a service to the colonies as well as a source of profit for printers like Franklin, who reprinted works of the classics and great European books to educate the American public.

Printers everywhere in America followed his lead. There are notorious examples of pirating. Matthew

NOAH WEBSTER

Engraving © The Bettmann Archive

Carey, an important American publisher, paid a London agent — a sort of literary spy — to send copies of unbound pages, or even proofs, to him in fast ships that could sail to America in a month. Carey's men would sail out to meet the incoming ships in the harbor and speed the pirated books into print using typesetters who divided the book into sections and worked in shifts around the clock. Such a pirated English book could be reprinted in a day and placed on the shelves for sale in American bookstores almost as fast as in England.

Because imported authorized editions were more expensive and could not compete with pirated ones, the copyright situation damaged foreign authors such as Sir Walter Scott and Charles Dickens, along with American authors. But at least the foreign authors had already been paid by their original publishers and were already well known. Americans such as James Fenimore Cooper not only failed to receive adequate payment, but they had to suffer seeing their works pirated under their noses. Cooper's first successful book, *The Spy* (1821), was pirated by four different printers within a month of its appearance.

Ironically, the copyright law of 1790, which allowed pirating, was nationalistic in intent. Drafted by Noah Webster, the great lexicographer who later compiled an American dictionary, the law protected only the work of American authors; it was felt that English writers should look out for themselves.

Bad as the law was, none of the early publishers were willing to have it changed because it proved profitable for them. Piracy starved the first generation of revolutionary American writers; not surprisingly, the generation after them produced even less work of merit. The high point of piracy, in 1815, corresponds with the low point of American writing. Nevertheless, the cheap and plentiful supply of pirated foreign books and classics in the first 50 years of the new country did educate Americans, including the first great writers, who began to make their appearance around 1825.

THE AMERICAN ENLIGHTENMENT

The 18th-century American Enlightenment was a movement marked by an emphasis on rationality rather than tradition, scientific inquiry instead of unquestioning religious dogma, and representative government in place of monarchy. Enlightenment thinkers and writers were devoted to the ideals of justice, liberty, and equality as the natural rights of man.

Benjamin Franklin (1706-1790)

Benjamin Franklin, whom the Scottish philosopher David Hume called America's "first great man of letters," embodied the Enlightenment ideal of humane rationality. Practical yet idealistic, hard-working and enormously successful, Franklin recorded his early life in his famous *Autobiography*. Writer, printer, publisher, scientist, philanthropist, and diplomat, he was the most famous and respected private figure of his time. He was the first great self-made man in America, a poor democrat born in an aristocratic age that his fine example helped to liberalize.

Franklin was a second-generation immigrant. His Puritan father, a chandler (candle-maker), came to Boston, Massachusetts, from England in 1683. In many ways Franklin's life illustrates the impact of the Enlightenment on a gifted individual. Self-educated but well-read in John Locke, Lord Shaftesbury, Joseph Addison, and other Enlightenment writers, Franklin learned from them to apply reason to his own life and to break with tradition — in particular the old-fashioned Puritan tradition — when it threatened to smother his ideals.

While a youth, Franklin taught himself languages, read widely, and practiced writing for the public. When he moved from Boston to Philadelphia, Pennsylvania, Franklin already had the kind of education associated with the upper classes. He also had the Puritan capacity for hard, careful work, constant self-scrutiny, and the desire to better himself. These qualities steadily propelled him to wealth, respectability, and honor. Never selfish, Franklin tried to help other ordinary people become successful by sharing his insights and initiating a characteristically American genre — the self-help book.

Franklin's *Poor Richard's Almanack*, begun in 1732 and published for many years, made Franklin prosperous and well-known throughout the colonies. In this annual book of useful encouragement, advice, and factual information, amusing characters such as old Father Abraham and Poor Richard exhort the reader in pithy, memorable sayings. In "The Way to Wealth," which originally appeared in the *Almanack*, Father Abraham, "a plain clean old Man, with white Locks," quotes Poor Richard at length. "A Word to the Wise is enough," he says. "God helps them that help themselves." "Early to Bed, and early to rise, makes a Man healthy, wealthy, and wise." Poor Richard is a psychologist ("Industry pays Debts, while Despair encreaseth them"), and he always counsels hard work ("Diligence is the Mother of Good Luck"). Do not be lazy, he advises, for "One To-day is worth two tomorrow." Sometimes he creates anecdotes to illustrate his points: "A little Neglect may breed great Mischief....For want of a Nail the Shoe was lost; for want of a Shoe the Horse was lost; and for want

Engraving courtesy Library of Congress

of a Horse the Rider was lost, being overtaken and slain by the Enemy, all for want of Care about a Horse-shoe Nail." Franklin was a genius at compressing a moral point: "What maintains one Vice, would bring up two Children." "A small leak will sink a great Ship." "Fools make Feasts, and wise Men eat them."

Franklin's *Autobiography* is, in part, another self-help book. Written to advise his son, it covers only the early years. The most famous section describes his scientific scheme of self-improvement. Franklin lists 13 virtues: temperance, silence, order, resolution, frugality, industry, sincerity, justice, moderation, cleanliness, tranquility, chastity, and humility. He elaborates on each with a maxim; for example, the temperance maxim is "Eat not to Dullness. Drink not to Elevation." A pragmatic scientist, Franklin put the idea of perfectibility to the test, using himself as the experimental subject.

To establish good habits, Franklin invented a reusable calendrical record book in which he worked on one virtue each week, recording each lapse with a black spot. His theory prefigures psychological behaviorism, while his systematic method of notation anticipates modern behavior modification. The project of self-improvement blends the Enlightenment belief in perfectibility with the Puritan habit of moral self-scrutiny.

Franklin saw early that writing could best advance his ideas, and he therefore deliberately perfected his supple prose style, not as an end in itself but as a tool. "Write with the learned. Pronounce with the vulgar," he advised. A scientist, he followed the Royal (scientific) Society's 1667 advice to use "a close, naked, natural way of speaking; positive expressions, clear senses, a native easiness, bringing all things as near the mathematical plainness as they can."

Despite his prosperity and fame, Franklin never lost his democratic sensibility, and he was an important figure at the 1787 convention at which the U.S. Constitution was drafted. In his later years, he was president of an antislavery association. One of his last efforts was to promote universal public education.

Hector St. John de Crèvecoeur (1735-1813)

Another Enlightenment figure is Hector St. John de Crèvecoeur, whose *Letters from an American Farmer* (1782) gave Europeans a glowing idea of opportunities for peace, wealth, and pride in America. Neither an American nor a farmer, but a French aristocrat who owned a plantation outside New York City before the Revolution, Crèvecoeur enthusiastically praised the colonies for their industry, tolerance, and growing prosperity in 12 letters that depict America as an agrarian paradise — a vision that would inspire Thomas Jefferson, Ralph Waldo Emerson, and many other writers up to the present.

Crèvecoeur was the earliest European to develop a considered view of America and the new American character. The first to exploit the "melting pot" image of America, in a famous passage he asks:

What then is the American, this new man? He is either a European, or the descendant of a European, hence that strange mixture of blood, which you will find in no other country. I could point out to you a family whose grandfather was an Englishman, whose wife was Dutch, whose son married a French woman, and whose present four sons have now four wives of different nations....Here individuals of all nations are melted into a new race of men, whose labors and posterity will one day cause changes in the world.

THE POLITICAL PAMPHLET:
Thomas Paine (1737-1809)

The passion of Revolutionary literature is found in pamphlets, the most popular form of political literature of the day. Over 2,000 pamphlets were published during the Revolution. The pamphlets thrilled patriots and threatened loyalists; they filled the role of drama, as they were often read aloud in public to excite audiences. American soldiers read them aloud in their camps; British Loyalists threw them into public bonfires.

Thomas Paine's pamphlet *Common Sense* sold over 100,000 copies in the first three months of its publication. It is still rousing today. "The cause of America is in a great measure the cause of all mankind," Paine wrote, voicing the idea of American exceptionalism still strong in the United States — that in some fundamental sense, since America is a democratic experiment and a country theoretically open to all immigrants, the fate of America foreshadows the fate of humanity at large.

Political writings in a democracy had to be clear to appeal to the voters. And to have informed voters, universal education was promoted by many of the founding fathers. One indication of the vigorous, if simple, literary life was the proliferation of newspapers. More newspapers were read in America during the Revolution than anywhere else in the world. Immigration also mandated a simple style. Clarity was vital to a newcomer, for whom

THOMAS PAINE

Portrait courtesy Library of Congress

English might be a second language. Thomas Jefferson's original draft of the Declaration of Independence is clear and logical, but his committee's modifications made it even simpler. *The Federalist Papers*, written in support of the Constitution, are also lucid, logical arguments, suitable for debate in a democratic nation.

NEOCLASSISM: EPIC, MOCK EPIC, AND SATIRE

Unfortunately, "literary" writing was not as simple and direct as political writing. When trying to write poetry, most educated authors stumbled into the pitfall of elegant neoclassicism. The epic, in particular, exercised a fatal attraction. American literary patriots felt sure that the great American Revolution naturally would find expression in the epic — a long, dramatic narrative poem in elevated language, celebrating the feats of a legendary hero.

Many writers tried but none succeeded. Timothy Dwight, (1752-1817), one of the group of writers known as the Hartford Wits, is an example. Dwight, who eventually became the president of Yale University, based his epic, *The Conquest of Canaan* (1785), on the Biblical story of Joshua's struggle to enter the Promised Land. Dwight cast General Washington, commander of the American army and later the first president of the United States, as Joshua in his allegory and borrowed the couplet form that Alexander Pope used to translate Homer. Dwight's epic was as boring as it was ambitious. English critics demolished it; even Dwight's friends, such as John Trumbull (1750-1831), remained unenthusiastic. So much thunder and lightning raged in the melodramatic battle scenes that Trumbull proposed that the epic be provided with lightning rods.

Not surprisingly, satirical poetry fared much better than serious verse. The mock epic genre encouraged American poets to use their natural voices and did not lure them into a bog of pretentious and predictable patriotic sentiments and faceless conventional poetic epithets out of the Greek poet Homer and the Roman poet Virgil by way of the English poets.

In mock epics like John Trumbull's goodhumored *M'Fingal* (1776-1782), stylized emotions and conventional turns of phrase are ammunition for good satire, and the bombastic oratory of the Revolution is itself ridiculed. Modeled on the British poet Samuel Butler's *Hudibras*, the mock epic derides a Tory, M'Fingal. It is often pithy, as when noting of condemned criminals facing hanging:

No man e'er felt the halter draw.
With good opinion of the law.

M'Fingal went into over 30 editions, was reprinted for a half-century, and was appreciated in England as well as America. Satire appealed to Revolutionary audiences partly because it contained social comment and criticism, and political topics and social problems were the main subjects of the day. The first American comedy to be performed, *The Contrast* (produced 1787) by Royall Tyler (1757-1826), humorously contrasts Colonel Manly, an American officer, with Dimple, who imitates English fashions. Naturally, Dimple is made to look ridiculous. The play introduces the first Yankee character, Jonathan.

Another satirical work, the novel *Modern Chivalry*, published by Hugh Henry Brackenridge

in installments from 1792 to 1815, memorably lampoons the excesses of the age. Brackenridge (1748-1816), a Scottish immigrant raised on the American frontier, based his huge, picaresque novel on Don Quixote; it describes the misadventures of Captain Farrago and his stupid, brutal, yet appealingly human, servant Teague O'Regan.

POET OF THE AMERICAN REVOLUTION: *Philip Freneau (1752-1832)*

One poet, Philip Freneau, incorporated the new stirrings of European Romanticism and escaped the imitativeness and vague universality of the Hartford Wits. The key to both his success and his failure was his passionately democratic spirit combined with an inflexible temper.

The Hartford Wits, all of them undoubted patriots, reflected the general cultural conservatism of the educated classes. Freneau set himself against this holdover of old Tory attitudes, complaining of "the writings of an aristocratic, speculating faction at Hartford, in favor of monarchy and titular distinctions." Although Freneau received a fine education and was as well acquainted with the classics as any Hartford Wit, he embraced liberal and democratic causes.

From a Huguenot (radical French Protestant) background, Freneau fought as a militiaman during the Revolutionary War. In 1780, he was captured and imprisoned in two British ships, where he almost died before his family managed to get him released. His poem "The British Prison Ship" is a bitter condemnation of the cruelties of the British, who wished "to stain the world with gore." This piece and other revolutionary works, including "Eutaw Springs," "American Liberty," "A Political Litany," "A Midnight Consultation," and "George the Third's Soliloquy," brought him fame as the "Poet of the American Revolution."

Freneau edited a number of journals during his life, always mindful of the great cause of democracy. When Thomas Jefferson helped him establish the militant, anti-Federalist *National Gazette* in 1791, Freneau became the first powerful, crusading newspaper editor in America, and the literary predecessor of William Cullen Bryant, William Lloyd Garrison, and H.L. Mencken.

As a poet and editor, Freneau adhered to his democratic ideals. His popular poems, published in newspapers for the average reader, regularly celebrated American subjects. "The Virtue of Tobacco" concerns the indigenous plant, a mainstay of the southern economy, while "The Jug of Rum" celebrates the alcoholic drink of the West Indies, a crucial commodity of early American trade and a major New World export. Common American characters lived in "The Pilot of Hatteras," as well as in poems about quack doctors and bombastic evangelists.

Freneau commanded a natural and colloquial style appropriate to a genuine democracy, but he could also rise to refined neoclassic lyricism in often-anthologized works such as "The Wild Honey Suckle" (1786), which evokes a sweet-smelling native shrub. Not until the "American Renaissance" that began in the 1820s would American poetry surpass the heights that Freneau had scaled 40 years earlier.

Additional groundwork for later literary achievement was laid during the early years. Nationalism inspired publications in many fields, leading to a new appreciation of things American. Noah

The 18th-century American Enlightenment was a movement marked by an emphasis on rationality rather than tradition, scientific inquiry instead of unquestioning religious dogma, and representative government in place of monarchy. Enlightenment thinkers and writers were devoted to the ideals of justice, liberty, and equality as the natural rights of man.

Webster (1758-1843) devised an American *Dictionary*, as well as an important reader and speller for the schools. His *Spelling Book* sold more than 100 million copies over the years. Updated Webster's dictionaries are still standard today. The *American Geography*, by Jedidiah Morse, another landmark reference work, promoted knowledge of the vast and expanding American land itself. Some of the most interesting, if nonliterary, writings of the period are the journals of frontiersmen and explorers such as Meriwether Lewis (1774-1809) and Zebulon Pike (1779-1813), who wrote accounts of expeditions across the Louisiana Territory, the vast portion of the North American continent that Thomas Jefferson purchased from Napoleon in 1803.

WRITERS OF FICTION

The first important fiction writers widely recognized today, Charles Brockden Brown, Washington Irving, and James Fenimore Cooper, used American subjects, historical perspectives, themes of change, and nostalgic tones. They wrote in many prose genres, initiated new forms, and found new ways to make a living through literature. With them, American literature began to be read and appreciated in the United States and abroad.

Charles Brockden Brown (1771-1810)

Already mentioned as the first professional American writer, Charles Brockden Brown was inspired by the English writers Mrs. Radcliffe and English William Godwin. (Radcliffe was known for her terrifying Gothic novels; a novelist and social reformer, Godwin was the father of Mary Shelley, who wrote *Frankenstein* and married English poet Percy Bysshe Shelley.)

Driven by poverty, Brown hastily penned four haunting novels in two years: *Wieland* (1798), *Arthur Mervyn* (1799), *Ormond* (1799), and *Edgar Huntley* (1799). In them, he developed the genre of American Gothic. The Gothic novel was a popular genre of the day featuring exotic and wild settings, disturbing psychological depth, and much suspense. Trappings included ruined castles or abbeys, ghosts, mysterious secrets, threatening figures, and solitary maidens who survive by their wits and spiritual strength. At their best, such novels offer tremendous suspense and hints of magic, along with profound explorations of the human soul in extremity. Critics suggest that Brown's Gothic sensibility expresses deep anxieties about the inadequate social institutions of the new nation.

Brown used distinctively American settings. A man of ideas, he dramatized scientific theories, developed a personal theory of fiction, and championed high literary standards despite personal poverty. Though flawed, his works are darkly powerful. Increasingly, he is seen as the precursor of romantic writers like Edgar Allan Poe, Herman Melville, and Nathaniel Hawthorne. He expresses subconscious fears that the outwardly optimistic Enlightenment period drove underground.

Washington Irving (1789-1859)

The youngest of 11 children born to a well-to-do New York merchant family, Washington Irving became a cultural and diplomatic ambassador to Europe, like Benjamin Franklin and Nathaniel Hawthorne. Despite his talent, he probably would not have become a full-time professional writer, given the lack of financial rewards, if a series of fortuitous incidents had not thrust writing as a profession upon him. Through friends, he was able to publish his *Sketch Book* (1819-1820) simultaneously in England and America, obtaining copyrights and payment in both countries.

The *Sketch Book of Geoffrye Crayon* (Irving's pseudonym) contains his two best remembered stories, "Rip Van Winkle" and "The Legend of Sleepy Hollow." "Sketch" aptly describes Irving's delicate, elegant, yet seemingly casual style, and "crayon" suggests his ability as a colorist or creator of rich, nuanced tones and emotional effects. In the *Sketch Book*, Irving transforms the Catskill mountains along the Hudson River north of New York City into a fabulous, magical region.

American readers gratefully accepted Irving's imagined "history" of the Catskills, despite the fact (unknown to them) that he had adapted his stories from a German source. Irving gave America something it badly needed in the brash, materialistic early years: an imaginative way of relating to the new land.

No writer was as successful as Irving at humanizing the land, endowing it with a name and a face and a set of legends. The story of "Rip Van Winkle," who slept for 20 years, waking to find the colonies had become independent, eventually became folklore. It was adapted for the stage, went into the oral tradition, and was gradually accepted as authentic American legend by generations of Americans.

Irving discovered and helped satisfy the raw new nation's sense of history. His numerous works may be seen as his devoted attempts to build the new nation's soul by recreating history and giving it living, breathing, imaginative life. For subjects, he chose the most dramatic aspects of American history: the discovery of the New World, the first president and national hero, and the westward exploration. His earliest work was a sparkling, satirical *History of New York* (1809) under the Dutch, ostensibly written by Diedrich Knickerbocker (hence the name of Irving's friends and New York writers of the day, the "Knickerbocker School").

James Fenimore Cooper (1789-1851)

James Fenimore Cooper, like Irving, evoked a sense of the past and gave it a local habitation and a name. In Cooper, though, one finds the powerful myth of a golden age and the poignance of its loss. While Irving and other American writers before and after him scoured Europe in search of its legends, castles, and great themes, Cooper grasped the essential myth of America: that it was timeless, like the wilderness. American history was a trespass on the eternal; European history in America was a reenactment of the fall in the Garden of Eden. The cyclical realm of nature was glimpsed only in the act of destroying it: The wilderness disappeared in front of American eyes, vanishing before the oncoming pioneers like a mirage. This is Cooper's basic tragic vision of the ironic destruction of the wilderness, the new Eden that had attracted the colonists in the first place.

Personal experience enabled Cooper to write vividly of the transformation of the wilderness and of other subjects such as the sea and the clash of peoples from different

JAMES FENIMORE COOPER

Photo courtesy Library of Congress

cultures. The son of a Quaker family, he grew up on his father's remote estate at Otsego Lake (now Cooperstown) in central New York State. Although this area was relatively peaceful during Cooper's boyhood, it had once been the scene of an Indian massacre. Young Fenimore Cooper grew up in an almost feudal environment. His father, Judge Cooper, was a landowner and leader. Cooper saw frontiersmen and Indians at Otsego Lake as a boy; in later life, bold white settlers intruded on his land.

Natty Bumppo, Cooper's renowned literary character, embodies his vision of the frontiersman as a gentleman, a Jeffersonian "natural aristocrat." Early in 1823, in *The Pioneers*, Cooper had begun to discover Bumppo. Natty is the first famous frontiersman in American literature and the literary forerunner of countless cowboy and backwoods heroes. He is the idealized, upright individualist who is better than the society he protects. Poor and isolated, yet pure, he is a touchstone for ethical values and prefigures Herman Melville's Billy Budd and Mark Twain's Huck Finn.

Based in part on the real life of American pioneer Daniel Boone — who was a Quaker like Cooper — Natty Bumppo, an outstanding woodsman like Boone, was a peaceful man adopted by an Indian tribe. Both Boone and the fictional Bumppo loved nature and freedom. They constantly kept moving west to escape the oncoming settlers they had guided into the wilderness, and they became legends in their own lifetimes. Natty is also chaste, high-minded, and deeply spiritual: He is the Christian knight of medieval romances transposed to the virgin forest and rocky soil of America.

The unifying thread of the five novels collectively known as the *Leather-Stocking Tales* is the life of Natty Bumppo. Cooper's finest achievement, they constitute a vast prose epic with the North American continent as setting, Indian tribes as characters, and great wars and westward migration as social background. The novels bring to life frontier America from 1740 to 1804.

Cooper's novels portray the successive waves of the frontier settlement: the original wilderness inhabited by Indians; the arrival of the first whites as scouts, soldiers, traders, and frontiersmen; the coming of the poor, rough settler families; and the final arrival of the middle class, bringing the first professionals — the judge, the physician, and the banker. Each incoming wave displaced the earlier: Whites displaced the Indians, who retreated westward; the "civilized" middle classes who erected schools, churches, and jails displaced the lower-class individualistic frontier folk, who moved further west, in turn displacing the Indians who had preceded them. Cooper evokes the endless, inevitable wave of settlers, seeing not only the gains but the losses.

Cooper's novels reveal a deep tension between the lone individual

PHILLIS WHEATLEY

Engraving © The Bettmann Archive

and society, nature and culture, spirituality and organized religion. In Cooper, the natural world and the Indian are fundamentally good — as is the highly civilized realm associated with his most cultured characters. Intermediate characters are often suspect, especially greedy, poor white settlers who are too uneducated or unrefined to appreciate nature or culture. Like Rudyard Kipling, E.M. Forster, Herman Melville, and other sensitive observers of widely varied cultures interacting with each other, Cooper was a cultural relativist. He understood that no culture had a monopoly on virtue or refinement.

Cooper accepted the American condition while Irving did not. Irving addressed the American setting as a European might have — by importing and adapting European legends, culture, and history. Cooper took the process a step farther. He created American settings and new, distinctively American characters and themes. He was the first to sound the recurring tragic note in American fiction.

WOMEN AND MINORITIES

Although the colonial period produced several women writers of note, the revolutionary era did not further the work of women and minorities, despite the many schools, magazines, newspapers, and literary clubs that were springing up. Colonial women such as Anne Bradstreet, Anne Hutchinson, Ann Cotton, and Sarah Kemble Knight exerted considerable social and literary influence in spite of primitive conditions and dangers; of the 18 women who came to America on the ship *Mayflower* in 1620, only four survived the first year. When every able-bodied person counted and conditions were fluid, innate talent could find expression. But as cultural institutions became formalized in the new republic, women and minorities gradually were excluded from them.

Phillis Wheatley (c. 1753-1784)

Given the hardships of life in early America, it is ironic that some of the best poetry of the period was written by an exceptional slave woman. The first African-American author of importance in the United States, Phillis Wheatley was born in Africa and brought to Boston, Massachusetts, when she was about seven, where she was purchased by the pious and wealthy tailor John Wheatley to be a companion for his wife. The Wheatleys recognized Phillis's remarkable intelligence and, with the help of their daughter, Mary, Phillis learned to read and write.

Wheatley's poetic themes are religious, and her style, like that of Philip Freneau, is neoclassical. Among her best-known poems are "To S.M., a Young African Painter, on Seeing His Works," a poem of praise and encouragement for another talented black, and a short poem showing her strong religious sensitivity filtered through her experience of Christian conversion. This poem unsettles some contemporary critics — whites because they find it conventional, and blacks because the poem does not protest the immorality of slavery. Yet the work is a sincere expression; it confronts white racism and asserts spiritual equality. Indeed, Wheatley was the first to address such issues confidently in verse, as in "On Being Brought from Africa to America":

'Twas mercy brought me from my Pagan land
Taught my benighted soul to understand
That there's a God, that there's a Savior too;
Once I redemption neither sought nor knew.
Some view our sable race with scornful eye,
"Their colour is a diabolic dye."
Remember, Christians, negroes, black as Cain,
May be refin'd, and join th' angelic train.

Other Women Writers

A number of accomplished Revolutionary-era women writers have been rediscovered by feminist scholars. Susanna Rowson (c. 1762-1824) was one of America's first professional novelists. Her seven novels included the best-selling seduction story *Charlotte Temple* (1791). She treats feminist and abolitionist themes and depicts American Indians with respect.

Another long-forgotten novelist was Hannah Foster (1758-1840), whose best-selling novel *The Coquette* (1797) was about a young woman torn between virtue and temptation. Rejected by her sweetheart, a cold man of the church, she is seduced, abandoned, bears a child, and dies alone.

Judith Sargent Murray (1751-1820) published under a man's name to secure serious attention for her works. Mercy Otis Warren (1728-1814) was a poet, historian, dramatist, satirist, and patriot. She held pre-Revolutionary gatherings in her home, attacked the British in her racy plays, and wrote the only contemporary radical history of the American revolution.

Letters between women such as Mercy Otis Warren and Abigail Adams, and letters generally, are important documents of the period. For example, Abigail Adams wrote to her husband, John Adams (later the second president of the United States), in 1776 urging that women's independence be guaranteed in the future U.S. constitution. ▧

CHAPTER 3

THE ROMANTIC PERIOD, 1820-1860: ESSAYISTS AND POETS

The Romantic movement, which originated in Germany but quickly spread to England, France, and beyond, reached America around the year 1820, some 20 years after William Wordsworth and Samuel Taylor Coleridge had revolutionized English poetry by publishing *Lyrical Ballads*. In America as in Europe, fresh new vision electrified artistic and intellectual circles. Yet there was an important difference: Romanticism in America coincided with the period of national expansion and the discovery of a distinctive American voice. The solidification of a national identity and the surging idealism and passion of Romanticism nurtured the masterpieces of "the American Renaissance."

Romantic ideas centered around art as inspiration, the spiritual and aesthetic dimension of nature, and metaphors of organic growth. Art, rather than science, Romantics argued, could best express universal truth. The Romantics underscored the importance of expressive art for the individual and society. In his essay "The Poet" (1844), Ralph Waldo Emerson, perhaps the most influential writer of the Romantic era, asserts:

For all men live by truth, and stand in need of expression. In love, in art, in avarice, in politics, in labor, in games, we study to utter our painful secret. The man is only half himself, the other half is his expression.

The development of the self became a major theme; self-awareness, a primary method. If, according to Romantic theory, self and nature were one, self-awareness was not a selfish dead end but a mode of knowledge opening up the universe. If one's self were one with all humanity, then the individual had a moral duty to reform social inequalities and relieve human suffering. The idea of "self" — which suggested selfishness to earlier generations — was redefined. New compound words with positive meanings emerged: "self-realization," "self-expression," "self-reliance."

As the unique, subjective self became important, so did the realm of psychology. Exceptional artistic effects and techniques were developed to evoke heightened psychological states. The "sublime" — an effect of beauty in grandeur (for example, a view from a mountaintop) — produced feelings of awe, reverence, vastness, and a power beyond human comprehension.

Romanticism was affirmative and appropriate for most American poets and creative essayists. America's vast mountains, deserts, and tropics embodied the sublime. The Romantic spirit seemed particularly suited to American democracy: It stressed individualism, affirmed the value of the common person, and looked to the inspired imagination for its aesthetic and ethical values. Certainly the New England Transcendentalists — Ralph Waldo Emerson, Henry David Thoreau, and their associates — were inspired to a new optimistic affirmation by the Romantic movement. In New England, Romanticism fell upon fertile soil.

TRANSCENDENTALISM

The Transcendentalist movement was a reaction against 18th-century rationalism and a manifestation of the general humanitarian trend of 19th-century thought. The movement was based on a fundamental belief in the unity of the world and God. The soul of each individual was thought to be identical with the world — a microcosm of the world itself. The doctrine of self-reliance and individualism developed through the belief in the identification of the individual soul with God.

Transcendentalism was intimately connected with Concord, a small New England village 32 kilometers west of Boston. Concord was the first inland settlement of the original Massachusetts Bay Colony. Surrounded by forest, it was and remains a peaceful town close enough to Boston's lectures, bookstores, and colleges to be intensely cultivated, but far enough away to be serene. Concord was the site of the first battle of the American Revolution, and Ralph Waldo Emerson's poem commemorating the battle, "Concord Hymn," has one of the most famous opening stanzas in American literature:

> By the rude bridge that arched
> the flood
> Their flag to April's breeze
> unfurled,
> Here once the embattled farmers
> stood
> And fired the shot heard round
> the world.

Concord was the first rural artist's colony, and the first place to offer a spiritual and cultural alternative to American materialism. It was a place of high-minded conversation and simple living (Emerson and Henry David Thoreau both had vegetable gardens). Emerson, who moved to Concord in 1834, and Thoreau are most closely associat-

RALPH
WALDO EMERSON

Photo courtesy
National Portrait Gallery,
Smithsonian Institution

ed with the town, but the locale also attracted the novelist Nathaniel Hawthorne, the feminist writer Margaret Fuller, the educator (and father of novelist Louisa May Alcott) Bronson Alcott, and the poet William Ellery Channing. The Transcendental Club was loosely organized in 1836 and included, at various times, Emerson, Thoreau, Fuller, Channing, Bronson Alcott, Orestes Brownson (a leading minister), Theodore Parker (abolitionist and minister), and others.

The Transcendentalists published a quarterly magazine, *The Dial*, which lasted four years and was first edited by Margaret Fuller and later by Emerson. Reform efforts engaged them as well as literature. A number of Transcendentalists were abolitionists, and some were involved in experimental utopian communities such as nearby Brook Farm (described in Hawthorne's *The Blithedale Romance*) and Fruitlands.

Unlike many European groups, the Transcendentalists never issued a manifesto. They insisted on individual differences — on the unique viewpoint of the individual. American Transcendental Romantics pushed radical individualism to the extreme. American writers often saw themselves as lonely explorers outside society and convention. The American hero — like Herman Melville's Captain Ahab, or Mark Twain's Huck Finn, or Edgar Allan Poe's Arthur Gordon Pym — typically faced risk, or even certain destruction, in the pursuit of metaphysical self-discovery. For the Romantic American writer, nothing was a given. Literary and social conventions, far from being helpful, were dangerous. There was tremendous pressure to discover an authentic literary form, content, and voice — all at the same time. It is clear from the many masterpieces produced in the three decades before the U.S. Civil War (1861-65) that American writers rose to the challenge.

Ralph Waldo Emerson (1803-1882)

Ralph Waldo Emerson, the towering figure of his era, had a religious sense of mission. Although many accused him of subverting Christianity, he explained that, for him "to be a good minister, it was necessary to leave the church." The address he delivered in 1838 at his alma mater, the Harvard Divinity School, made him unwelcome at Harvard for 30 years. In it, Emerson accused the church of acting "as if God were dead" and of emphasizing dogma while stifling the spirit.

Emerson's philosophy has been called contradictory, and it is true that he consciously avoided building a logical intellectual system because such a rational system would have negated his Romantic belief in intuition and flexibility. In his essay "Self-Reliance," Emerson remarks: "A foolish consistency is the hobgoblin of little minds." Yet he is remarkably consistent in his call for the birth of American individualism inspired by nature. Most of his major ideas — the need for a new national vision, the use of personal experience, the notion of the cosmic Over-Soul, and the doctrine of compensation — are suggested in his first publication, *Nature* (1836). This essay opens:

Our age is retrospective. It builds the sepulchres of the fathers. It writes biographies, histories, criticism. The foregoing generations beheld God and nature face to face; we, through their eyes. Why should not we

also enjoy an original relation to the universe? Why should not we have a poetry of insight and not of tradition, and a religion by revelation to us, and not the history of theirs. Embosomed for a season in nature, whose floods of life stream around and through us, and invite us by the powers they supply, to action proportioned to nature, why should we grope among the dry bones of the past...? The sun shines today also. There is more wool and flax in the fields. There are new lands, new men, new thoughts. Let us demand our own works and laws and worship.

Emerson loved the aphoristic genius of the 16th-century French essayist Montaigne, and he once told Bronson Alcott that he wanted to write a book like Montaigne's, "full of fun, poetry, business, divinity, philosophy, anecdotes, smut." He complained that Alcott's abstract style omitted "the light that shines on a man's hat, in a child's spoon."

Spiritual vision and practical, aphoristic expression make Emerson exhilarating; one of the Concord Transcendentalists aptly compared listening to him with "going to heaven in a swing." Much of his spiritual insight comes from his readings in Eastern religion, especially Hinduism, Confucianism, and Islamic Sufism. For example, his poem "Brahma" relies on Hindu sources to assert a cosmic order beyond the limited perception of mortals:

If the red slayer think he slay
Or the slain think he is slain,
They know not well the subtle ways
I keep, and pass, and turn again.

Far or forgot to me is near
Shadow and sunlight are the same;
The vanished gods to me appear;
And one to me are shame and fame.

They reckon ill who leave me out;
When me they fly, I am the wings;
I am the doubter and the doubt,
And I the hymn the Brahmin sings

The strong gods pine for my
    abode,
And pine in vain the sacred Seven,
But thou, meek lover of the good!
Find me, and turn thy back on
    heaven.

This poem, published in the first number of the *Atlantic Monthly* magazine (1857), confused readers unfamiliar with Brahma, the highest Hindu god, the eternal and infinite soul of the universe. Emerson had this advice for his readers: "Tell them to say Jehovah instead of Brahma."

The British critic Matthew Arnold said the most important writings in English in the 19th century had been Wordsworth's poems and Emerson's essays. A great prosepoet, Emerson influenced a long line of American poets, including Walt Whitman, Emily Dickinson, Edwin Arlington Robinson, Wallace Stevens, Hart Crane, and Robert Frost. He is also credited with influencing the philosophies of John Dewey, George Santayana, Friedrich Nietzsche, and William James.

Henry David Thoreau (1817-1862)

Henry David Thoreau, of French and Scottish descent, was born in Concord and made it his permanent home. From a poor family, like

HENRY DAVID THOREAU

Photo © The Bettmann
Archive

Emerson, he worked his way through Harvard. Throughout his life, he reduced his needs to the simplest level and managed to live on very little money, thus maintaining his independence. In essence, he made living his career. A nonconformist, he attempted to live his life at all times according to his rigorous principles. This attempt was the subject of many of his writings.

Thoreau's masterpiece, *Walden, or, Life in the Woods* (1854), is the result of two years, two months, and two days (from 1845 to 1847) he spent living in a cabin he built at Walden Pond on property owned by Emerson. In *Walden*, Thoreau consciously shapes this time into one year, and the book is carefully constructed so the seasons are subtly evoked in order. The book also is organized so that the simplest earthly concerns come first (in the section called "Economy," he describes the expenses of building a cabin); by the ending, the book has progressed to meditations on the stars.

In *Walden*, Thoreau, a lover of travel books and the author of several, gives us an anti-travel book that paradoxically opens the inner frontier of self-discovery as no American book had up to this time. As deceptively modest as Thoreau's ascetic life, it is no less than a guide to living the classical ideal of the good life. Both poetry and philosophy, this long poetic essay challenges the reader to examine his or her life and live it authentically. The building of the cabin, described in great detail, is a concrete metaphor for the careful building of a soul. In his journal for January 30, 1852, Thoreau explains his preference for living rooted in one place: "I am afraid to travel much or to famous places, lest it might completely dissipate the mind."

Thoreau's method of retreat and concentration resembles Asian meditation techniques. The resemblance is not accidental: like Emerson and Whitman, he was influenced by Hindu and Buddhist philosophy. His most treasured possession was his library of Asian classics, which he shared with Emerson. His eclectic style draws on Greek and Latin classics and is crystalline, punning, and as richly metaphorical as the English metaphysical writers of the late Renaissance.

In *Walden*, Thoreau not only tests the theories of Transcendentalism, he re-enacts the collective American experience of the 19th century: living on the frontier. Thoreau felt that his contribution would be to renew a sense of the wilderness in language. His journal has an undated entry from 1851:

English literature from the days of the minstrels to the Lake Poets, Chaucer and Spenser and Shakespeare and Milton included, breathes no quite fresh and in this sense, wild strain. It is an essentially tame and civilized literature, reflecting Greece and Rome. Her wilderness is a green-

WALT WHITMAN

wood, her wildman a Robin Hood. There is plenty of genial love of nature in her poets, but not so much of nature herself. Her chronicles inform us when her wild animals, but not the wildman in her, became extinct. There was need of America.

Walden inspired William Butler Yeats, a passionate Irish nationalist, to write "The Lake Isle of Innisfree," while Thoreau's essay "Civil Disobedience," with its theory of passive resistance based on the moral necessity for the just individual to disobey unjust laws, was an inspiration for Mahatma Gandhi's Indian independence movement and Martin Luther King's struggle for black Americans' civil rights in the 20th century.

Thoreau is the most attractive of the Transcendentalists today because of his ecological consciousness, do-it-yourself independence, ethical commitment to abolitionism, and political theory of civil disobedience and peaceful resistance. His ideas are still fresh, and his incisive poetic style and habit of close observation are still modern.

Walt Whitman (1819-1892)

Born on Long Island, New York, Walt Whitman was a part-time carpenter and man of the people, whose brilliant, innovative work expressed the country's democratic spirit. Whitman was largely self-taught; he left school at the age of

11 to go to work, missing the sort of traditional education that made most American authors respectful imitators of the English. His *Leaves of Grass* (1855), which he rewrote and revised throughout his life, contains "Song of Myself," the most stunningly original poem ever written by an American. The enthusiastic praise that Emerson and a few others heaped on this daring volume confirmed Whitman in his poetic vocation, although the book was not a popular success.

A visionary book celebrating all creation, *Leaves of Grass* was inspired largely by Emerson's writings, especially his essay "The Poet," which predicted a robust, open-hearted, universal kind of poet uncannily like Whitman himself. The poem's innovative, unrhymed, free-verse form, open celebration of sexuality, vibrant democratic sensibility, and extreme Romantic assertion that the poet's self was one with the poem, the universe, and the reader permanently altered the course of American poetry.

Leaves of Grass is as vast, energetic, and natural as the American continent; it was the epic generations of American critics had been calling for, although they did not recognize it. Movement ripples through "Song of Myself" like restless music:

My ties and ballasts leave me...
I skirt sierras, my palms cover continents
I am afoot with my vision.

The poem bulges with myriad concrete sights and sounds. Whitman's birds are not the conventional "winged spirits" of poetry. His "yellow-crown'd heron comes to the edge of the marsh at night and feeds upon small crabs." Whitman seems to project himself into everything that he sees or imagines. He is mass man, "Voyaging to every port to dicker and adventure, / Hurrying with the modern crowd as eager and fickle as any." But he is equally the suffering individual,

"The mother of old, condemn'd for a witch, burnt with dry wood, her children gazing on....I am the hounded slave, I wince at the bite of the dogs....I am the mash'd fireman with breast-bone broken...."

More than any other writer, Whitman invented the myth of democratic America. "The Americans of all nations at any time upon the earth have probably the fullest poetical nature. The United States is essentially the greatest poem." When Whitman wrote this, he daringly turned upside down the general opinion that America was too brash and new to be poetic. He invented a timeless America of the free imagination, peopled with pioneering spirits of all nations. D.H. Lawrence, the British novelist and poet, accurately called him the poet of the "open road."

Whitman's greatness is visible in many of his poems, among them "Crossing Brooklyn Ferry," "Out of the Cradle Endlessly Rocking," and "When Lilacs Last in the Dooryard Bloom'd," a moving elegy on the death of Abraham Lincoln. Another important work is his long essay "Democratic Vistas" (1871), written during the unrestrained materialism of industrialism's "Gilded Age." In this essay, Whitman justly criticizes America for its "mighty, many-threaded wealth and industry" that mask an underlying "dry and flat Sahara" of soul. He calls for a new kind of literature to revive the American population ("Not the book needs so much to be the complete thing, but the reader of the book does"). Yet ultimately, Whitman's main claim to immortality lies in "Song of Myself." Here he places the Romantic self at the center of the consciousness of the poem:

I celebrate myself, and sing myself,
And what I assume you shall assume,
For every atom belonging to me
   as good belongs to you.

Whitman's voice electrifies even modern readers with his proclamation of the unity and vital force of all creation. He was enormously innovative. From him spring the poem as autobiography, the American Everyman as bard, the reader as creator, and the still-contemporary discovery of "experimental," or organic, form.

THE BRAHMIN POETS

In their time, the Boston Brahmins (as the patrician, Harvard-educated class came to be called) supplied the most respected and genuinely cultivated literary arbiters of the United States. Their lives fitted a pleasant pattern of wealth and leisure directed by the strong New England work ethic and respect for learning.

In an earlier Puritan age, the Boston Brahmins would have been ministers; in the 19th century, they became professors, often at Harvard. Late in life they sometimes became ambassadors or received honorary degrees from European institutions. Most of them travelled or were educated in Europe: They were familiar with the ideas and books of Britain, Germany, and France, and often Italy and Spain. Upper class in background but democratic in sympathy, the Brahmin poets carried their genteel, European-oriented views to every section of the United States, through public lectures at the 3,000 lyceums (centers for public lectures) and in the pages of two influential Boston magazines, the

HENRY WADSWORTH LONGFELLOW

North American Review and the *Atlantic Monthly.*

The writings of the Brahmin poets fused American and European traditions and sought to create a continuity of shared Atlantic experience. These scholar-poets attempted to educate and elevate the general populace by introducing a European dimension to American literature. Ironically, their overall effect was conservative. By insisting on European things and forms, they retarded the growth of a distinctive American consciousness. Well-meaning men, their conservative backgrounds blinded them to the daring innovativeness of Thoreau, Whitman (whom they refused to meet socially), and Edgar Allan Poe (whom even Emerson regarded as the "jingle man"). They were pillars of what was called the "genteel tradition" that three generations of American realists had to battle. Partly because of their benign but bland influence, it was almost 100 years before the distinctive American genius of Whitman, Melville, Thoreau, and Poe was generally recognized in the United States.

Henry Wadsworth Longfellow (1807-1882)

The most important Boston Brahmin poets were Henry Wadsworth Longfellow, Oliver Wendell Holmes, and James Russell Lowell. Longfellow, professor of modern languages at Harvard, was the best-known American poet of his day. He was responsible for the misty, ahistorical, legendary sense of the past that merged American and European traditions. He wrote three long narrative poems popularizing native legends in European meters — "Evangeline" (1847), "The Song of Hiawatha" (1855), and "The Courtship of Miles Standish" (1858).

Longfellow also wrote textbooks on modern languages and a travel book entitled *Outre-Mer*, retelling foreign legends and patterned after Washington Irving's *Sketch Book*. Although conventionality, sentimentality, and facile handling mar the long poems, haunting short lyrics like "The Jewish Cemetery at Newport" (1854), "My Lost Youth" (1855), and "The Tide Rises, The Tide Falls" (1880) continue to give pleasure.

James Russell Lowell (1819-1891)

James Russell Lowell, who became professor of modern languages at Harvard after Longfellow retired, is the Matthew Arnold of American literature. He began as a poet but gradually lost his poetic ability, ending as a respected critic and educator. As editor of the *Atlantic* and co-editor of the *North American Review*, Lowell exercised enormous influence. Lowell's *A Fable for Critics* (1848) is a funny and apt appraisal of American writers, as in his comment: "There comes Poe, with his raven, like Barnaby Rudge / Three-fifths of him genius and two-fifths sheer fudge."

Under his wife's influence, Lowell became a liberal reformer, abolitionist, and supporter of women's suffrage and laws ending child labor. His *Biglow Papers, First Series* (1847-48), creates Hosea Biglow, a shrewd but uneducated village poet who argues for reform in dialect poetry. Benjamin Franklin and Phillip Freneau had used intelligent villagers as mouthpieces for social commentary. Lowell writes in the same vein, linking the colonial "character" tradition with the new realism and regionalism based on dialect that flowered in the 1850s and came to fruition in Mark Twain.

Oliver Wendell Holmes (1809-1894)

Oliver Wendell Holmes, a celebrated physician and professor of anatomy and physiology at Harvard, is the hardest of the three well-known Brahmins to categorize because his work is marked by a refreshing versatility. It encompasses collections of humorous essays (for example, *The Autocrat of the Breakfast-Table*, 1858), novels (*Elsie Venner*, 1861), biographies (*Ralph Waldo Emerson*, 1885), and verse that could be sprightly ("The Deacon's Masterpiece, or, The Wonderful One-Hoss Shay"), philosophical ("The Chambered Nautilus"), or fervently patriotic ("Old Ironsides").

Born in Cambridge, Massachusetts, the suburb of Boston that is home to Harvard, Holmes was the son of a prominent local minister. His mother was a descendant of the poet Anne Bradstreet. In his time, and more so thereafter, he symbolized wit, intelligence, and charm not as a discoverer or a trailblazer, but rather as an exemplary interpreter of everything from society and language to medicine and human nature.

TWO REFORMERS

New England sparkled with intellectual energy in the years before the Civil War. Some of the stars that shine more brightly today than the famous constellation of Brahmins were dimmed by poverty or accidents of gender or race in their own time. Modern readers increasingly value the work of abolitionist John Greenleaf Whittier and feminist and social reformer Margaret Fuller.

John Greenleaf Whittier (1807-1892)

John Greenleaf Whittier, the most active poet of the era, had a background very similar to Walt Whitman's. He was born and raised on a modest Quaker farm in Massachusetts, had little formal education, and worked as a journalist. For decades before it became popular, he was an ardent abolitionist. Whittier is respected for anti-slavery poems such as "Ichabod," and his poetry is sometimes viewed as an early example of regional realism.

Whittier's sharp images, simple constructions, and ballad-like tetrameter couplets have the simple earthy texture of Robert Burns. His best work, the long poem "Snow Bound," vividly recreates the poet's deceased family members and friends as he remembers them from childhood, huddled cozily around the blazing hearth during one of New England's blustering snowstorms. This simple, religious, intensely personal poem, coming after the long nightmare of the Civil War, is an elegy for the dead and a healing hymn. It affirms the eternity of the spirit, the timeless power of love in the memory, and the undiminished beauty of nature, despite violent outer political storms.

Margaret Fuller (1810-1850)

Margaret Fuller, an outstanding essayist, was born and raised in Cambridge, Massachusetts. From a modest financial background, she was educated at home by her father (women were not allowed to attend Harvard) and became a child prodigy in the classics and modern literatures. Her special passion was German Romantic literature, especially Goethe, whom she translated.

The first professional woman journalist of note in America, Fuller wrote influential book reviews and reports on social issues such as the treatment of women prisoners and the insane. Some of these essays

EMILY DICKINSON

Daguerreotype courtesy
Harper & Bros.

were published in her book *Papers on Literature and Art* (1846). A year earlier, she had her most significant book, *Woman in the Nineteenth Century*. It originally had appeared in the Transcendentalist magazine, *The Dial*, which she edited from 1840 to 1842.

Fuller's *Woman in the Nineteenth Century* is the earliest and most American exploration of women's role in society. Often applying democratic and Transcendental principles, Fuller thoughtfully analyzes the numerous subtle causes and evil consequences of sexual discrimination and suggests positive steps to be taken. Many of her ideas are strikingly modern. She stresses the importance of "self-dependence," which women lack because "they are taught to learn their rule from without, not to unfold it from within."

Fuller is finally not a feminist so much as an activist and reformer dedicated to the cause of creative human freedom and dignity for all:

...Let us be wise and not impede the soul....Let us have one creative energy....Let it take what form it will, and let us not bind it by the past to man or woman, black or white.

EMILY DICKINSON (1830-1886)

Emily Dickinson is, in a sense, a link between her era and the literary sensitivities of the turn of the century. A radical individualist, she

34

was born and spent her life in Amherst, Massachusetts, a small Calvinist village. She never married, and she led an unconventional life that was outwardly uneventful but was full of inner intensity. She loved nature and found deep inspiration in the birds, animals, plants, and changing seasons of the New England countryside.

Dickinson spent the latter part of her life as a recluse, due to an extremely sensitive psyche and possibly to make time for writing (for stretches of time she wrote about one poem a day). Her day also included homemaking for her attorney father, a prominent figure in Amherst who became a member of Congress.

Dickinson was not widely read, but knew the Bible, the works of William Shakespeare, and works of classical mythology in great depth. These were her true teachers, for Dickinson was certainly the most solitary literary figure of her time. That this shy, withdrawn village woman, almost unpublished and unknown, created some of the greatest American poetry of the 19th century has fascinated the public since the 1950s, when her poetry was rediscovered.

Dickinson's terse, frequently imagistic style is even more modern and innovative than Whitman's. She never uses two words when one will do, and combines concrete things with abstract ideas in an almost proverbial, compressed style. Her best poems have no fat; many mock current sentimentality, and some are even heretical. She sometimes shows a terrifying existential awareness. Like Poe, she explores the dark and hidden part of the mind, dramatizing death and the grave. Yet she also celebrated simple objects — a flower, a bee. Her poetry exhibits great intelligence and often evokes the agonizing paradox of the limits of the human consciousness trapped in time. She had an excellent sense of humor, and her range of subjects and treatment is amazingly wide. Her poems are generally known by the numbers assigned them in Thomas H. Johnson's standard edition of 1955. They bristle with odd capitalizations and dashes.

A nonconformist, like Thoreau she often reversed meanings of words and phrases and used paradox to great effect. From 435:

Much Madness is divinest sense —
To a discerning Eye —
Much Sense — the starkest Madness —
'Tis the Majority
In this, as All, prevail —
Assent — and you are sane —
Demur — you're straightway dangerous
And handled with a chain —

Her wit shines in the following poem (288), which ridicules ambition and public life:

I'm Nobody! Who are you?
Are you — Nobody — Too?
Then there's a pair of us?
Don't tell! they'd advertise — you know!
How dreary — to be — Somebody!
How public — like a Frog —
To tell one's name — the livelong June —
To an admiring Bog!

Dickinson's 1,775 poems continue to intrigue critics, who often disagree about them. Some stress her mystical side, some her sensitivity to nature; many note her odd, exotic appeal. One modern critic, R.P. Blackmur, comments that Dickinson's poetry sometimes feels as if "a cat came at us speaking English." Her clean, clear, chiseled poems are some of the most fascinating and challenging in American literature. ■

CHAPTER 4

THE ROMANTIC PERIOD, 1820-1860: FICTION

Walt Whitman, Nathaniel Hawthorne, Herman Melville, Edgar Allan Poe, Emily Dickinson, and the Transcendentalists represent the first great literary generation produced in the United States. In the case of the novelists, the Romantic vision tended to express itself in the form Hawthorne called the "romance," a heightened, emotional, and symbolic form of the novel. Romances were not love stories, but serious novels that used special techniques to communicate complex and subtle meanings.

Instead of carefully defining realistic characters through a wealth of detail, as most English or continental novelists did, Hawthorne, Melville, and Poe shaped heroic figures larger than life, burning with mythic significance. The typical protagonists of the American Romance are haunted, alienated individuals. Hawthorne's Arthur Dimmesdale or Hester Prynne in *The Scarlet Letter*, Melville's Ahab in *Moby-Dick*, and the many isolated and obsessed characters of Poe's tales are lonely protagonists pitted against unknowable, dark fates that, in some mysterious way, grow out of their deepest unconscious selves. The symbolic plots reveal hidden actions of the anguished spirit.

One reason for this fictional exploration into the hidden recesses of the soul is the absence of settled, traditional community life in America. English novelists — Jane Austen, Charles Dickens (the great favorite), Anthony Trollope, George Eliot, William Thackeray — lived in a complex, well-articulated, traditional society and shared with their readers attitudes that informed their realistic fiction. American novelists were faced with a history of strife and revolution, a geography of vast wilderness, and a fluid and relatively classless democratic society. American novels frequently reveal a revolutionary absence of tradition. Many English novels show a poor main character rising on the economic and social ladder, perhaps because of a good marriage or the discovery of a hidden aristocratic past. But this buried plot does not challenge the aristocratic social structure of England. On the contrary, it confirms it. The rise of the main character satisfies the wish fulfillment of the mainly middle-class readers.

In contrast, the American novelist had to depend on his or her own devices. America was, in part, an undefined, constantly moving frontier populated by immigrants speaking foreign languages and following strange and crude ways of life. Thus the main character in American literature might find himself alone among cannibal tribes, as in Melville's *Typee*, or exploring a wilderness like James Fenimore Cooper's Leatherstocking, or witnessing lonely visions from the grave, like Poe's solitary individuals, or meeting the devil walking in the forest, like Hawthorne's Young Goodman Brown. Virtually all the great American protagonists have been "loners." The democratic American individual had, as it were, to invent himself.

The serious American novelist had to invent new forms as well — hence the sprawling, idiosyncratic shape of Melville's novel *Moby-Dick*, and Poe's dreamlike, wandering *Narrative of Arthur Gordon Pym*. Few American novels achieve formal perfection, even today. Instead of borrowing tested literary methods, Americans tend to invent new creative techniques. In America, it is not enough to be a traditional and definable social unit, for the old and traditional gets left behind; the new, innovative force is the center of attention.

THE ROMANCE

The Romance form is dark and forbidding, indicating how difficult it is to create an identity without a stable society. Most of the Romantic heroes die in the end: All the sailors except Ishmael are drowned in *Moby-Dick*, and the sensitive but sinful minister Arthur Dimmesdale dies at the end of *The Scarlet Letter.* The self-divided, tragic note in American literature becomes dominant in the novels, even before the Civil War of the 1860s manifested the greater social tragedy of a society at war with itself.

Nathaniel Hawthorne (1804-1864)

Nathaniel Hawthorne, a fifth-generation American of English descent, was born in Salem, Massachusetts, a wealthy seaport north of Boston that specialized in East India trade. One of his ancestors had been a judge in an earlier century, during trials in Salem of women accused of being witches. Hawthorne used the idea of a curse on the family of an evil judge in his novel *The House of the Seven Gables.*

Many of Hawthorne's stories are set in Puritan New England, and his greatest novel, *The Scarlet Letter* (1850), has become the classic portrayal of Puritan America. It tells of the passionate, forbidden love affair linking a sensitive, reli-

NATHANIEL HAWTHORNE

Photo courtesy OWI

gious young man, the Reverend Arthur Dimmesdale, and the sensuous, beautiful townsperson, Hester Prynne. Set in Boston around 1650 during early Puritan colonization, the novel highlights the Calvinistic obsession with morality, sexual repression, guilt and confession, and spiritual salvation.

For its time, *The Scarlet Letter* was a daring and even subversive book. Hawthorne's gentle style, remote historical setting, and ambiguity softened his grim themes and contented the general public, but sophisticated writers such as Ralph Waldo Emerson and Herman Melville recognized the book's "hellish" power. It treated issues that were usually suppressed in 19th-century America, such as the impact of the new, liberating democratic experience on individual behavior, especially on sexual and religious freedom.

The book is superbly organized and beautifully written. Appropriately, it uses allegory, a technique the early Puritan colonists themselves practiced.

Hawthorne's reputation rests on his other novels and tales as well. In *The House of the Seven Gables* (1851), he again returns to New England's history. The crumbling of the "house" refers to a family in Salem as well as to the actual structure. The theme concerns an inherited curse and its resolution through love. As one critic has noted, the idealistic protagonist Holgrave voices Hawthorne's own democratic distrust of old aristocratic families: "The truth is, that once in every half-century, at least, a family should be merged into the great, obscure mass of humanity, and forget about its ancestors."

Hawthorne's last two novels were less successful. Both use modern settings, which hamper the magic of romance. *The Blithedale Romance* (1852) is interesting for its portrait of the socialist, utopian Brook Farm community. In the book, Hawthorne criticizes egotistical, power-hungry social reformers whose deepest instincts are not genuinely democratic. *The Marble Faun* (1860), though set in Rome, dwells on the Puritan themes of sin, isolation, expiation, and salvation.

These themes, and his characteristic settings in Puritan colonial New England, are trademarks of many of Hawthorne's best-known shorter stories: "The Minister's Black Veil," "Young Goodman Brown," and "My Kinsman, Major Molineux." In the last of these, a naïve young man from the country comes to the city — a common route in urbanizing 19th-century America — to seek help from his powerful relative, whom he has never met. Robin has great difficulty finding the major, and finally joins in a strange night riot in which a man who seems to be a disgraced criminal is comically and cruelly driven out of town. Robin laughs loudest of all until he realizes that this "criminal" is none other than the man he sought — a representative of the British who has just been overthrown by a revolutionary American mob. The story confirms the bond of sin and suffering shared by all humanity. It also stresses the theme of the self-made man: Robin must learn, like every democratic American, to prosper from his own hard work, not from special favors from wealthy relatives.

"My Kinsman, Major Molineux" casts light on one of the most striking elements in Hawthorne's fiction: the lack of functioning families in his works. Although Cooper's *Leather-Stocking Tales* manage to introduce families into the least

likely wilderness places, Hawthorne's stories and novels repeatedly show broken, cursed, or artificial families and the sufferings of the isolated individual.

The ideology of revolution, too, may have played a part in glorifying a sense of proud yet alienated freedom. The American Revolution, from a psychohistorical viewpoint, parallels an adolescent rebellion away from the parent-figure of England and the larger family of the British Empire. Americans won their independence and were then faced with the bewildering dilemma of discovering their identity apart from old authorities. This scenario was played out countless times on the frontier, to the extent that, in fiction, isolation often seems the basic American condition of life. Puritanism and its Protestant offshoots may have further weakened the family by preaching that the individual's first responsibility was to save his or her own soul.

Herman Melville (1819-1891)

Herman Melville, like Nathaniel Hawthorne, was a descendant of an old, wealthy family that fell abruptly into poverty upon the death of the father. Despite his patrician upbringing, proud family traditions, and hard work, Melville found himself in poverty with no college education. At 19 he went to sea. His interest in sailors' lives grew naturally out of his own experiences, and most of his early novels grew out of his voyages. In these we see the young Melville's wide, democratic experience and hatred of tyranny and injustice. His first book, *Typee*, was based on his time spent among the supposedly cannibalistic but hospitable tribe of the Taipis in the Marquesas Islands of the South Pacific. The book praises the islanders and their natural, harmonious life, and criticizes the Christian missionaries, who Melville found less genuinely civilized than the people they came to convert.

Moby-Dick; or, The Whale, Melville's masterpiece, is the epic story of the whaling ship

Pequod and its "ungodly, god-like man," Captain Ahab, whose obsessive quest for the white whale Moby-Dick leads the ship and its men to destruction. This work, a realistic adventure novel, contains a series of meditations on the human condition. Whaling, throughout the book, is a grand metaphor for the pursuit of knowledge. Realistic catalogues and descriptions of whales and the whaling industry punctuate the book, but these carry symbolic connotations. In chapter 15, "The Right Whale's Head," the narrator says that the Right Whale is a Stoic and the Sperm Whale is a Platonian, referring to two classical schools of philosophy.

Although Melville's novel is philosophical, it is also tragic. Despite his heroism, Ahab is doomed and perhaps damned in the end. Nature, however beautiful, remains alien and potentially deadly. In *Moby-Dick*, Melville challenges Emerson's optimistic idea that humans can understand nature. Moby-Dick, the great white whale, is an inscrutable, cosmic existence that dominates the novel, just as he obsesses Ahab. Facts about the whale and whaling cannot explain Moby-Dick; on the contrary, the facts themselves tend to become symbols, and every fact is obscurely related in a cosmic web to every other fact. This idea of correspondence (as Melville calls it in the "Sphinx" chapter) does not, however, mean that humans can "read" truth in nature, as it does in Emerson. Behind Melville's accumulation of facts is a mystic vision

HERMAN MELVILLE

— but whether this vision is evil or good, human or inhuman, is never explained.

The novel is modern in its tendency to be self-referential, or reflexive. In other words, the novel often is about itself. Melville frequently comments on mental processes such as writing, reading, and understanding. One chapter, for instance, is an exhaustive survey in which the narrator attempts a classification but finally gives up, saying that nothing great can ever be finished ("God keep me from ever completing anything. This whole book is but a draught — nay, but the draught of a draught. O Time, Strength, Cash and Patience"). Melville's notion of the literary text as an imperfect version or an abandoned draft is quite contemporary.

Ahab insists on imaging a heroic, timeless world of absolutes in which he can stand above his men. Unwisely, he demands a finished text, an answer. But the novel shows that just as there are no finished texts, there are no final answers except, perhaps, death.

Certain literary references resonate throughout the novel. Ahab, named for an Old Testament king, desires a total, Faustian, god-like knowledge. Like Oedipus in Sophocles' play, who pays tragically for wrongful knowledge, Ahab is struck blind before he is wounded in the leg and finally killed. *Moby-Dick* ends with the word "orphan." Ishmael, the narrator, is an orphan-like wanderer. The name Ishmael emanates from the Book of Genesis in the Old Testament — he was the son of Abraham and Hagar (servant to Abraham's wife, Sarah). Ishmael and Hagar were cast into the wilderness by Abraham.

Other examples exist. Rachel (one of the patriarch Jacob's wives) is the name of the boat that rescues Ishmael at book's end. Finally, the metaphysical whale reminds Jewish and Christian readers of the Biblical story of Jonah, who was tossed overboard by fellow sailors who considered him an object of ill fortune. Swallowed by a "big fish," according to the biblical text, he lived for a time in its belly before being returned to dry land through God's intervention. Seeking to flee from punishment, he only brought more suffering upon himself.

Historical references also enrich the novel. The ship *Pequod* is named for an extinct New England Indian tribe; thus the name suggests that the boat is doomed to destruction. Whaling was in fact a major industry, especially in New England: It supplied oil as an energy source, especially for lamps. Thus the whale does literally "shed light" on the universe. Whaling was also inherently expansionist and linked with the idea of manifest destiny, since it required Americans to sail round the world in search of whales (in fact, the present state of Hawaii came under American domination because it was used as the major refueling base for American whaling ships). The *Pequod's* crew members represent all races and various religions, suggesting the idea of America as a universal state of mind as well as a melting pot. Finally, Ahab embodies the tragic version of democratic American individualism. He asserts his dignity as an individual and dares to oppose the inexorable external forces of the universe.

The novel's epilogue tempers the tragic destruction of the ship. Throughout, Melville stresses the importance of friendship and the multicultural human community. After the ship sinks, Ishmael is saved by the engraved coffin made by his close friend, the heroic tatooed harpooner and Polynesian prince Queequeg. The coffin's primitive, mythological designs incorporate the history of the cosmos. Ishmael is rescued from death by an object of death. From death life emerges, in the end.

Moby-Dick has been called a "natural epic" — a magnificent dramatization of the human spirit set in primitive nature — because of its hunter myth, its initiation theme, its Edenic island symbolism, its positive treatment of pre-technological peoples, and its quest for rebirth. In setting humanity alone in nature, it is eminently American. The French writer and politician Alexis de Tocqueville had predicted, in the 1835 work *Democracy in America*, that this theme would arise in America as a result of its democracy:

> The destinies of mankind, man himself taken aloof from his country and his age and standing in the presence of Nature and God, with his passions, his doubts, his rare propensities and inconceivable wretchedness, will become the chief, if not the sole, theme of (American) poetry.

Tocqueville reasons that, in a democracy, literature would dwell on "the hidden depths of the immaterial nature of man" rather than on mere appearances or superficial distinctions such as class and status. Certainly both *Moby-Dick* and *Typee*, like *Adventures of Huckleberry Finn* and *Walden*, fit this description. They are celebrations of nature and pastoral subversions of class-oriented, urban civilization.

Edgar Allan Poe (1809-1849)

Edgar Allan Poe, a southerner, shares with Melville a darkly metaphysical vision mixed with elements of realism, parody, and burlesque. He refined the short story genre and invented detective fiction. Many of his stories prefigure the genres of science fiction, horror, and fantasy so popular today.

Poe's short and tragic life was plagued with insecurity. Like so many other major 19th-century American writers, Poe was orphaned at an early age. Poe's strange marriage in 1835 to his first cousin Virginia Clemm, who was not yet 14, has been interpreted as an attempt to find the stable family life he lacked.

Poe believed that strangeness was an essential ingredient of beauty, and his writing is often exotic. His stories and poems are populated with doomed, introspective aristocrats (Poe, like many other southerners, cherished an aristocratic ideal). These gloomy characters never seem to work or socialize; instead they bury themselves in dark, moldering castles symbolically decorated with bizarre rugs and draperies that hide the real world of sun, windows, walls, and floors. The hidden rooms reveal ancient libraries, strange art works, and eclectic oriental objects. The aristocrats play musical instruments or read ancient books while they brood on tragedies, often the deaths of loved ones. Themes of death-in-life, especially being buried alive or returning like a vampire from the grave, appear in many of his works, including "The Premature Burial," "Ligeia," "The Cask of Amontillado," and "The Fall of the House of Usher." Poe's twilight realm between life and death and his gaudy, Gothic settings are not merely decorative. They reflect

EDGAR ALLAN POE

the overcivilized yet deathly interior of his characters' disturbed psyches. They are symbolic expressions of the unconscious, and thus are central to his art.

Poe's verse, like that of many southerners, was very musical and strictly metrical. His best-known poem, in his own lifetime and today, is "The Raven" (1845). In this eerie poem, the haunted, sleepless narrator, who has been reading and mourning the death of his "lost Lenore" at midnight, is visited by a raven (a bird that eats dead flesh, hence a symbol of death) who perches above his door and ominously repeats the poem's famous refrain, "nevermore." The poem ends in a frozen scene of death-in-life:

And the Raven, never flitting,
   still
is sitting, *still* is sitting
On the pallid bust of Pallas just
above my chamber door;
And his eyes have all the
   seeming of
a demon's that is dreaming,
And the lamp-light o'er him
streaming throws his shadow
   on the floor;
And my soul from out
   that shadow
that lies floating on the floor
   Shall be lifted — nevermore!

Poe's stories — such as those cited above — have been described as tales of horror. Stories like "The Gold Bug" and "The Purloined Letter" are more tales of ratiocination, or reasoning. The horror tales prefigure works by such American authors of horror fantasy as H.P. Lovecraft and Stephen King, while the tales of ratiocination are harbingers of the detective fiction of Dashiell Hammett, Raymond Chandler, Ross Macdonald, and John D. MacDonald. There is a hint, too, of what was to follow as science fiction. All of these stories reveal Poe's fascination with the mind and the unsettling scientific knowledge that was radically secularizing the 19th-century world view.

In every genre, Poe explores the psyche. Profound psychological insights glint throughout the stories. "Who has not, a hundred times, found himself committing a vile or silly action, for no other reason than because he knows he should not," we read in "The Black Cat." To explore the exotic and strange aspect of psychological processes, Poe delved into accounts of madness and extreme emotion. The painfully deliberate style and elaborate explanation in the stories heighten the sense of the horrible by making the events seem vivid and plausible.

Poe's combination of decadence and romantic primitivism appealed enormously to Europeans, particularly to the French poets Stéphane Mallarmé, Charles Baudelaire, Paul Valéry, and Arthur Rimbaud. But Poe is not un-American, despite his aristocratic disgust with democracy, preference for the exotic, and themes of dehumanization. On the contrary, he is almost a textbook example of Tocqueville's prediction that American democracy would produce works that lay bare the deepest, hidden parts of the psyche. Deep anxiety and psychic insecurity seem to have occurred earlier in America than in Europe, for Europeans at least had a firm, complex social structure that gave them psychological security. In America, there was no compensating security; it was every man for himself. Poe accurately described the underside of the American dream of the self-made man and showed the price of materialism and excessive competition — loneliness, alienation, and images of death-in-life.

Poe's "decadence" also reflects the devaluation of symbols that occurred in the 19th century — the tendency to mix art objects promiscuously from many eras and places, in the process stripping them of their identity and reducing them to merely decorative items in a collection. The resulting chaos of styles was particularly noticeable in the United States, which often lacked traditional styles of its own. The jumble reflects the loss of coherent systems of thought as immigration, urbanization, and industrialization uprooted families and traditional ways. In art, this confusion of symbols fueled the grotesque, an idea that Poe explicitly made his theme in his classic collection of stories *Tales of the Grotesque and Arabesque* (1840).

WOMEN WRITERS AND REFORMERS

American women endured many inequalities in the 19th century: They were denied the vote, barred from professional schools and most higher education, forbidden to speak in public and even attend public conventions, and unable to own property. Despite these obstacles, a strong women's network sprang up. Through letters, personal friendships, formal meetings, women's newspapers, and books, women furthered social change. Intellectual women drew parallels between themselves and slaves. They courageously demanded fundamental reforms, such as the abolition of slavery and women's suffrage, despite social ostracism and sometimes financial ruin. Their works were the vanguard of intellectual expression of a larger women's literary tradition that included the sentimental novel. Women's sentimental novels, such as Harriet Beecher Stowe's *Uncle Tom's Cabin*, were enormously popular. They appealed to the emotions and often dramatized contentious social issues, particularly those touching the family and women's roles and responsibilities.

Abolitionist Lydia Child (1802-1880), who greatly influenced Margaret Fuller, was a leader of this network. Her successful 1824 novel *Hobomok* shows the need for racial and religious toleration. Its setting — Puritan Salem, Massachusetts — anticipated Nathaniel Hawthorne. An activist, Child founded a private girls' school, founded and edited the first journal for children in the United States, and published the first anti-slavery tract, *An Appeal in Favor of that Class of Americans Called Africans*, in 1833. This daring work made her notorious and ruined her financially. Her *History of the Condition of Women in Various Ages and Nations* (1855) argues for women's equality by pointing to their historical achievements.

Angelina Grimké (1805-1879) and Sarah Grimké (1792-1873) were born into a large family of wealthy slaveowners in elegant Charleston, South Carolina. These sisters moved to the North to defend the rights of blacks and women. As speakers for the New York Anti-Slavery Society, they were the first women to publicly lecture to audiences, including men. In letters, essays, and studies, they drew parallels between racism and sexism.

Elizabeth Cady Stanton (1815-1902), abolitionist and women's rights activist, lived for a time in Boston, where she befriended Lydia Child. With Lucretia Mott, she organized the 1848 Seneca Falls Convention for Women's rights; she also drafted its *Declaration of Sentiments*. Her "Woman's Declaration of Independence" begins "men and women are created equal" and includes a resolution to give women the right to vote. With Susan B. Anthony, Elizabeth Cady Stanton campaigned for suffrage in the 1860s and 1870s, formed the anti-slavery Women's Loyal National League and the National Woman Suffrage Association, and co-edited the weekly newspaper *Revolution*. President of the Woman Suffrage Association for 21 years, she led the struggle for women's rights. She gave public lectures in several states, partly to support the education of her seven children.

After her husband died, Cady Stanton deepened her analysis of inequality between the sexes. Her book *The Woman's Bible* (1895) discerns a deep-seated anti-female bias in Judaeo-Christian tradition. She lectured on such subjects as divorce, women's rights, and religion until her death at 86, just after writing a letter to President Theodore Roosevelt supporting the women's vote. Her numerous works — at first pseudonymous, but later under her own name — include three co-authored volumes of *History of Woman Suffrage* (1881-1886) and a candid, humorous autobiography.

Sojourner Truth (c. 1797-1883) epitomized the endurance and charisma of this extraordinary group of women. Born a slave in New York, she grew up speaking Dutch. She escaped from slavery in 1827, settling with a son and daughter in the supportive Dutch-American Van Wagener family, for whom she worked as a servant. They helped her win a legal battle for her son's freedom, and she took their name. Striking out on her own, she worked with a preacher to convert prostitutes to Christianity and lived in a progressive communal home. She was christened "Sojourner Truth" for the mystical voices and visions she began to experience. To spread the truth of these visionary teachings, she sojourned alone, lecturing, singing gospel songs, and preaching abolitionism through many states over three decades. Encouraged by Elizabeth Cady Stanton, she advocated women's suffrage. Her life is told in the *Narrative of Sojourner Truth* (1850), an autobiographical account transcribed and edited by Olive Gilbert. Illiterate her whole life, she spoke Dutch-accented English. Sojourner Truth is said to have bared her breast at a women's rights convention when she was accused of really being a man. Her answer to a man who said that women were the weaker sex has become legendary:

> I have ploughed and planted, and gathered into bars, and no man could head me! And ain't I a woman? I could work as much and eat as much as a man — when I could get it —and bear the lash as well! And ain't I a woman? I have borne thirteen children, and seen them most all sold off to slavery, and when I cried out with my mother's grief, none but Jesus heard me! And ain't I a woman?

This humorous and irreverent orator has been compared to the great blues singers. Harriet Beecher Stowe and many others found wisdom in this visionary black woman, who could declare, "Lord, Lord, I can love even de white folk!"

Harriet Beecher Stowe (1811-1896)

Harriet Beecher Stowe's novel *Uncle Tom's Cabin; or, Life Among the Lowly* was the most popular American book of the 19th century. First published serially in the *National Era* magazine (1851-1852), it was an immediate success. Forty different publishers printed it in England alone, and it was quickly translated into 20 languages, receiving the praise of such authors as Georges Sand in France, Heinrich Heine in Germany, and Ivan Turgenev in Russia. Its passionate appeal for an end to slavery in the United States inflamed the debate that, within a decade, led to the U.S.

HARRIET BEECHER STOWE

Photo courtesy Culver Pictures, Inc.

Civil War (1861-1865).

Reasons for the success of *Uncle Tom's Cabin* are obvious. It reflected the idea that slavery in the United States, the nation that purportedly embodied democracy and equality for all, was an injustice of colossal proportions.

Stowe herself was a perfect representative of old New England Puritan stock. Her father, brother, and husband all were well-known, learned Protestant clergymen and reformers. Stowe conceived the idea of the novel — in a vision of an old, ragged slave being beaten — as she participated in a church service. Later, she said that the novel was inspired and "written by God." Her motive was the religious passion to reform life by making it more godly. The romantic period had ushered in an era of feeling: The virtues of family and love reigned supreme. Stowe's novel attacked slavery precisely because it violated domestic values.

Uncle Tom, the slave and central character, is a true Christian martyr who labors to convert his kind master, St. Clare, prays for St. Clare's soul as he dies, and is killed defending slave women. Slavery is depicted as evil not for political or philosophical reasons but mainly because it divides families, destroys normal parental love, and is inherently un-Christian. The most touching scenes show an agonized slave mother unable to help her screaming child and a father sold away from his family.

These were crimes against the sanctity of domestic love.

Stowe's novel was not originally intended as an attack on the South; in fact, Stowe had visited the South, liked southerners, and portrayed them kindly. Southern slaveowners are good masters and treat Tom well. St. Clare personally abhors slavery and intends to free all of his slaves. The evil master Simon Legree, on the other hand, is a northerner and the villain. Ironically, the novel was meant to reconcile the North and South, which were drifting toward the Civil War a decade away. Ultimately, though, the book was used by abolitionists and others as a polemic against the South.

Harriet Jacobs (1818-1896)

Born a slave in North Carolina, Harriet Jacobs was taught to read and write by her mistress. On her mistress's death, Jacobs was sold to a white master who tried to force her to have sexual relations. She resisted him, finding another white lover by whom she had two children, who went to live with her grandmother. "It seems less degrading to give one's self than to submit to compulsion," she candidly wrote. She escaped from her owner and started a rumor that she had fled North.

Terrified of being caught and sent back to slavery and punishment, she spent almost seven years hidden in her master's town, in the tiny dark attic of her grandmother's house. She was sustained

FREDERICK DOUGLASS

Photo-ambrotype courtesy
National Portrait Gallery,
Smithsonian Institution

by glimpses of her beloved children seen through holes that she drilled through the ceiling. She finally escaped to the North, settling in Rochester, New York, where Frederick Douglass was publishing the anti-slavery newspaper *North Star* and near which (in Seneca Falls) a women's rights convention had recently met. There Jacobs became friends with Amy Post, a Quaker feminist abolitionist, who encouraged her to write her autobiography. *Incidents in the Life of a Slave Girl*, published under the pseudonym "Linda Brent" in 1861, was edited by Lydia Child. It outspokenly condemned the sexual exploitation of black slave women. Jacobs's book, like Douglass's, is part of the slave narrative genre extending back to Olaudah Equiano in colonial times.

Harriet Wilson (1807-1870)

Harriet Wilson was the first African-American to publish a novel in the United States — *Our Nig: or, Sketches from the life of a Free Black, in a two-storey white house, North. Showing that Slavery's Shadows Fall Even There* (1859). The novel realistically dramatizes the marriage between a white woman and a black man, and also depicts the difficult life of a black servant in a wealthy Christian household. Formerly thought to be autobiographical, it is now understood to be a work of fiction.

Like Jacobs, Wilson did not publish under her own name (*Our Nig* was ironic), and her work was overlooked until recently. The same can be said of the work of most of the women writers of the era. Noted African-American scholar Henry Louis Gates, Jr. — in his role of spearheading the black fiction project — reissued *Our Nig* in 1983.

Frederick Douglass (1817-1895)

The most famous black American anti-slavery leader and orator of the era, Frederick Douglass was born a slave on a Maryland plantation. It was his good fortune to be sent to relatively liberal Baltimore as a young man, where he learned to read and write. Escaping to Massachusetts in 1838, at age 21, Douglass was helped by abolitionist editor William Lloyd Garrison and began to lecture for anti-slavery societies.

In 1845, he published his *Narrative of the Life of Frederick Douglass, An American Slave* (second version 1855, revised in 1892), the best and most popular of many "slave narratives." Often dictated by illiterate blacks to white abolitionists and used as propaganda, these slave narratives were well-known in the years just before the Civil War. Douglass's narrative is vivid and highly literate, and it gives unique insights into the mentality of slavery and the agony that institution caused among blacks.

The slave narrative was the first black literary prose genre in the United States. It helped blacks in the difficult task of establishing an African-American identity in white America, and it has continued to exert an important influence on black fictional techniques and themes throughout the 20th century. The search for identity, anger against discrimination, and sense of living an invisible, hunted, underground life unacknowledged by the white majority, have recurred in the works of such 20th-century black American authors as Richard Wright, James Baldwin, Ralph Ellison, and Toni Morrison. ▪

CHAPTER 5

THE RISE OF REALISM: 1860-1914

The U.S. Civil War (1861-1865) between the industrial North and the agricultural, slave-owning South was a watershed in American history. The innocent optimism of the young democratic nation gave way, after the war, to a period of exhaustion. American idealism remained but was rechanneled. Before the war, idealists championed human rights, especially the abolition of slavery; after the war, Americans increasingly idealized progress and the self-made man. This was the era of the millionaire manufacturer and the speculator, when Darwinian evolution and the "survival of the fittest" seemed to sanction the sometimes unethical methods of the successful business tycoon.

Business boomed after the war. War production had boosted industry in the North and given it prestige and political clout. It also gave industrial leaders valuable experience in the management of men and machines. The enormous natural resources — iron, coal, oil, gold, and silver — of the American land benefitted business. The new intercontinental rail system, inaugurated in 1869, and the transcontinental telegraph, which began operating in 1861, gave industry access to materials, markets, and communications. The constant influx of immigrants provided a seemingly endless supply of inexpensive labor as well. Over 23 million foreigners — German, Scandinavian, and Irish in the early years, and increasingly Central and Southern Europeans thereafter — flowed into the United States between 1860 and 1910. Chinese, Japanese, and Filipino contract laborers were imported by Hawaiian plantation owners, railroad companies, and other American business interests on the West Coast.

In 1860, most Americans lived on farms or in small villages, but by 1919 half of the population was concentrated in about 12 cities. Problems of urbanization and industrialization appeared: poor and overcrowded housing, unsanitary conditions, low pay (called "wage slavery"), difficult working conditions, and inadequate restraints on business. Labor unions grew, and strikes brought the plight of working people to national awareness. Farmers, too, saw themselves struggling against the "money interests" of the East, the so-called robber barons like J.P. Morgan and John D. Rockefeller. Their eastern banks tightly controlled mortgages and credit so vital to western development and agriculture, while railroad companies charged high prices to transport farm products to the cities. The farmer gradually became an object of ridicule, lampooned as an unsophisticated "hick" or "rube." The ideal American of the post-Civil War period became the millionaire. In 1860, there were fewer than 100 millionaires; by 1875, there were more than 1,000.

From 1860 to 1914, the United States was transformed from a small, young, agricultural ex-colony to a huge, modern, industrial nation. A debtor nation in 1860, by 1914 it had become the world's wealthiest state, with a population that had more than doubled, rising from 31 million in 1860 to 76 million in 1900. By World War I, the United States had become a major world power.

As industrialization grew, so did alienation. Characteristic American novels of the period — Stephen Crane's *Maggie: A Girl of the Streets,* Jack London's *Martin Eden,* and later Theodore Dreiser's *An American Tragedy* — depict the damage of economic forces and alienation on the weak or vulnerable individual. Survivors, like Twain's Huck Finn, Humphrey Vanderveyden in London's *The Sea-Wolf*, and Dreiser's opportunistic Sister Carrie, endure through inner strength involving kindness, flexibility, and, above all, individuality.

SAMUEL CLEMENS (MARK TWAIN) (1835-1910)

Samuel Clemens, better known by his pen name of Mark Twain, grew up in the Mississippi River frontier town of Hannibal, Missouri. Ernest Hemingway's famous statement that all of American literature comes from one great book, Twain's *Adventures of Huckleberry Finn*, indicates this author's towering place in the tradition. Early 19th-century American writers tended to be too flowery, sentimental, or ostentatious — partially because they were still trying to prove that they could write as elegantly as the English. Twain's style, based on vigorous, realistic, colloquial American speech, gave American writers a new appreciation of their national voice. Twain was the first major author to come from the interior of the country, and he captured its distinctive, humorous slang and iconoclasm.

For Twain and other American writers of the late 19th century, realism was not merely a literary technique: It was a way of speaking truth and exploding worn-out conventions. Thus it was profoundly liberating and potentially at odds

SAMUEL CLEMENS
(MARK TWAIN)

illustration by
Thaddeus A. Miksinski, Jr.

with society. The most well-known example is Huck Finn, a poor boy who decides to follow the voice of his conscience and help a Negro slave escape to freedom, even though Huck thinks this means that he will be damned to hell for breaking the law.

Twain's masterpiece, which appeared in 1884, is set in the Mississippi River village of St. Petersburg. The son of an alcoholic bum, Huck has just been adopted by a respectable family when his father, in a drunken stupor, threatens to kill him. Fearing for his life, Huck escapes, feigning his own death. He is joined in his escape by another outcast, the slave Jim, whose owner, Miss Watson, is thinking of selling him down the river to the harsher slavery of the deep South. Huck and Jim float on a raft down the majestic Mississippi, but are sunk by a steamboat, separated, and later reunited. They go through many comical and dangerous shore adventures that show the variety, generosity, and sometimes cruel irrationality of society. In the end, it is discovered that Miss Watson had already freed Jim, and a respectable family is taking care of the wild boy Huck. But Huck grows impatient with civilized society and plans to escape to "the territories" — Indian lands. The ending gives the reader the counter-version of the classic American success myth: the open road leading to the pristine wilderness, away from the morally corrupting influences of "civilization." James Fenimore

Cooper's novels, Walt Whitman's hymns to the open road, William Faulkner's *The Bear,* and Jack Kerouac's *On the Road* are other literary examples.

Huckleberry Finn has inspired countless literary interpretations. Clearly, the novel is a story of death, rebirth, and initiation. The escaped slave, Jim, becomes a father figure for Huck; in deciding to save Jim, Huck grows morally beyond the bounds of his slave-owning society. It is Jim's adventures that initiate Huck into the complexities of human nature and give him moral courage.

The novel also dramatizes Twain's ideal of the harmonious community: "What you want, above all things, on a raft is for everybody to be satisfied and feel right and kind toward the others." Like Melville's ship the *Pequod*, the raft sinks, and with it that special community. The pure, simple world of the raft is ultimately overwhelmed by progress — the steamboat — but the mythic image of the river remains, as vast and changing as life itself.

The unstable relationship between reality and illusion is Twain's characteristic theme, the basis of much of his humor. The magnificent yet deceptive, constantly changing river is also the main feature of his imaginative landscape. In *Life on the Mississippi*, Twain recalls his training as a young steamboat pilot when he writes: "I went to work now to learn the shape of the river; and of all the eluding and ungraspable objects that ever I tried to get mind or hands on, that was the chief."

Twain's moral sense as a writer echoes his pilot's responsibility to steer the ship to safety. Samuel Clemens's pen name, "Mark Twain," is the phrase Mississippi boatmen used to signify two fathoms (3.6 meters) of water, the depth needed for a boat's safe passage. Twain's serious purpose combined with a rare genius for humor and style keep Twain's writing fresh and appealing.

FRONTIER HUMOR AND REALISM

Two major literary currents in 19th-century America merged in Mark Twain: popular frontier humor and local color, or "regionalism." These related literary approaches began in the 1830s — and had even earlier roots in local oral traditions. In ragged frontier villages, on riverboats, in mining camps, and around cowboy campfires far from city amusements, storytelling flourished. Exaggeration, tall tales, incredible boasts, and comic workingmen heroes enlivened frontier literature. These humorous forms were found in many frontier regions — in the "old Southwest" (the present-day inland South and the lower Midwest), the mining frontier, and the Pacific Coast. Each region had its colorful characters around whom stories collected: Mike Fink, the Mississippi riverboat brawler; Casey Jones, the brave railroad engineer; John Henry, the steel-driving African-American; Paul Bunyan, the giant logger whose fame was helped along by advertising; westerners Kit Carson, the Indian fighter, and Davy Crockett, the scout. Their exploits were exaggerated and enhanced in ballads, newspapers, and magazines. Sometimes, as with Kit Carson and Davy Crockett, these stories were strung together into book form.

Twain, Faulkner, and many other writers, particularly southerners, are indebted to frontier pre-Civil War humorists such as Johnson Hooper, George Washington Harris, Augustus Longstreet, Thomas Bangs Thorpe, and Joseph Baldwin. From them and the American frontier folk came the wild proliferation of comical new American words: "absquatulate" (leave), "flabbergasted" (amazed), "rampagious" (unruly, rampaging). Local boasters, or "ring-tailed roarers," who asserted they were half horse, half alligator, also underscored the boundless energy of the frontier. They drew strength from natural hazards that would terrify lesser men. "I'm a regular tornado," one swelled, "tough as hickory and long-winded as a nor'wester. I can strike a blow like a falling tree, and every lick makes a gap in the crowd that lets in an acre of sunshine."

LOCAL COLORISTS

Like frontier humor, local color writing has old roots but produced its best works long after the Civil War. Obviously, many pre-war writers, from Henry David Thoreau and Nathaniel Hawthorne to James Greenleaf Whittier and James Russell Lowell, paint striking portraits of specific American regions. What sets the colorists apart is their self-conscious and exclusive interest in rendering a given location, and their scrupulously factual, realistic technique.

Bret Harte (1836-1902) is remembered as the author of adventurous stories such as "The Luck of Roaring Camp" and "The Outcasts of Poker Flat," set along the western mining frontier. As the first great success in the local colorist school, Harte for a brief time was perhaps the best-known writer in America — such was the appeal of his romantic version of the gun-slinging West. Outwardly realistic, he was one of the first to introduce low-life characters — cunning gamblers, gaudy prostitutes, and uncouth robbers — into serious literary works. He got away with this (as had Charles Dickens in England, who greatly admired Harte's work) by showing in the end that these seeming derelicts really had hearts of gold.

Several women writers are remembered for their fine depictions

SARAH ORNE JEWETT

Photo © The Bettmann Archive

of New England: Mary Wilkins Freeman (1852-1930), Harriet Beecher Stowe (1811-1896), and especially Sarah Orne Jewett (1849-1909). Jewett's originality, exact observation of her Maine characters and setting, and sensitive style are best seen in her fine story "The White Heron" in *Country of the Pointed Firs* (1896). Harriet Beecher Stowe's local color works, especially *The Pearl of Orr's Island* (1862), depicting humble Maine fishing communities, greatly influenced Jewett. Nineteenth-century women writers formed their own networks of moral support and influence, as their letters show. Women made up the major audience for fiction, and many women wrote popular novels, poems, and humorous pieces.

All regions of the country celebrated themselves in writing influenced by local color. Some of it included social protest, especially toward the end of the century, when social inequality and economic hardship were particularly pressing issues. Racial injustice and inequality between the sexes appear in the works of southern writers such as George Washington Cable (1844-1925) and Kate Chopin (1851-1904), whose powerful novels set in Cajun/French Louisiana transcend the local color label. Cable's *The Grandissimes* (1880) treats racial injustice with great artistry; like Kate Chopin's daring novel *The Awakening* (1899), about a woman's doomed attempt to find her own identity through passion, it was ahead of its time. In *The Awakening*, a young married woman with attractive children and an indulgent and successful husband gives up family, money, respectability, and eventually her life in search of self-realization. Poetic evocations of ocean, birds (caged and freed), and music endow this short novel with unusual intensity and complexity.

Often paired with *The Awakening* is the fine story "The Yellow Wallpaper" (1892) by Charlotte Perkins Gilman (1860-1935). Both works were forgotten for a time, but rediscovered by feminist literary critics late in the 20th century. In Gilman's story, a condescending doctor drives his wife mad by confining her in a room to "cure" her of nervous exhaustion. The imprisoned wife projects her entrapment onto the wallpaper, in the design of which she sees imprisoned women creeping behind bars.

MIDWESTERN REALISM

For many years, the editor of the important *Atlantic Monthly* magazine, William Dean Howells (1837-1920) published realistic local color writing by Bret Harte, Mark Twain, George Washington Cable, and others. He was the champion of realism, and his novels, such as *A Modern Instance* (1882), *The Rise of Silas Lapham* (1885), and *A Hazard of New Fortunes* (1890), carefully interweave social circumstances with the emotions of ordinary middle-class Americans.

WILLIAM DEAN HOWELLS

Photo © The Bettmann Archive

Love, ambition, idealism, and temptation motivate his characters; Howells was acutely aware of the moral corruption of business tycoons during the Gilded Age of the 1870s. Howells's *The Rise of Silas Lapham* uses an ironic title to make this point. Silas Lapham became rich by cheating an old business partner; and his immoral act deeply disturbed his family, though for years Lapham could not see that he had acted improperly. In the end, Lapham is morally redeemed, choosing bankruptcy rather than unethical success. Silas Lapham is, like Huckleberry Finn, an unsuccess story: Lapham's business fall is his moral rise. Toward the end of his life, Howells, like Twain, became increasingly active in political causes, defending the rights of labor union organizers and deploring American colonialism in the Philippines.

COSMOPOLITAN NOVELISTS
Henry James (1843-1916)

Henry James once wrote that art, especially literary art, "makes life, makes interest, makes importance." James's fiction and criticism is the most highly conscious, sophisticated, and difficult of its era. With Twain, James is generally ranked as the greatest American novelist of the second half of the 19th century.

James is noted for his "international theme" — that is, the complex relationships between naïve Americans and cosmopolitan Europeans. What his biographer Leon

Edel calls James's first, or "international," phase encompassed such works as *Transatlantic Sketches* (travel pieces, 1875), *The American* (1877), *Daisy Miller* (1879), and a masterpiece, *The Portrait of a Lady* (1881). In *The American*, for example, Christopher Newman, a naïve but intelligent and idealistic self-made millionaire industrialist, goes to Europe seeking a bride. When her family rejects him because he lacks an aristocratic background, he has a chance to revenge himself; in deciding not to, he demonstrates his moral superiority.

James's second period was experimental. He exploited new subject matters — feminism and social reform in *The Bostonians* (1886) and political intrigue in *The Princess Casamassima* (1885). He also attempted to write for the theater, but failed embarrassingly when his play *Guy Domville* (1895) was booed on the first night.

In his third, or "major," phase James returned to international subjects, but treated them with increasing sophistication and psychological penetration. The complex and almost mythical *The Wings of the Dove* (1902), *The Ambassadors* (1903) (which James felt was his best novel), and *The Golden Bowl* (1904) date from this major period. If the main theme of Twain's work is appearance and reality, James's constant concern is perception. In James, only self-awareness and clear perception of others yields wisdom and self-sacrificing

HENRY JAMES

love. As James develops, his novels become more psychological and less concerned with external events. In James's later works, the most important events are all psychological — usually moments of intense illumination that show characters their previous blindness. For example, in *The Ambassadors*, the idealistic, aging Lambert Strether uncovers a secret love affair and, in doing so, discovers a new complexity to his inner life. His rigid, upright, morality is humanized and enlarged as he discovers a capacity to accept those who have sinned.

Edith Wharton (1862-1937)

Like James, Edith Wharton grew up partly in Europe and eventually made her home there. She was descended from a wealthy, established family in New York society and saw firsthand the decline of this cultivated group and, in her view, the rise of boorish, nouveau-riche business families. This social transformation is the background of many of her novels.

Like James, Wharton contrasts Americans and Europeans. The core of her concern is the gulf separating social reality and the inner self. Often a sensitive character feels trapped by unfeeling characters or social forces. Edith Wharton had personally experienced such entrapment, as a young writer suffering a long nervous breakdown partly due to the conflict in roles between writer and wife.

Wharton's best novels include *The House of Mirth* (1905), *The Custom of the Country* (1913), *Summer* (1917), *The Age of Innocence* (1920), and the beautifully crafted novella *Ethan Frome* (1911).

NATURALISM AND MUCKRAKING

Wharton's and James's dissections of hidden sexual and financial motivations at work in society link them with writers who seem superficially quite different: Stephen Crane, Jack London, Frank Norris, Theodore Dreiser, and Upton Sinclair. Like the cosmopolitan novelists, but much more explicitly, these naturalists used realism to relate the individual to society. Often they exposed social problems and were influenced by Darwinian thought and the related philosophical doctrine of determinism, which views individuals as the helpless pawns of economic and social forces beyond their control.

Naturalism is essentially a literary expression of determinism. Associated with bleak, realistic depictions of lower-class life, determinism denies religion as a motivating force in the world and instead perceives the universe as a machine. Eighteenth-century Enlightenment thinkers had also imagined the world as a machine, but as a perfect one, invented by God and tending toward progress and human betterment. Naturalists imagined society, instead, as a blind machine, godless and out of control.

STEPHEN CRANE

Photo courtesy
Library of Congress

The 19th-century American historian Henry Adams constructed an elaborate theory of history involving the idea of the dynamo, or machine force, and entropy, or decay of force. Instead of progress, Adams sees inevitable decline in human society.

Stephen Crane, the son of a clergyman, put the loss of God most succinctly:

A man said to the universe:
"Sir, I exist!"
"However," replied the universe,
"The fact has not created in me
A sense of obligation."

Like Romanticism, naturalism first appeared in Europe. It is usually traced to the works of Honoré de Balzac in the 1840s and seen as a French literary movement associated with Gustave Flaubert, Edmond and Jules Goncourt, Émile Zola, and Guy de Maupassant. It daringly opened up the seamy underside of society and such topics as divorce, sex, adultery, poverty, and crime.

Naturalism flourished as Americans became urbanized and aware of the importance of large economic and social forces. By 1890, the frontier was declared officially closed. Most Americans resided in towns, and business dominated even remote farmsteads.

Stephen Crane (1871-1900)

Stephen Crane, born in New Jersey, had roots going back to Revolutionary War soldiers, clergymen, sheriffs, judges, and farmers who had lived a century earlier. Primarily a journalist who also wrote fiction, essays, poetry, and plays, Crane saw life at its rawest, in slums and on battlefields. His short stories — in particular, "The Open Boat," "The Blue Hotel," and "The Bride Comes to Yellow Sky" — exemplified that literary form. His haunting Civil War novel, *The Red Badge of Courage*, was published to great acclaim in 1895, but he barely had time to bask in the attention before he died, at 29, having neglected his health. He was virtually forgotten during the first two decades of the 20th century, but was resurrected through a laudatory biography by Thomas Beer in 1923. He has enjoyed continued success ever since — as a champion of the common man, a realist, and a symbolist.

Crane's *Maggie: A Girl of the Streets* (1893) is one of the best, if not the earliest, naturalistic American novels. It is the harrowing story of a poor, sensitive young girl whose uneducated, alcoholic parents utterly fail her. In love and eager to escape her violent home life, she allows herself to be seduced into living with a young man, who soon deserts her. When her self-righteous mother rejects her, Maggie becomes a prostitute to survive, but soon commits suicide out of despair. Crane's earthy subject matter and his objective, scientific style, devoid of moralizing, earmark *Maggie* as a naturalist work.

Jack London (1876-1916)

A poor, self-taught worker from California, the naturalist Jack London was catapulted from poverty to fame by his first collection of stories, *The Son of the Wolf* (1900), set largely in the Klondike region of Alaska and the Canadian Yukon. Other of his best-sellers, including *The Call of the Wild* (1903) and *The Sea-Wolf* (1904), made him the highest paid writer in the United States of his time.

The autobiographical novel *Martin Eden* (1909) depicts the inner stresses of the American dream as London experienced them during his meteoric rise from obscure poverty to wealth and fame. Eden, an impoverished but intelligent and hardworking sailor and laborer, is determined to become a writer. Eventually, his writing makes him rich and well-known, but Eden realizes that the woman he loves cares only for his money and fame. His despair over her inability to love causes him to lose faith in human nature. He also suffers from class alienation, for he no longer belongs to the working class, while he rejects the materialistic values of the wealthy whom he worked so hard to join. He sails for the South Pacific and commits suicide by jumping into the sea. Like many of the best novels of its time, *Martin Eden* is an unsuccess story. It looks ahead to F. Scott Fitzgerald's *The Great Gatsby* in its revelation of despair amid great wealth.

Theodore Dreiser (1871-1945)

The 1925 work *An American Tragedy* by Theodore Dreiser, like London's *Martin Eden*, explores the dangers of the American dream. The novel relates, in great detail, the life of Clyde Griffiths, a boy of weak will and little self-awareness. He grows up in great poverty in a family of wandering evangelists, but dreams of wealth and the love of beautiful women. A rich uncle employs him in his factory. When his girlfriend Roberta becomes pregnant, she demands that he marry her. Meanwhile, Clyde has fallen in love with a wealthy society girl who represents success, money, and social acceptance. Clyde carefully plans to drown Roberta on a boat trip, but at the last minute he begins to change his mind; however, she accidentally falls out of the boat. Clyde, a good swimmer, does not save her, and she drowns. As Clyde is brought to justice, Dreiser replays his story in reverse, masterfully using the vantage points of prosecuting and defense attorneys to analyze each step and motive that led the mild-mannered Clyde, with a highly religious background and good family connections, to commit murder.

Despite his awkward style, Dreiser, in *An American Tragedy*, displays crushing authority. Its precise details build up an overwhelming sense of tragic inevitability. The novel is a scathing portrait of the American success myth gone sour, but it is also a universal story about the stresses of urbanization, modernization, and alienation. Within it roam the romantic and dangerous fantasies of the dispossessed.

An American Tragedy is a reflection of the dissatisfaction, envy, and despair that afflicted many poor and working people in America's competitive, success-driven society. As American industrial power soared, the glittering lives of the wealthy in newspapers and photographs sharply contrasted with the drab lives of ordinary farmers and city workers. The media fanned rising expectations and unreasonable desires. Such problems, common to modernizing nations, gave rise to muckraking journalism — penetrating investigative reporting that documented social problems and provided an important impetus to social reform.

The great tradition of American investigative journalism had its beginning in this period, during which national magazines such as *McClures* and *Collier's* published Ida M. Tarbell's *History of the Standard Oil Company* (1904), Lincoln Steffens's *The Shame of the Cities* (1904), and other hard-hit-

THEODORE DREISER

Photo © The Bettmann Archive

ting exposés. Muckraking novels used eye-catching journalistic techniques to depict harsh working conditions and oppression. Populist Frank Norris's *The Octopus* (1901) exposed big railroad companies, while socialist Upton Sinclair's *The Jungle* (1906) painted the squalor of the Chicago meat-packing houses. Jack London's dystopia *The Iron Heel* (1908) anticipates George Orwell's *1984* in predicting a class war and the takeover of the government.

Another more artistic response was the realistic portrait, or group of portraits, of ordinary characters and their frustrated inner lives. The collection of stories *Main-Travelled Roads* (1891), by William Dean Howells's protégé, Hamlin Garland (1860-1940), is a portrait gallery of ordinary people. It shockingly depicted the poverty of midwestern farmers who were demanding agricultural reforms. The title suggests the many trails westward that the hardy pioneers followed and the dusty main streets of the villages they settled.

Close to Garland's *Main-Travelled Roads* is *Winesburg, Ohio*, by Sherwood Anderson (1876-1941), begun in 1916. This is a loose collection of stories about residents of the fictitious town of Winesburg seen through the eyes of a naïve young newspaper reporter, George Willard, who eventually leaves to seek his fortune in the city. Like *Main-Travelled Roads* and other naturalistic works of the period, *Winesburg, Ohio* emphasizes the quiet poverty, loneliness, and despair in small-town America.

THE "CHICAGO SCHOOL" OF POETRY

Three Midwestern poets who grew up in Illinois and shared the midwestern concern with ordinary people are Carl Sandburg, Vachel Lindsay, and Edgar Lee Masters. Their poetry often concerns obscure individuals; they developed techniques — realism, dramatic renderings — that reached out to a larger readership. They are part of the Midwestern, or Chicago School, that arose before World War I to challenge the East Coast literary establishment. The "Chicago Renaissance" was a watershed in American culture: It demonstrated that America's interior had matured.

Edgar Lee Masters (1868-1950)

By the turn of the century, Chicago had become a great city, home of innovative architecture and cosmopolitan art collections. Chicago was also the home of Harriet Monroe's *Poetry*, the most important literary magazine of the day.

Among the intriguing contemporary poets the journal printed was Edgar Lee Masters, author of the daring *Spoon River Anthology* (1915), with its new "unpoetic" colloquial style, frank presentation of sex, critical view of village life, and intensely imagined inner lives of ordinary people.

Spoon River Anthology is a collection of portraits presented as colloquial epitaphs (words found inscribed on gravestones) summing up the lives of individual villagers as if in their own words. It presents a panorama of a country village through its cemetery: 250 people buried there speak, revealing their deepest secrets. Many of the people are related; members of about 20 families speak of their failures and dreams in free-verse monologues that are surprisingly modern.

Carl Sandburg (1878-1967)

A friend once said, "Trying to write briefly about Carl Sandburg is like trying to picture the Grand Canyon in one black-and-white snapshot." Poet, historian, biographer, novelist, musician, essayist — Sandburg, son of a railroad blacksmith, was all of these and more. A journalist by profession, he wrote a massive biography of Abraham Lincoln that is one of the classic works of the 20th century.

To many, Sandburg was a latter-day Walt Whitman, writing expansive, evocative urban and patriotic poems and simple, childlike rhymes and ballads. He traveled about reciting and recording his poetry, in a lilting, mellifluously toned voice that was a kind of singing. At heart he was totally unassuming, notwithstanding his national fame. What he wanted from life, he once said, was "to be out of jail...to eat regular..to get what I write printed,...a little love at home and a little nice affection hither and yon over the American landscape,...(and) to sing every day."

A fine example of his themes and his Whitmanesque style is the poem "Chicago" (1914):

Hog Butcher for the World,
Tool Maker, Stacker of Wheat,
Player with Railroads and the
Nation's Freight Handler;
Stormy, husky, brawling,
City of the Big Shoulders...

Vachel Lindsay (1879-1931)

Vachel Lindsay was a celebrant of small-town midwestern populism and creator of strong, rhythmic poetry designed to be declaimed aloud. His work forms a curious link between the popular, or folk, forms of poetry, such as Christian gospel songs and vaudeville (popular theater) on the one hand, and advanced modernist poetics on the other. An extremely popular public reader in his day, Lindsay's readings prefigure "Beat" poetry readings of the post-World War II era that were accompanied by jazz.

To popularize poetry, Lindsay developed what he called a "higher vaudeville," using music and strong rhythm. Racist by today's standards, his famous poem "The Congo" (1914) celebrates the history of Africans by mingling jazz, poetry, music, and chanting. At the same time, he immortalized such figures on the American landscape as Abraham Lincoln ("Abraham Lincoln Walks at Midnight") and John Chapman ("Johnny Appleseed"), often blending facts with myth.

Edwin Arlington Robinson (1869-1935)

Edwin Arlington Robinson is the best U.S. poet of the late 19th century. Like Edgar Lee Masters, he is known for short, ironic character studies of ordinary individuals. Unlike Masters, Robinson uses traditional metrics. Robinson's imaginary Tilbury Town, like Masters's Spoon River, contains lives of quiet desperation.

Some of the best known of Robinson's dramatic monologues are "Luke Havergal" (1896), about a forsaken lover; "Miniver Cheevy" (1910), a portrait of a romantic dreamer; and "Richard Cory" (1896), a somber portrait of a wealthy man who commits suicide:

WILLA CATHER

Whenever Richard Cory went
    down town,
We people on the pavement
    looked at him:
He was a gentleman from sole to
    crown,
Clean favored, and imperially slim,

And he was always quietly
    arrayed,
And he was always human when
    he talked;
But still he fluttered pulses
    when he said,
"Good-morning," and he glittered when he walked.

And he was rich — yes, richer
    than a king —
And admirably schooled in every
    grace:
In fine, we thought that he was
    everything
To make us wish that we were in
    his place.

So on we worked, and waited for
    the light,
And went without the meat, and
    cursed the bread;
And Richard Cory, one calm summer night,
Went home and put a bullet
    through his head.

"Richard Cory" takes its place alongside *Martin Eden, An American Tragedy,* and *The Great Gatsby* as a powerful warning against the overblown success myth that had come to plague Americans in the era of the millionaire.

TWO WOMEN REGIONAL NOVELISTS

Novelists Ellen Glasgow (1873-1945) and Willa Cather (1873-1947) explored women's lives, placed in brilliantly evoked regional settings. Neither novelist set out to address specifically female issues; their early works usually treat male protagonists, and only as they gained artistic confidence and maturity did they turn to depictions of women's lives. Glasgow and Cather can only be regarded as "women writers" in a descriptive sense, for their works resist categorization.

Glasgow was from Richmond, Virginia, the old capital of the Southern Confederacy. Her realistic novels examine the transformation of the South from a rural to an industrial economy. Mature works such as *Virginia* (1912) focus on the southern experience, while later novels like *Barren Ground* (1925) — acknowledged as her best — dramatize gifted women attempting to surmount the claustrophobic, traditional southern code of domesticity, piety, and dependence for women.

Cather, another Virginian, grew up on the Nebraska prairie among pioneering immigrants — later immortalized in *O Pioneers!* (1913), *My Antonia* (1918), and her well-known story "Neighbour Rosicky" (1928). During her lifetime she became increasingly alienated from the materialism of modern life and wrote of alternative visions in the American Southwest and in the

BOOKER
T. WASHINGTON

past. *Death Comes for the Archbishop* (1927) evokes the idealism of two 16th-century priests establishing the Catholic Church in the New Mexican desert. Cather's works commemorate important aspects of the American experience outside the literary mainstream — pioneering, the establishment of religion, and women's independent lives.

THE RISE OF BLACK AMERICAN LITERATURE

The literary achievement of African-Americans was one of the most striking literary developments of the post-Civil War era. In the writings of Booker T. Washington, W.E.B. Du Bois, James Weldon Johnson, Charles Waddell Chesnutt, Paul Laurence Dunbar, and others, the roots of black American writing took hold, notably in the forms of autobiography, protest literature, sermons, poetry, and song.

Booker T. Washington (1856-1915)

Booker T. Washington, educator and the most prominent black leader of his day, grew up as a slave in Franklin County, Virginia, born to a white slave-holding father and a slave mother. His fine, simple autobiography, *Up From Slavery* (1901), recounts his successful struggle to better himself. He became renowned for his efforts to improve the lives of African-Americans; his policy of accommodation with whites — an attempt to involve the recently freed black American in the mainstream of American society — was outlined in his famous Atlanta Exposition Address (1895).

W.E.B. Du Bois (1868-1963)

Born in New England and educated at Harvard University and the University of Berlin (Germany), W.E.B. Du Bois authored "Of Mr. Booker T. Washington and Others," an essay later collected in his landmark book *The Souls of Black Folk* (1903). Du Bois carefully demonstrates that despite his many accomplishments, Washington had, in effect, accepted segregation — that is, the unequal and separate treatment of black Americans — and that segregation would inevitably lead to inferiority, particularly in education. Du Bois, a founder of the National Association for the Advancement of Colored People (NAACP), also wrote sensitive appreciations of the African-American traditions and culture; his work helped black intellectuals rediscover their rich folk literature and music.

James Weldon Johnson (1871-1938)

Like Du Bois, the poet James Weldon Johnson found inspiration in African-American spirituals.

His poem "O Black and Unknown Bards" (1917) asks:

Heart of what slave poured out such melody
As "Steal Away to Jesus?" On its strains
His spirit must have nightly floated free,
Though still about his hands he felt his chains.

Of mixed white and black ancestry, Johnson explored the complex issue of race in his fictional *Autobiography of an Ex-Colored Man* (1912), about a mixed-race man who "passes" (is accepted) for white. The book effectively conveys the black American's concern with issues of identity in America.

Charles Waddell Chesnutt (1858-1932)

Charles Waddell Chesnutt, author of two collections of stories, *The Conjure Woman* (1899) and *The Wife of His Youth* (1899), several novels, including *The Marrow of Tradition* (1901), and a biography of Frederick Douglass, was ahead of his time. His stories dwell on racial themes, but avoid predictable endings and generalized sentiment; his characters are distinct individuals with complex attitudes about many things, including race. Chesnutt often shows the strength of the black community and affirms ethical values and racial solidarity. ■

CHAPTER

6

MODERNISM AND EXPERIMENTATION: 1914-1945

Many historians have characterized the period between the two world wars as the United States' traumatic "coming of age," despite the fact that U.S. direct involvement was relatively brief (1917-1918) and its casualties many fewer than those of its European allies and foes. John Dos Passos expressed America's postwar disillusionment in the novel *Three Soldiers* (1921), when he noted that civilization was a "vast edifice of sham, and the war, instead of its crumbling, was its fullest and most ultimate expression." Shocked and permanently changed, Americans returned to their homeland but could never regain their innocence.

Nor could soldiers from rural America easily return to their roots. After experiencing the world, many now yearned for a modern, urban life. New farm machines such as planters, harvesters, and binders had drastically reduced the demand for farm jobs; yet despite their increased productivity, farmers were poor. Crop prices, like urban workers' wages, depended on unrestrained market forces heavily influenced by business interests: Government subsidies for farmers and effective workers' unions had not yet become established. "The chief business of the American people is business," President Calvin Coolidge proclaimed in 1925, and most agreed.

In the postwar "Big Boom," business flourished, and the successful prospered beyond their wildest dreams. For the first time, many Americans enrolled in higher education — in the 1920s college enrollment doubled. The middle-class prospered; Americans began to enjoy the world's highest national average income in this era, and many people purchased the ultimate status symbol — an automobile. The typical urban American home glowed with electric lights and boasted a radio that connected the house with the outside world, and perhaps a telephone, a camera, a typewriter, or a sewing machine. Like the businessman protagonist of Sinclair Lewis's novel *Babbitt* (1922), the average American approved of these machines because they were modern and because most were American inventions and American-made.

Americans of the "Roaring Twenties" fell in love with other modern entertainments. Most people went to the movies once a week. Although Prohibition — a nationwide ban on the production, transport, and sale of alcohol instituted through the 18th Amendment to the U.S. Constitution — began in 1919, underground "speak-easies" and nightclubs proliferated, featuring jazz music, cocktails, and daring modes of dress and dance. Dancing, moviegoing, automobile touring, and radio were national crazes. American women, in particular, felt liberated. Many had left farms and villages for homefront duty in American cities during World War I, and had become resolutely modern. They cut their hair short ("bobbed"), wore short "flapper" dresses, and gloried in the right to vote assured by the 19th Amendment to the Constitution, passed in 1920. They boldly spoke their mind and took public roles in society.

Western youths were rebelling, angry and disillusioned with the savage war, the older generation they held responsible, and difficult postwar economic conditions that, ironically, allowed Americans with dollars — like writers F. Scott Fitzgerald, Ernest Hemingway, Gertrude Stein, and Ezra Pound — to live abroad handsomely on very little money. Intellectual currents, particularly Freudian psychology and to a lesser extent Marxism (like the earlier Darwinian theory of evolution), implied a "godless" world view and contributed to the breakdown of traditional values. Americans abroad absorbed these views and brought them back to the United States where they took root, firing the imagination of young writers and artists. William Faulkner, for example, a 20th-century American novelist, employed Freudian elements in all his works, as did virtually all serious American fiction writers after World War I.

Despite outward gaiety, modernity, and unparalleled material prosperity, young Americans of the 1920s were "the lost generation" — so named by literary portraitist Gertrude Stein. Without a stable, traditional structure of values, the individual lost a sense of identity. The secure, supportive family life; the familiar, settled community; the natural and eternal rhythms of nature that guide the planting and harvesting on a farm; the sustaining sense of patriotism; moral values inculcated by religious beliefs and observations — all seemed undermined by World War I and its aftermath.

Numerous novels, notably Hemingway's *The Sun Also Rises* (1926) and Fitzgerald's *This Side of Paradise* (1920), evoke the extravagance and disillusionment of the lost generation. In T.S. Eliot's influential long poem *The Waste Land* (1922), Western civilization is symbolized by a bleak desert in desperate need of rain (spiritual renewal).

The world depression of the 1930s affected most of the population of the United States. Workers lost their jobs, and factories shut down; businesses and banks failed; farmers, unable to harvest, transport, or sell their crops, could not pay their debts and lost their farms. Midwestern droughts turned the "breadbasket" of America into a dust bowl. Many farmers left the Midwest for California in search of jobs, as vividly described in John Steinbeck's *The Grapes of Wrath* (1939). At the peak of the Depression, one-third of all Americans were out of work. Soup kitchens, shanty towns, and armies of hobos — unemployed men illegally riding freight trains — became part of national life. Many saw the Depression as a punishment for sins of excessive materialism and loose living. The dust storms that blackened the midwestern sky, they believed, constituted an Old Testament judgment: the "whirlwind by day and the darkness at noon."

The Depression turned the world upside down. The United States had preached a gospel of business in the 1920s; now, many Americans supported a more active role for government in the New Deal programs of President Franklin D. Roosevelt. Federal money created jobs in public works, conservation, and rural electrification. Artists and intellectuals were paid to create murals and state handbooks. These remedies helped, but only the industrial build-up of World War II renewed prosperity. After Japan attacked the United States at Pearl Harbor on December 7, 1941, disused shipyards and factories came to bustling life mass-producing ships, airplanes, jeeps, and supplies. War production and experimentation led to new technologies, including the nuclear bomb. Witnessing the first experimental nuclear blast, Robert Oppenheimer, leader of an international team of nuclear scientists, prophetically quoted a Hindu poem: "I am become Death, the shatterer of worlds."

MODERNISM

The large cultural wave of Modernism, which gradually emerged in Europe and the United States in the early years of the 20th century, expressed a sense of modern life through art as a sharp break from the past, as well as from Western civilization's classical traditions. Modern life seemed radically different from traditional life — more scientific, faster, more technological, and more mechanized. Modernism embraced these changes.

In literature, Gertrude Stein (1874-1946) developed an analogue to modern art. A resident of Paris and an art collector (she and her brother Leo purchased works of the artists Paul Cézanne, Paul Gauguin, Pierre Auguste Renoir, Pablo Picasso, and many others), Stein once explained that she and Picasso were doing the same thing, he in art and she in writing. Using simple, concrete words as counters, she developed an abstract, experimental prose poetry. The childlike quality of Stein's simple vocabulary recalls the bright, primary colors of modern art, while her repetitions echo the repeated shapes of abstract visual compositions. By dislocating grammar and punctuation, she achieved new "abstract" meanings as in her influential collection *Tender Buttons* (1914), which views objects from different angles, as in a cubist painting:

A Table A Table means does it not my
dear it means a whole steadiness.
Is it likely that a change. A table
means more than a glass
even a looking glass is tall.

Meaning, in Stein's work, was often subordinated to technique, just as subject was less important than shape in abstract visual art. Subject and technique became inseparable in both the visual and literary art of the period. The idea of form as the equivalent of content, a cornerstone of post-World War II art and literature, crystallized in this period.

Technological innovation in the world of factories and machines inspired new attentiveness to technique in the arts. To take one example: Light, particularly electrical light, fascinated modern artists and writers. Posters and advertisements of the period are full of images of floodlit skyscrapers and light rays shooting out from automobile headlights, moviehouses, and watch-towers to illumine a forbidding outer darkness suggesting ignorance and old-fashioned tradition.

Photography began to assume the status of a fine art allied with the latest scientific developments. The photographer Alfred Stieglitz opened a salon in New York City, and by 1908 he was showing the latest European works, including pieces by Picasso and other European friends of Gertrude Stein. Stieglitz's salon influenced numerous writers and artists, including William Carlos Williams, who was one of the most influential American poets of the 20th century. Williams cultivated a photographic clarity of image; his aesthetic dictum was "no ideas but in things."

Vision and viewpoint became an essential aspect of the modernist novel as well. No longer was it sufficient to write a straightforward third-person narrative or (worse yet) use a pointlessly intrusive narrator. The way the story was told became as important as the story itself.

Henry James, William Faulkner, and many other American writers experimented with fictional points of view (some are still doing so). James often restricted the information in the novel to what a single character would have known. Faulkner's novel *The Sound and The Fury* (1929) breaks up the narrative into four sections, each giving the viewpoint of a different character (including a mentally retarded boy).

To analyze such modernist novels and poetry, a school of "New Criticism" arose in the United States, with a new critical vocabulary. New Critics hunted the "epiphany" (moment in which a character suddenly sees the transcendent truth of a situation, a term derived from a holy saint's appearance to mortals); they "examined" and "clarified" a work, hoping to "shed light" upon it through their "insights."

POETRY 1914-1945:
EXPERIMENTS IN FORM
Ezra Pound (1885-1972)

Ezra Pound was one of the most influential American poets of this century. From 1908 to 1920, he resided in London where he associated with many writers, including William Butler Yeats, for whom he worked as a secretary, and T.S. Eliot, whose *Waste Land* he drastically edited and improved. He was a link between the United States and Britain, acting as contributing editor to Harriet Monroe's important Chicago magazine *Poetry* and spearheading the new school of poetry known as Imagism, which advocated a clear, highly visual presentation. After Imagism, he championed various poetic approaches. He eventually moved to Italy, where he became caught up in Italian Fascism.

Pound furthered Imagism in letters, essays, and an anthology. In a letter to Monroe in 1915, he argues for a modern-sounding, visual poetry that avoids "clichés and set phrases." In "A Few Don'ts of an Imagiste" (1913), he defined "image" as something that "presents an intellectual and emotional complex in an instant of time." Pound's 1914 anthology of 10 poets, *Des Imagistes*, offered examples of Imagist poetry by outstanding poets, including William Carlos Williams, H.D. (Hilda Doolittle), and Amy Lowell.

Pound's interests and reading were universal. His adaptations and brilliant, if sometimes flawed,

T.S. ELIOT

Photo courtesy Acme Photos

translations introduced new literary possibilities from many cultures to modern writers. His life-work was *The Cantos*, which he wrote and published until his death. They contain brilliant passages, but their allusions to works of literature and art from many eras and cultures make them difficult. Pound's poetry is best known for its clear, visual images, fresh rhythms, and muscular, intelligent, unusual lines, such as, in Canto LXXXI, "The ant's a centaur in his dragon world," or in poems inspired by Japanese haiku, such as "In a Station of the Metro" (1916):

> The apparition of these faces in
>   the crowd;
> Petals on a wet, black bough.

T.S. Eliot (1888-1965)

Thomas Stearns Eliot was born in St. Louis, Missouri, to a well-to-do family with roots in the northeastern United States. He received the best education of any major American writer of his generation at Harvard College, the Sorbonne, and Merton College of Oxford University. He studied Sanskrit and Oriental philosophy, which influenced his poetry. Like his friend Pound, he went to England early and became a towering figure in the literary world there. One of the most respected poets of his day, his modernist, seemingly illogical or abstract iconoclastic poetry had revolutionary impact. He also wrote influential essays and dramas, and championed the importance of literary and social traditions for the modern poet.

As a critic, Eliot is best remembered for his formulation of the "objective correlative," which he described, in *The Sacred Wood*, as a means of expressing emotion through "a set of objects, a situation, a chain of events" that would be the "formula" of that particular emotion. Poems such as "The Love Song of J. Alfred Prufrock" (1915) embody this approach, when the ineffectual, elderly Prufrock thinks to himself that he has "measured out his life in coffee spoons," using coffee spoons to reflect a humdrum existence and a wasted lifetime.

The famous beginning of Eliot's "Prufrock" invites the reader into tawdry alleys that, like modern life, offer no answers to the questions life poses:

> Let us go then, you and I,
> When the evening is spread
>   out against the sky
> Like a patient etherized upon
>   a table;
> Let us go, through certain half-
>   deserted streets,
> The muttering retreats
> Of restless nights in one-night
>   cheap hotels
> And sawdust restaurants with
>   oyster-shells:
> Streets that follow like a
>   tedious argument
> Of insidious intent
> To lead you to an overwhelm-
>   ing question...
> Oh, do not ask, "What is it?"

Robert Frost

Let us go and make our visit.

Similar imagery pervades *The Waste Land* (1922), which echoes Dante's Inferno to evoke London's thronged streets around the time of World War I:

> Unreal City,
> Under the brown fog of a winter
>   dawn,
> A crowd flowed over London
>   Bridge, so many
> I had not thought death had
>   undone so many... (I, 60-63)

The Waste Land's vision is ultimately apocalyptic and worldwide:

> Cracks and reforms and bursts
>   in the violet air
> Falling towers
> Jerusalem, Athens, Alexandria
> Vienna London
> Unreal (V, 373-377)

Eliot's other major poems include "Gerontion" (1920), which uses an elderly man to symbolize the decrepitude of Western society; "The Hollow Men" (1925), a moving dirge for the death of the spirit of contemporary humanity; *Ash-Wednesday* (1930), in which he turns explicitly toward the Church of England for meaning in human life; and *Four Quartets* (1943), a complex, highly subjective, experimental meditation on transcendent subjects such as time, the nature of self, and spiritual awareness. His poetry, especially his daring, innovative early work, has influenced generations.

Robert Frost (1874-1963)

Robert Lee Frost was born in California but raised on a farm in the northeastern United States until the age of 10. Like Eliot and Pound, he went to England, attracted by new movements in poetry there. A charismatic public reader, he was renowned for his tours. He read an original work at the inauguration of President John F. Kennedy in 1961 that helped spark a national interest in poetry. His popularity is easy to explain: He wrote of traditional farm life, appealing to a nostalgia for the old ways. His subjects are universal — apple picking, stone walls, fences, country roads. Frost's approach was lucid and accessible: He rarely employed pedantic allusions or ellipses. His frequent use of rhyme also appealed to the general audience.

Frost's work is often deceptively simple. Many poems suggest a deeper meaning. For example, a quiet snowy evening by an almost hypnotic rhyme scheme may suggest the not entirely unwelcome approach of death. From: "Stopping by Woods on a Snowy Evening" (1923):

Whose woods these are I think I know.
His house is in the village, though;
He will not see me stopping here
To watch his woods fill up with snow.

My little horse must think it queer
To stop without a farmhouse near
Between the woods and frozen lake
The darkest evening of the year.

He gives his harness bells a shake
To ask if there is some mistake.
The only other sound's the sweep
Of easy wind and downy flake.

The woods are lovely, dark and deep,
But I have promises to keep,
And miles to go before I sleep,
And miles to go before I sleep.

Wallace Stevens (1879-1955)

Born in Pennsylvania, Wallace Stevens was educated at Harvard College and New York University Law School. He practiced law in New York City from 1904 to 1916, a time of great artistic and poetic activity there. On moving to Hartford, Connecticut, to become an insurance executive in 1916, he continued writing poetry. His life is remarkable for its compartmentalization: His associates in the insurance company did not know that he was a major poet. In private he continued to develop extremely complex ideas of aesthetic order throughout his life in aptly named books such as *Harmonium* (enlarged edition 1931), *Ideas of Order*

WALLACE STEVENS

(1935), and *Parts of a World* (1942). Some of his best known poems are "Sunday Morning," "Peter Quince at the Clavier," "The Emperor of Ice-Cream," "Thirteen Ways of Looking at a Blackbird," and "The Idea of Order at Key West."

Stevens's poetry dwells upon themes of the imagination, the necessity for aesthetic form and the belief that the order of art corresponds with an order in nature. His vocabulary is rich and various: He paints lush tropical scenes but also manages dry, humorous, and ironic vignettes.

Some of his poems draw upon popular culture, while others poke fun at sophisticated society or soar into an intellectual heaven. He is known for his exuberant word play: "Soon, with a noise like tambourines / Came her attendant Byzantines."

Stevens's work is full of surprising insights. Sometimes he plays tricks on the reader, as in "Disillusionment of Ten O'Clock" (1931):

The houses are haunted
By white night-gowns.
None are green,
Or purple with green rings,
Or green with yellow rings,
Or yellow with blue rings.
None of them are strange,
With socks of lace
And beaded ceintures.
People are not going
To dream of baboons and periwinkles.
Only, here and there, an old sailor,
Drunk and asleep in his boots,
Catches tigers
In red weather.

This poem seems to complain about unimaginative lives (plain white night-gowns), but actually conjures up vivid images in the reader's mind. At the end a drunken sailor, oblivious to the proprieties, does "catch tigers" — at least in his dream. The poem shows that the human imagination — of reader or sailor — will always find a creative outlet.

William Carlos Williams (1883-1963)

William Carlos Williams was a practicing pediatrician throughout his life; he delivered over 2,000 babies and wrote poems on his prescription pads. Williams was a classmate of poets Ezra Pound and Hilda Doolittle, and his early poetry reveals the influence of Imagism. He later went on to champion the use of colloquial speech; his ear for the natural rhythms of American English helped free American poetry from the iambic meter that had dominated English verse since the Renaissance. His sympathy for ordinary working people, children, and everyday events in modern urban settings make his poetry attractive and accessible. "The Red Wheelbarrow" (1923), like a Dutch still life, finds interest and beauty in everyday objects:

So much depends
upon

a red wheel
barrow

glazed with rain
water

beside the white
chickens.

Williams cultivated a relaxed, natural poetry. In his hands, the poem was not to become a perfect object of art as in Stevens, or the carefully recreated Wordsworthian incident as in Frost. Instead, the poem was to capture an instant of time like an unposed snapshot — a concept he derived from photographers and artists he met at galleries like Stieglitz's in New York City. Like photographs, his poems often hint at hidden possibilities or attractions, as in "The Young Housewife" (1917):

At ten a.m. the young housewife
moves about in negligee behind
the wooden walls of her
    huband's house.
I pass solitary in my car.

Then again she comes to the
    curb,
to call the ice-man, fish-man,
    and stands
shy, uncorseted, tucking in
stray ends of hair, and I
    compare her
To a fallen leaf.

The noiseless wheels of my car
rush with a crackling sound over
dried leaves as I bow and pass
    smiling.

He termed his work "objectivist"
to suggest the importance of concrete, visual objects. His work often
captured the spontaneous, emotive
pattern of experience, and influenced the "Beat" writing of the
early 1950s.

Like Eliot and Pound, Williams
tried his hand at the epic form, but
while their epics employ literary
allusions directed to a small number of highly educated readers,
Williams instead writes for a more
general audience. Though he studied abroad, he elected to live in the
United States. His epic, *Paterson*
(five vols., 1946-1958), celebrates
his hometown of Paterson, New
Jersey, as seen by an autobiographical "Dr. Paterson." In it, Williams
juxtaposed lyric passages, prose,
letters, autobiography, newspaper

ROBINSON JEFFERS

accounts, and historical facts. The
layout's ample white space suggests the open road theme of
American literature and gives a
sense of new vistas even open to
the poor people who picnic in the
public park on Sundays. Like
Whitman's persona in *Leaves of
Grass*, Dr. Paterson moves freely
among the working people:

-late spring,
a Sunday afternoon!

- and goes by the footpath to the
cliff (counting: the proof)

himself among others
- treads there the same stones
on which their feet slip as they
    climb,
paced by their dogs!

laughing, calling to each other -

Wait for me!
(II, i, 14-23)

BETWEEN THE WARS
Robinson Jeffers (1887-1962)

Numerous American poets of
stature and genuine vision
arose in the years between
the world wars, among them poets
from the West Coast, women, and
African-Americans. Like the novelist John Steinbeck, Robinson
Jeffers lived in California and wrote
of the Spanish rancheros and Indians and their mixed traditions,
and of the haunting beauty of the
land. Trained in the classics and
well-read in Freud, he re-created

themes of Greek tragedy set in the rugged coastal seascape. He is best known for his tragic narratives such as *Tamar* (1924), *Roan Stallion* (1925), *The Tower Beyond Tragedy* (1924) — a recreation of Aeschylus's *Agamemnon* — and *Medea* (1946), a re-creation of the tragedy by Euripides.

Edward Estlin Cummings (1894-1962)

Edward Estlin Cummings, commonly known as e.e. cummings, wrote attractive, innovative verse distinguished for its humor, grace, celebration of love and eroticism, and experimentation with punctuation and visual format on the page. A painter, he was the first American poet to recognize that poetry had become primarily a visual, not an oral, art; his poems used much unusual spacing and indentation, as well as dropping all use of capital letters.

Like Williams, Cummings also used colloquial language, sharp imagery, and words from popular culture. Like Williams, he took creative liberties with layout. His poem "in Just —" (1920) invites the reader to fill in the missing ideas:

in Just —

Spring   when the world is mud -
luscious the little
lame balloonman

LANGSTON HUGHES

whistles far and wee

and eddieandbill come
running from marbles and
piracies and it's
spring...

Hart Crane (1899-1932)

Hart Crane was a tormented young poet who committed suicide at age 33 by leaping into the sea. He left striking poems, including an epic, *The Bridge* (1930), which was inspired by the Brooklyn Bridge, in which he ambitiously attempted to review the American cultural experience and recast it in affirmative terms. His luscious, overheated style works best in short poems such as "Voyages" (1923, 1926) and "At Melville's Tomb" (1926), whose ending is a suitable epitaph for Crane:

monody shall not wake the
mariner.
This fabulous shadow only the
sea keeps.

Marianne Moore (1887-1972)

Marianne Moore once wrote that poems were "imaginary gardens with real toads in them." Her poems are conversational, yet elaborate and subtle in their syllabic versification, drawing upon extremely precise description and historical and scientific fact. A "poet's poet," she influenced such later poets as her young friend Elizabeth Bishop.

Langston Hughes (1902-1967)

One of many talented poets of the Harlem Renaissance of the 1920s — in the company of James Weldon Johnson, Claude McKay, Countee Cullen, and others — was Langston Hughes. He embraced African-American jazz rhythms and was one of the first black writers to attempt to make a profitable career out of his writing. Hughes incorporated blues, spirituals, colloquial speech, and folkways in his poetry.

An influential cultural organizer, Hughes published numerous black anthologies and began black theater groups in Los Angeles and Chicago, as well as New York City. He also wrote effective journalism, creating the character Jesse B. Semple ("simple") to express social commentary. One of his most beloved poems, "The Negro Speaks of Rivers" (1921, 1925), embraces his African — and universal — heritage in a grand epic catalogue. The poem suggests that, like the great rivers of the world, African culture will endure and deepen:

I've known rivers:
I've known rivers ancient as the
world and older than the
flow of human blood in
human veins.

My soul has grown deep like the
rivers.

I bathed in the Euphrates when

dawns were young.
I built my hut near the Congo
and it lulled me to sleep.
I looked upon the Nile and
raised the pyramids above it.
I heard the singing of the
Mississippi when Abe Lincoln
went down to New Orleans,
and I've seen its muddy
bosom turn all golden in the
sunset

I've known rivers
Ancient, dusky rivers.

My soul has grown deep like
the rivers.

PROSE WRITING, 1914-1945: AMERICAN REALISM

Although American prose between the wars experimented with viewpoint and form, Americans wrote more realistically, on the whole, than did Europeans. Novelist Ernest Hemingway wrote of war, hunting, and other masculine pursuits in a stripped, plain style; William Faulkner set his powerful southern novels spanning generations and cultures firmly in Mississippi heat and dust; and Sinclair Lewis delineated bourgeois lives with ironic clarity.

The importance of facing reality became a dominant theme in the 1920s and 1930s: Writers such as F. Scott Fitzgerald and the playwright Eugene O'Neill repeatedly portrayed the tragedy awaiting those who live in flimsy dreams.

F. Scott Fitzgerald
(1896-1940)

Francis Scott Key Fitzgerald's life resembles a fairy tale. During World War I, Fitzgerald enlisted in the U.S. Army and fell in love with a rich and beautiful girl, Zelda Sayre, who lived near Montgomery, Alabama, where he was stationed. Zelda broke off their engagement because he was relatively poor. After he was discharged at war's end, he went to seek his literary fortune in New York City in order to marry her.

His first novel, *This Side of Paradise* (1920), became a bestseller, and at 24 they married. Neither of them was able to withstand the stresses of success and fame, and they squandered their money. They moved to France to economize in 1924 and returned seven years later. Zelda became mentally unstable and had to be institutionalized; Fitzgerald himself became an alcoholic and died young as a movie screenwriter.

Fitzgerald's secure place in American literature rests primarily on his novel *The Great Gatsby* (1925), a brilliantly written, economically structured story about the American dream of the self-made man. The protagonist, the mysterious Jay Gatsby, discovers the devastating cost of success in terms of personal fulfillment and love. Other fine works include *Tender Is the Night* (1934), about a young psychiatrist whose life is doomed by his marriage to an unstable woman, and some stories in the collections *Flappers and Philosophers* (1920), *Tales of the Jazz Age* (1922), and *All the Sad Young Men* (1926). More than any other writer, Fitzgerald captured the glittering, desperate life of the 1920s; *This Side of Paradise* was heralded as the voice of modern American youth. His second novel, *The Beautiful and the Damned* (1922), continued his exploration of the self-destructive extravagance of his times.

Fitzgerald's special qualities include a dazzling style perfectly suited to his theme of seductive glamour. A famous section from *The Great Gatsby* masterfully summarizes a long passage of time: "There was music from my neighbor's house through the summer nights. In his blue gardens men and girls came and went like moths among the whisperings and the champagne and the stars."

Ernest Hemingway
(1899-1961)

Few writers have lived as colorfully as Ernest Hemingway, whose career could have come out of one of his adventurous novels. Like Fitzgerald, Dreiser, and many other fine novelists of the 20th century, Hemingway came from the U.S. Midwest. Born in Illinois, Hemingway spent childhood vacations in Michigan on hunting and fishing trips. He volunteered for an ambulance unit in France during World War I, but was wounded and hospitalized for six months. After the war, as a war correspondent based in

ERNEST HEMINGWAY

Photo courtesy
Pix Publishing, Inc.

Paris, he met expatriate American writers Sherwood Anderson, Ezra Pound, F. Scott Fitzgerald, and Gertrude Stein. Stein, in particular, influenced his spare style.

After his novel *The Sun Also Rises* (1926) brought him fame, he covered the Spanish Civil War, World War II, and the fighting in China in the 1940s. On a safari in Africa, he was badly injured when his small plane crashed; still, he continued to enjoy hunting and sport fishing, activities that inspired some of his best work. *The Old Man and the Sea* (1952), a short poetic novel about a poor, old fisherman who heroically catches a huge fish devoured by sharks, won him the Pulitzer Prize in 1953; the next year he received the Nobel Prize. Discouraged by a troubled family background, illness, and the belief that he was losing his gift for writing, Hemingway shot himself to death in 1961.

Hemingway is arguably the most popular American novelist of this century. His sympathies are basically apolitical and humanistic, and in this sense he is universal. His simple style makes his novels easy to comprehend, and they are often set in exotic surroundings. A believer in the "cult of experience," Hemingway often involved his characters in dangerous situations in order to reveal their inner natures; in his later works, the danger sometimes becomes an occasion for masculine assertion.

Like Fitzgerald, Hemingway be-

WILLIAM FAULKNER

came a spokesperson for his generation. But instead of painting its fatal glamour as did Fitzgerald, who never fought in World War I, Hemingway wrote of war, death, and the "lost generation" of cynical survivors. His characters are not dreamers but tough bullfighters, soldiers, and athletes. If intellectual, they are deeply scarred and disillusioned.

His hallmark is a clean style devoid of unnecessary words. Often he uses understatement: In *A Farewell to Arms* (1929) the heroine dies in childbirth saying "I'm not a bit afraid. It's just a dirty trick." He once compared his writing to icebergs: "There is seven-eighths of it under water for every part that shows."

Hemingway's fine ear for dialogue and exact description shows in his excellent short stories, such as "The Snows of Kilimanjaro" and "The Short Happy Life of Francis Macomber." Critical opinion, in fact, generally holds his short stories equal or superior to his novels. His best novels include *The Sun Also Rises*, about the demoralized life of expatriates after World War I; *A Farewell to Arms*, about the tragic love affair of an American soldier and an English nurse during the war; *For Whom the Bell Tolls* (1940), set during the Spanish Civil War; and *The Old Man and the Sea.*

William Faulkner (1897-1962)

Born to an old southern family, William Harrison Faulkner was raised in Oxford, Mississippi, where he lived most of his life. Faulkner created an entire imaginative landscape, Yoknapatawpha County, mentioned in numerous novels, along with several families with interconnections extending back for generations. Yoknapatawpha County, with its capital, "Jefferson," is closely modeled on Oxford, Mississippi, and its surroundings. Faulkner re-creates the history of the land and the various races — Indian, African-American, Euro-American, and various mixtures — who have lived on it. An innovative writer, Faulkner experimented brilliantly with narrative chronology, different points of view and voices (including those of outcasts, children, and illiterates), and a rich and demanding baroque style built of extremely long sentences full of complicated subordinate parts.

The best of Faulkner's novels include *The Sound and the Fury* (1929) and *As I Lay Dying* (1930), two modernist works experimenting with viewpoint and voice to probe southern families under the stress of losing a family member; *Light in August* (1932), about complex and violent relations between a white woman and a black man; and *Absalom, Absalom!* (1936), perhaps his finest, about the rise of a self-made plantation owner and his tragic fall through racial prejudice and a failure to love.

Most of these novels use different characters to tell parts of the story and demonstrate how meaning resides in the manner of telling,

SINCLAIR LEWIS

Photo courtesy
Pix Publishing, Inc.

as much as in the subject at hand. The use of various viewpoints makes Faulkner more self-referential, or "reflexive," than Hemingway or Fitzgerald; each novel reflects upon itself, while it simultaneously unfolds a story of universal interest. Faulkner's themes are southern tradition, family, community, the land, history and the past, race, and the passions of ambition and love. He also created three novels focusing on the rise of a degenerate family, the Snopes clan: *The Hamlet* (1940), *The Town* (1957), and *The Mansion* (1959).

NOVELS OF SOCIAL AWARENESS

Since the 1890s, an undercurrent of social protest had coursed through American literature, welling up in the naturalism of Stephen Crane and Theodore Dreiser and in the clear messages of the muckraking novelists. Later socially engaged authors included Sinclair Lewis, John Steinbeck, John Dos Passos, Richard Wright, and the dramatist Clifford Odets. They were linked to the 1930s in their concern for the welfare of the common citizen and their focus on groups of people — the professions, as in Sinclair Lewis's archetypal *Arrowsmith* (a physician) or *Babbitt* (a local businessman); families, as in Steinbeck's *The Grapes of Wrath*; or urban masses, as Dos Passos accomplishes through his 11 major characters in his *U.S.A.* trilogy.

Sinclair Lewis (1885-1951)

Harry Sinclair Lewis was born in Sauk Centre, Minnesota, and graduated from Yale University. He took time off from school to work at a socialist community, Helicon Home Colony, financed by muckraking novelist Upton Sinclair. Lewis's *Main Street* (1920) satirized monotonous, hypocritical small-town life in Gopher Prairie, Minnesota. His incisive presentation of American life and his criticism of American materialism, narrowness, and hypocrisy brought him national and international recognition. In 1926, he was offered and declined a Pulizer Prize for *Arrowsmith* (1925), a novel tracing a doctor's efforts to maintain his medical ethics amid greed and corruption. In 1930, he became the first American to win the Nobel Prize for Literature.

Lewis's other major novels include *Babbitt* (1922). George Babbitt is an ordinary businessman living and working in Zenith, an ordinary American town. Babbitt is moral and enterprising, and a believer in business as the new scientific approach to modern life. Becoming restless, he seeks fulfilment but is disillusioned by an affair with a bohemian woman, returns to his wife, and accepts his lot. The novel added a new word to the American language — "babbittry," meaning narrow-minded, complacent, bourgeois ways. *Elmer Gantry* (1927) exposes revivalist religion in the United States, while *Cass Timberlane* (1945) studies the stresses that develop within the marriage of an older judge and his young wife.

John Dos Passos (1896-1970)

Like Sinclair Lewis, John Dos Passos began as a left-wing radical but moved to the right as he aged. Dos Passos wrote realistically, in line with the doctrine of socialist realism. His best work achieves a scientific objectivism and almost documentary effect. Dos Passos developed an experimental collage technique for his masterwork *U.S.A.*, consisting of *The 42nd Parallel* (1930), *1919* (1932), and *The Big Money* (1936). This sprawling collection covers the social history of the United States from 1900 to 1930 and exposes the moral corruption of materialistic American society through the lives of its characters.

Dos Passos's new techniques included "newsreel" sections taken from contemporary headlines, popular songs, and advertisements, as well as "biographies" briefly setting forth the lives of important Americans of the period, such as inventor Thomas Edison, labor organizer Eugene Debs, film star Rudolph Valentino, financier J.P. Morgan, and sociologist Thorstein Veblen. Both the newsreels and biographies lend Dos Passos's novels a documentary value; a third technique, the "camera eye," consists of stream of consciousness prose poems that offer a subjective response to the events described in the books.

JOHN STEINBECK

Photo courtesy
Pinney & Beecher

John Steinbeck (1902-1968)

Like Sinclair Lewis, John Steinbeck is held in higher critical esteem outside the United States than in it today, largely because he received the Nobel Prize for Literature in 1963 and the international fame it confers. In both cases, the Nobel Committee selected liberal American writers noted for their social criticism.

Steinbeck, a Californian, set much of his writing in the Salinas Valley near San Francisco. His best known work is the Pulitzer Prize-winning novel *The Grapes of Wrath* (1939), which follows the travails of a poor Oklahoma family that loses its farm during the Depression and travels to California to seek work. Family members suffer conditions of feudal oppression by rich landowners. Other works set in California include *Tortilla Flat* (1935), *Of Mice and Men* (1937), *Cannery Row* (1945), and *East of Eden* (1952).

Steinbeck combines realism with a primitivist romanticism that finds virtue in poor farmers who live close to the land. His fiction demonstrates the vulnerability of such people, who can be uprooted by droughts and are the first to suffer in periods of political unrest and economic depression.

THE HARLEM RENAISSANCE

During the exuberant 1920s, Harlem, the black community situated uptown in New York City, sparkled with passion and creativity. The sounds of its black

JEAN TOOMER

Photo © UPI/The Bettmann Archive

American jazz swept the United States by storm, and jazz musicians and composers like Duke Ellington became stars beloved across the United States and overseas. Bessie Smith and other blues singers presented frank, sensual, wry lyrics raw with emotion. Black spirituals became widely appreciated as uniquely beautiful religious music. Ethel Waters, the black actress, triumphed on the stage, and black American dance and art flourished with music and drama.

Among the rich variety of talent in Harlem, many visions coexisted. Carl Van Vechten's sympathetic 1926 novel of Harlem gives some idea of the complex and bittersweet life of black America in the face of economic and social inequality.

The poet Countee Cullen (1903-1946), a native of Harlem who was briefly married to W.E.B. Du Bois's daughter, wrote accomplished rhymed poetry, in accepted forms, which was much admired by whites. He believed that a poet should not allow race to dictate the subject matter and style of a poem. On the other end of the spectrum were African-Americans who rejected the United States in favor of Marcus Garvey's "Back to Africa" movement. Somewhere in between lies the work of Jean Toomer.

Jean Toomer (1894-1967)

Like Cullen, African-American fiction writer and poet Jean Toomer envisioned an American identity that would transcend race.

Perhaps for this reason, he brilliantly employed poetic traditions of rhyme and meter and did not seek out new "black" forms for his poetry. His major work, *Cane* (1923), is ambitious and innovative, however. Like Williams's *Paterson*, *Cane* incorporates poems, prose vignettes, stories, and autobiographical notes. In it, an African-American struggles to discover his selfhood within and beyond the black communities in rural Georgia, Washington, D.C., and Chicago, Illinois, and as a black teacher in the South. In *Cane*, Toomer's Georgia rural black folk are naturally artistic:

Their voices rise...the pine trees
    are guitars,
Strumming, pine-needles fall
    like sheets of rain...
Their voices rise...the chorus of
    the cane
Is caroling a vesper to the
    stars...(I, 21-24)

Cane contrasts the fast pace of African-American life in the city of Washington:

Money burns the pocket, pocket
    hurts,
Bootleggers in silken shirts,
Ballooned, zooming Cadillacs,
Whizzing, whizzing down the
    street-car tracks. (II, 1-4)

Richard Wright (1908-1960)

Richard Wright was born into a poor Mississippi sharecropping family that his father deserted

RICHARD WRIGHT

Photo courtesy
Howard University

when the boy was five. Wright was the first African-American novelist to reach a general audience, even though he had barely a ninth grade education. His harsh childhood is depicted in one of his best books, his autobiography, *Black Boy* (1945). He later said that his sense of deprivation, due to racism, was so great that only reading kept him alive.

The social criticism and realism of Sherwood Anderson, Theodore Dreiser, and Sinclair Lewis especially inspired Wright. During the 1930s, he joined the Communist party; in the 1940s, he moved to France, where he knew Gertrude Stein and Jean-Paul Sartre and became an anti-Communist. His outspoken writing blazed a path for subsequent African-American novelists.

His work includes *Uncle Tom's Children* (1938), a book of short stories, and the powerful and relentless novel *Native Son* (1940), in which Bigger Thomas, an uneducated black youth, mistakenly kills his white employer's daughter, gruesomely burns the body, and murders his black girlfriend — fearing she will betray him. Although some African-Americans have criticized Wright for portraying a black character as a murderer, Wright's novel was a necessary and overdue expression of the racial inequality that has been the subject of so much debate in the United States.

Zora Neale Hurston
(1903-1960)

Born in the small town of Eatonville, Florida, Zora Neale Hurston is known as one of the lights of the Harlem Renaissance. She first came to New York City at the age of 16 — having arrived as part of a traveling theatrical troupe. A strikingly gifted storyteller who captivated her listeners, she attended Barnard College, where she studied with anthropologist Franz Boaz and came to grasp ethnicity from a scientific perspective. Boaz urged her to collect folklore from her native Florida environment, which she did. The distinguished folklorist Alan Lomax called her *Mules and Men* (1935) "the most engaging, genuine, and skillfully written book in the field of folklore."

Hurston also spent time in Haiti, studying voodoo and collecting Caribbean folklore that was anthologized in *Tell My Horse* (1938). Her natural command of colloquial English puts her in the great tradition of Mark Twain. Her writing sparkles with colorful language and comic — or tragic — stories from the African-American oral tradition.

Hurston was an impressive novelist. Her most important work, *Their Eyes Were Watching God* (1937), is a moving, fresh depiction of a beautiful mulatto woman's maturation and renewed happiness as she moves through three marriages. The novel vividly evokes the lives of African-Americans working the land in the rural South. A har-

ZORA NEALE HURSTON

Photo © Carl Van Vechten, courtesy Yale University

binger of the women's movement, Hurston inspired and influenced such contemporary writers as Alice Walker and Toni Morrison through books such as her autobiography, *Dust Tracks on a Road* (1942).

LITERARY CURRENTS: THE FUGITIVES AND NEW CRITICISM

From the Civil War into the 20th century, the southern United States had remained a political and economic backwater ridden with racism and superstition, but, at the same time, blessed with rich folkways and a strong sense of pride and tradition. It had a somewhat unfair reputation for being a cultural desert of provincialism and ignorance.

Ironically, the most significant 20th-century regional literary movement was that of the Fugitives — led by poet-critic-theoretician John Crowe Ransom, poet Allen Tate, and novelist-poet-essayist Robert Penn Warren. This southern literary school rejected "northern" urban, commercial values, which they felt had taken over America. The Fugitives called for a return to the land and to American traditions that could be found in the South. The movement took its name from a literary magazine, *The Fugitive*, published from 1922 to 1925 at Vanderbilt University in Nashville, Tennessee, and with which Ransom, Tate, and Warren were all associated.

These three major Fugitive writers were also associated with New

Criticism, an approach to understanding literature through close readings and attentiveness to formal patterns (of imagery, metaphors, metrics, sounds, and symbols) and their suggested meanings. Ransom, leading theorist of the southern renaissance between the wars, published a book, *The New Criticism* (1941), on this method, which offered an alternative to previous extra-literary methods of criticism based on history and biography. New Criticism became the dominant American critical approach in the 1940s and 1950s because it proved to be well-suited to modernist writers such as Eliot and could absorb Freudian theory (especially its structural categories such as id, ego, and superego) and approaches drawing on mythic patterns.

20TH-CENTURY AMERICAN DRAMA

American drama imitated English and European theater until well into the 20th century. Often, plays from England or translated from European languages dominated theater seasons. An inadequate copyright law that failed to protect and promote American dramatists worked against genuinely original drama. So did the "star system," in which actors and actresses, rather than the actual plays, were given most acclaim. Americans flocked to see European actors who toured theaters in the United States. In addition, imported drama, like imported

Eugene O'Neill

Photo © The Bettmann Archive

wine, enjoyed higher status than indigenous productions.

During the 19th century, melodramas with exemplary democratic figures and clear contrasts between good and evil had been popular. Plays about social problems such as slavery also drew large audiences; sometimes these plays were adaptations of novels like *Uncle Tom's Cabin*. Not until the 20th century would serious plays attempt aesthetic innovation. Popular culture showed vital developments, however, especially in vaudeville (popular variety theater involving skits, clowning, music, and the like). Minstrel shows, based on African-American music and folkways, performed by white characters using "blackface" makeup, also developed original forms and expressions.

Eugene O'Neill (1888-1953)

Eugene O'Neill is the great figure of American theater. His numerous plays combine enormous technical originality with freshness of vision and emotional depth. O'Neill's earliest dramas concern the working class and poor; later works explore subjective realms, such as obsessions and sex, and underscore his reading in Freud and his anguished attempt to come to terms with his dead mother, father, and brother. His play *Desire Under the Elms* (1924) recreates the passions hidden within one family; *The Great God Brown* (1926) uncovers the unconsciousness of a wealthy businessman; and *Strange Interlude*

(1928), a winner of the Pulitzer Prize, traces the tangled loves of one woman. These powerful plays reveal different personalities reverting to primitive emotions or confusion under intense stress.

O'Neill continued to explore the Freudian pressures of love and dominance within families in a trilogy of plays collectively entitled *Mourning Becomes Electra* (1931), based on the classical *Oedipus* trilogy by Sophocles. His later plays include the acknowledged masterpieces *The Iceman Cometh* (1946), a stark work on the theme of death, and *Long Day's Journey Into Night* (1956) — a powerful, extended autobiography in dramatic form focusing on his own family and their physical and psychological deterioration, as witnessed in the course of one night. This work was part of a cycle of plays O'Neill was working on at the time of his death.

O'Neill redefined the theater by abandoning traditional divisions into acts and scenes (*Strange Interlude* has nine acts, and *Mourning Becomes Electra* takes nine hours to perform); using masks such as those found in Asian and ancient Greek theater; introducing Shakespearean monologues and Greek choruses; and producing special effects through lighting and sound. He is generally acknowledged to have been America's foremost dramatist. In 1936 he received the Nobel Prize for Literature — the first American playwright to be so honored.

Thornton Wilder (1897-1975)

Thornton Wilder is known for his plays *Our Town* (1938) and *The Skin of Our Teeth* (1942), and for his novel *The Bridge of San Luis Rey* (1927).

Our Town conveys positive American values. It has all the elements of sentimentality and nostalgia — the archetypal traditional small country town, the kindly parents and mischievous children, the young lovers. Still, the innovative elements such as ghosts, voices from the audience, and daring time shifts keep the play engaging. It is, in effect, a play about life and death in which the dead are reborn, at least for the moment.

Clifford Odets (1906-1963)

Clifford Odets, a master of social drama, came from an Eastern European, Jewish immigrant background. Raised in New York City, he became one of the original acting members of the Group Theater directed by Harold Clurman, Lee Strasberg, and Cheryl Crawford, which was committed to producing only native American dramas.

Odets's best-known play was *Waiting for Lefty* (1935), an experimental one-act drama that fervently advocated labor unionism. His *Awake and Sing!*, a nostalgic family drama, became another popular success, followed by *Golden Boy*, the story of an Italian immigrant youth who ruins his musical talent (he is a violinist) when he is seduced by the lure of money to become a boxer and injures his hands. Like Fitzgerald's *The Great Gatsby* and Drieser's *An American Tragedy*, the play warns against excessive ambition and materialism.

CHAPTER

AMERICAN POETRY, 1945-1990: THE ANTI-TRADITION

Traditional forms and ideas no longer seemed to provide meaning to many American poets in the second half of the 20th century. Events after World War II produced for many writers a sense of history as discontinuous: Each act, emotion, and moment was seen as unique. Style and form now seemed provisional, makeshift, reflexive of the process of composition and the writer's self-awareness. Familiar categories of expression were suspect; originality was becoming a new tradition.

The break from tradition gathered momentum during the 1957 obscenity trial of Allen Ginsberg's poem *Howl*. When the San Francisco customs office seized the book, its publisher, Lawrence Ferlinghetti's City Lights, brought a lawsuit. During that notorious court case, famous critics defended *Howl*'s passionate social criticism on the basis of the poem's redeeming literary merit. *Howl*'s triumph over the censors helped propel the rebellious Beat poets — especially Ginsberg and his friends Jack Kerouac and William Burroughs — to fame.

It is not hard to find historical causes for this dissociated sensibility in the United States. World War II itself, the rise of anonymity and consumerism in a mass urban society, the protest movements of the 1960s, the decade-long Vietnam conflict, the Cold War, environmental threats —

the catalog of shocks to American culture is long and varied. The change that most transformed American society, however, was the rise of the mass media and mass culture. First radio, then movies, and later an all-powerful, ubiquitous television presence changed American life at its roots. From a private, literate, elite culture based on the book and reading, the United States became a media culture attuned to the voice on the radio, the music of compact discs and cassettes, film, and the images on the television screen.

American poetry was directly influenced by the mass media and electronic technology. Films, videotapes, and tape recordings of poetry readings and interviews with poets became available, and new inexpensive photographic methods of printing encouraged young poets to self-publish and young editors to begin literary magazines — of which there were more than 2,000 by 1990.

At the same time, Americans became uncomfortably aware that technology, so useful as a tool, could be used to manipulate the culture. To Americans seeking alternatives, poetry seemed more relevant than before: It offered people a way to express subjective life and articulate the impact of technology and mass society on the individual.

A host of styles, some regional, some associated with famous schools or poets, vied for attention; post-World War II American poetry was decentralized, richly varied, and difficult to summarize. For the sake of discussion, however, it can be arranged along a spectrum, producing three overlapping camps — the traditional on one end, the idiosyncratic in the middle, and the experimental on the other end. Traditional poets have maintained or revitalized poetic traditions. Idiosyncratic poets have used both traditional and innovative techniques in creating unique voices. Experimental poets have courted new cultural styles.

TRADITIONALISM

Traditional writers include acknowledged masters of established forms and diction who wrote with a readily recognizable craft, often using rhyme or a set metrical pattern. Often they were from the U.S. eastern seaboard or the southern part of the country, and taught in colleges and universities. Richard Eberhart and Richard Wilbur; the older Fugitive poets John Crowe Ransom, Allen Tate, and Robert Penn Warren; such accomplished younger poets as John Hollander and Richard Howard; and the early Robert Lowell are examples. In the years after World War II, they became established and were frequently anthologized.

The previous chapter discussed the refinement, respect for nature, and profoundly conservative values of the Fugitives. These qualities grace much poetry oriented to traditional modes. Traditionalist poets were generally precise, realistic, and witty; many, like Richard Wilbur (1921-), were influenced by British metaphysical poets brought to favor by T.S. Eliot. Wilbur's most famous poem, "A World Without Objects Is a Sensible Emptiness" (1950), takes its title from Thomas Traherne, a 17th-century English metaphysical poet. Its vivid opening illustrates the clarity some poets found within rhyme and formal regularity:

> The tall camels of the spirit
> Steer for their deserts, passing the last
> groves loud
> With the sawmill shrill of the locust, to the
> whole honey of the arid
> Sun. They are slow, proud...

Traditional poets, unlike many experimentalists who distrusted "too poetic" diction, welcomed resounding poetic lines. Robert Penn Warren (1905-1989) ended one poem with the words: "To love so well the world that we may believe, in the end, in God." Allen Tate (1899-1979) ended a poem: "Sentinel of the grave who counts us all!" Traditional poets also at times used a somewhat rhetorical diction of obsolete or odd words, using many adjectives (for example, "sepulchral owl") and inversions, in which the natural, spoken word order of English is altered unnaturally. Sometimes the effect is noble, as in the line by Warren; other times, the poetry seems stilted and out of touch with real emotions, as in Tate's line: "Fatuously touched the hems of the hierophants."

Occasionally, as in Hollander, Howard, and James Merrill (1926-1995), self-conscious diction combines with wit, puns, and literary allusions. Merrill, who was innovative in his urban themes, unrhymed lines, personal subjects, and light conversational tone, shares a witty habit with the traditionalists in "The Broken Heart" (1966), writing about a marriage as if it were a cocktail:

> Always that same old story —
> Father Time and Mother Earth,
> A marriage on the rocks.

Obvious fluency and verbal pyrotechnics by some poets, including Merrill and John Ashbery, made them successful in traditional terms, although they redefined poetry in radically innovative ways. Stylistic gracefulness made some poets seem more traditional than they were, as in the case of Randall Jarrell (1914-1965) and A.R. Ammons (1926-2001). Ammons created intense dialogues between humanity and nature; Jarrell stepped into the trapped consciousness of the dispossessed — women, children, doomed soldiers, as in "The Death of the Ball Turret Gunner" (1945):

> From my mother's sleep I fell into the State,
> And I hunched in its belly till my wet fur froze.
> Six miles from earth, loosed from its dream
> of life,
> I woke to black flak and the nightmare
> fighters.

When I died they washed me out
of the turret with a hose.

Although many traditional poets used rhyme, not all rhymed poetry was traditional in subject or tone. Poet Gwendolyn Brooks (1917-2000) wrote of the difficulties of living — let alone writing — in urban slums. Her "Kitchenette Building" (1945) asks how

could a dream send up through
    onion fumes
Its white and violet, fight with
    fried potatoes
And yesterday's garbage ripening
    in the hall...

Many poets, including Brooks, Adrienne Rich, Richard Wilbur, Robert Lowell, and Robert Penn Warren, began writing traditionally, using rhyme and meters, but they abandoned these in the 1960s under the pressure of public events and a gradual trend toward open forms.

Robert Lowell (1917-1977)

The most influential poet of the period, Robert Lowell, began traditionally but was influenced by experimental currents. Because his life and work spanned the period between the older modernist masters like T.S. Eliot and the recent antitraditional writers, his career places the later experimentalism in a larger context.

Lowell fits the mold of the academic writer: white, male, Protestant by birth, well educated, and linked

ROBERT LOWELL

Photo © Nancy Crampton

with the political and social establishment. He was a descendant of the respected Boston Brahmin family that included the famous 19th-century poet James Russell Lowell and a 20th-century president of Harvard University.

Robert Lowell found an identity outside his elite background, however. He left Harvard to attend Kenyon College in Ohio, where he rejected his Puritan ancestry and converted to Catholicism. Jailed for a year as a conscientious objector in World War II, he later publicly protested the Vietnam conflict.

Lowell's early books, *Land of Unlikeness* (1944) and *Lord Weary's Castle* (1946), which won a Pulitzer Prize, revealed great control of traditional forms and styles, strong feeling, and an intensely personal yet historical vision. The violence and specificity of the early work is overpowering in poems like "Children of Light" (1946), a harsh condemnation of the Puritans who killed Indians and whose descendants burned surplus grain instead of shipping it to hungry people. Lowell writes: "Our fathers wrung their bread from stocks and stones / And fenced their gardens with the Redman's bones."

Lowell's next book, *The Mills of the Kavanaughs* (1951), contains moving dramatic monologues in which members of his family reveal their tenderness and failings. As always, his style mixes the human with the majestic. Often he uses traditional rhyme, but his colloquialism disguises it until it seems like background melody. It was experimental poetry, however, that gave Lowell his breakthrough into a creative individual idiom.

On a reading tour in the mid-1950s, Lowell heard some of the new experimental poetry for the first time. Allen Ginsberg's *Howl* and Gary Snyder's *Myths and Texts*, still unpublished, were being read and chanted, sometimes to jazz accompaniment, in coffee houses in North Beach, a section of San Francisco. Lowell felt that next to these, his own accomplished poems were too stilted, rhetorical, and encased in convention; when reading them aloud, he made spontaneous revisions toward a more colloquial diction. "My own poems seemed like prehistoric monsters dragged down into a bog and death by their ponderous armor," he wrote later. "I was reciting what I no longer felt."

At this point Lowell, like many poets after him, accepted the challenge of learning from the rival tradition in America — the school of William Carlos Williams. "It's as if no poet except Williams had really seen America or heard its language," Lowell wrote in 1962. Henceforth, Lowell changed his writing drastically, using the "quick changes of tone, atmosphere, and speed" that Lowell most appreciated in Williams.

Lowell dropped many of his obscure allusions; his rhymes became integral to the experience within the poem instead of superimposed on it. The stanzaic structure, too, collapsed; new improvisational forms arose. In *Life Studies* (1959),

SYLVIA PLATH

Photo © UPI / The Bettmann Archive

he initiated confessional poetry, a new mode in which he bared his most tormenting personal problems with great honesty and intensity. In essence, he not only discovered his individuality but celebrated it in its most difficult and private manifestations. He transformed himself into a contemporary, at home with the self, the fragmentary, and the form as process.

Lowell's transformation, a watershed for poetry after the war, opened the way for many younger writers. In *For the Union Dead* (1964), *Notebook 1967-68* (1969), and later books, he continued his autobiographical explorations and technical innovations, drawing upon his experience of psychoanalysis. Lowell's confessional poetry has been particularly influential. Works by John Berryman, Anne Sexton, and Sylvia Plath (the last two his students), to mention only a few, are impossible to imagine without Lowell.

IDIOSYNCRATIC POETS

Poets who developed unique styles drawing on tradition but extending it into new realms with a distinctively contemporary flavor, in addition to Plath and Sexton, include John Berryman, Theodore Roethke, Richard Hugo, Philip Levine, James Dickey, Elizabeth Bishop, and Adrienne Rich.

Sylvia Plath (1932-1963)

Sylvia Plath lived an outwardly exemplary life, attending Smith

College on scholarship, graduating first in her class, and winning a Fulbright grant to Cambridge University in England. There she met her charismatic husband-to-be, poet Ted Hughes, with whom she had two children and settled in a country house in England.

Beneath the fairy-tale success festered unresolved psychological problems evoked in her highly readable novel *The Bell Jar* (1963). Some of these problems were personal, while others arose from her sense of repressive attitudes toward women in the 1950s. Among these were the beliefs — shared by many women themselves — that women should not show anger or ambitiously pursue a career, and instead find fulfillment in tending their husbands and children. Professionally successful women like Plath felt that they lived a contradiction.

Plath's storybook life crumbled when she and Hughes separated and she cared for the young children in a London apartment during a winter of extreme cold. Ill, isolated, and in despair, Plath worked against the clock to produce a series of stunning poems before she committed suicide by gassing herself in her kitchen. These poems were collected in the volume *Ariel* (1965), two years after her death. Robert Lowell, who wrote the introduction, noted her poetry's rapid development from the time she and Anne Sexton had attended his poetry classes in 1958.

Plath's early poetry is well crafted and traditional, but her late poems exhibit a desperate bravura and proto-feminist cry of anguish. In "The Applicant" (1966), Plath exposes the emptiness in the current role of wife (who is reduced to an inanimate "it"):

A living doll, everywhere you look.
It can sew, it can cook.
It can talk, talk, talk.

It works, there is nothing wrong with it.
You have a hole, it's a poultice.

You have an eye, it's an image.
My boy, it's your last resort.
Will you marry it, marry it, marry it.

Plath dares to use a nursery rhyme language, a brutal directness. She has a knack for using bold images from popular culture. Of a baby she writes, "Love set you going like a fat gold watch." In "Daddy," she imagines her father as the Dracula of cinema: "There's a stake in your fat black heart / And the villagers never liked you."

Anne Sexton (1928-1974)

Like Sylvia Plath, Anne Sexton was a passionate woman who attempted to be wife, mother, and poet on the eve of the women's movement in the United States. Like Plath, she suffered from mental illness and ultimately committed suicide.

Sexton's confessional poetry is more autobiographical than Plath's and lacks the craftedness Plath's earlier poems exhibit. Sexton's poems appeal powerfully to the emotions, however. They thrust taboo subjects into close focus. Often they daringly introduce female topics such as childbearing, the female body, or marriage seen from a woman's point of view. In poems like "Her Kind" (1960), Sexton identifies with a witch burned at the stake:

I have ridden in your cart, driver,
waved my nude arms at villages going by,
learning the last bright routes, survivor
where your flames still bite my thigh
and my ribs crack where your wheels wind.
A woman like that is not ashamed to die.
I have been her kind.

The titles of her works indicate their concern with madness and death. They include *To Bedlam and Part Way Back* (1960), *Live or Die* (1966), and the posthumous book *The Awful Rowing Toward God* (1975).

John Berryman (1914-1972)

John Berryman's life paralleled Robert Lowell's in some respects. Born in Oklahoma, Berryman was educated in the Northeast — at prep school and at Columbia University, and later was a fellow at Princeton University. Specializing in traditional forms and meters, he was inspired by early American history and wrote self-critical, confessional poems in his *Dream Songs* (1969) that feature a grotesque autobiographical character named Henry and reflections on his own teaching routine, chronic alcoholism, and ambition.

Like his contemporary, Theodore Roethke, Berryman developed a supple, playful, but profound style enlivened by phrases from folklore, children's rhymes, clichés, and slang. Berryman writes, of Henry, "He stared at ruin. Ruin stared straight back." Elsewhere, he wittily writes, "Oho alas alas / When will indifference come, I moan and rave."

Theodore Roethke (1908-1963)

The son of a greenhouse owner, Theodore Roethke evolved a special language evoking the "greenhouse world" of tiny insects and unseen roots: "Worm, be with me. / This is my hard time." His love poems in *Words for the Wind* (1958) celebrate beauty and desire with innocent passion. One poem begins: "I knew a woman, lovely in her bones, / When small birds sighed, she would sigh back at them." Sometimes his poems seem like nature's short-

JAMES DICKEY

Photo © Nancy Crampton

hand or ancient riddles: "Who stunned the dirt into noise? / Ask the mole, he knows."

Richard Hugo (1923-1982)

Richard Hugo, a native of Seattle, Washington, studied under Theodore Roethke. He grew up poor in dismal urban environments and excelled at communicating the hopes, fears, and frustrations of working people against the backdrop of the northwestern United States.

Hugo wrote nostalgic, confessional poems in bold iambics about shabby, forgotten small towns in his part of the United States; he wrote of shame, failure, and rare moments of acceptance through human relationships. He focused the reader's attention on minute, seemingly inconsequential details in order to make more significant points. "What Thou Lovest Well, Remains American" (1975) ends with a person carrying memories of his old hometown as if they were food:

> in case you're stranded in some
> odd empty town
> and need hungry lovers for
> friends, and need feel
> you are welcome in the street
> club they have formed.

Philip Levine (1928-)

Philip Levine, born in Detroit, Michigan, deals directly with the economic sufferings of workers through keen observation, rage, and painful irony. Like Hugo, his background is urban and poor. He has been the voice for the lonely individual caught up in industrial America. Much of his poetry is somber and reflects an anarchic tendency amid the realization that systems of government will endure.

In one poem, Levine likens himself to a fox who survives in a dangerous world of hunters through his courage and cunning. In terms of his rhythmic pattern, he has traveled a path from traditional meters in his early works to a freer, more open line in his later poetry as he expresses his lonely protest against the evils of the contemporary world.

James Dickey (1923-1997)

James Dickey, a novelist and essayist as well as poet, was a native of Georgia. At Vanderbilt University he studied under Agrarian poet and critic Donald Davidson, who encouraged Dickey's sensitivity to his southern heritage. Like Randall Jarrell, Dickey flew in World War II and wrote of the agony of war.

As a novelist and poet, Dickey was often concerned with strenuous effort, "outdoing, desperately / Outdoing what is required." He yearned for revitalizing contact with the world — a contact he sought in nature (animals, the wild), sexuality, and physical exertion. Dickey's novel *Deliverance* (1970), set in a southern wilderness river canyon, explores the struggle for survival and the dark side of male bonding. When filmed with the poet himself playing a southern sheriff, the novel and film increased his renown. While *Selected Poems* (1998)

ELIZABETH BISHOP

Photo © UPI/The Bettmann Archive

includes later work, Dickey's reputation rests largely on his early collection *Poems 1957-1967* (1967).

Elizabeth Bishop (1911-1979) and Adrienne Rich (1929-)

Among women poets of the idiosyncratic group, Elizabeth Bishop and Adrienne Rich have garnered the most respect in recent years. Bishop's crystalline intelligence and interest in remote landscapes and metaphors of travel appeal to readers for their exactitude and subtlety. Like her mentor Marianne Moore, Bishop wrote highly crafted poems in a descriptive style that contains hidden philosophical depths. The description of the ice-cold North Atlantic in "At the Fishhouses" (1955) could apply to Bishop's own poetry: "It is like what we imagine knowledge to be: / dark, salt, clear, moving, utterly free."

With Moore, Bishop may be placed in a "cool" female poetic tradition harking back to Emily Dickinson, in comparison with the "hot" poems of Plath, Sexton, and Adrienne Rich. Though Rich began by writing poems in traditional form and meter, her works, particularly those written after she became an ardent feminist in the 1980s, embody strong emotions.

Rich's special genius is the metaphor, as in her extraordinary work "Diving Into the Wreck" (1973), evoking a woman's search for identity in terms of diving down to a wrecked ship. Rich's poem "The Roofwalker" (1961), dedicated to poet Denise Levertov, imagines poetry writing, for women, as a dangerous craft. Like men building a roof, she feels "exposed, larger than life, / and due to break my neck."

EXPERIMENTAL POETRY

The force behind Robert Lowell's mature achievement and much of contemporary poetry lies in the experimentation begun in the 1950s by a number of poets. They may be divided into five loose schools, identified by Donald Allen in *The New American Poetry, 1945-1960* (1960), the first anthology to present the work of poets who were previously neglected by the critical and academic communities.

Inspired by jazz and abstract expressionist painting, most of the experimental writers are a generation younger than Lowell. They have tended to be bohemian, counterculture intellectuals who disassociated themselves from universities and outspokenly criticized "bourgeois" American society. Their poetry is daring, original, and sometimes shocking. In its search for new values, it claims affinity with the archaic world of myth, legend, and traditional societies such as those of the American Indian. The forms are looser, more spontaneous, organic; they arise from the subject matter and the feeling of the poet as the poem is written, and from the natural pauses of the spoken language. As Allen Ginsberg noted in "Improvised Poetics," "first thought best thought."

The Black Mountain School

The Black Mountain School centered around Black Mountain College, an experimental liberal arts college in Asheville, North Carolina, where poets Charles Olson, Robert Duncan, and Robert Creeley taught in the early 1950s. Ed Dorn, Joel Oppenheimer, and Jonathan Williams studied there, and Paul Blackburn, Larry Eigner, and Denise Levertov published work in the school's magazines *Origin* and *Black Mountain Review*. The Black Mountain School is linked with Charles Olson's theory of "projective verse," which insisted on an open form based on the spontaneity of the breath pause in speech and the typewriter line in writing.

Robert Creeley (1926-2005), who writes with a terse, minimalist style, was one of the major Black Mountain poets. In "The Warning" (1955), Creeley imagines the violent, loving imagination:

> For love — I would
> split open your head and put
> a candle in
> behind the eyes.
>
> Love is dead in us
> if we forget
> the virtues of an amulet
> and quick surprise

The San Francisco School

The work of the San Francisco School owes much to Eastern philosophy and religion, as well as to Japanese and Chinese poetry. This is not surprising because the influence of the Orient has always been strong in the U.S. West. The land around San Francisco — the Sierra Nevada Mountains and the jagged seacoast — is lovely and majestic, and poets from that area tend to have a deep feeling for nature. Many of their poems are set in the mountains or take place on backpacking trips. The poetry looks to nature instead of literary tradition as a source of inspiration.

San Francisco poets include Jack Spicer, Lawrence Ferlinghetti, Robert Duncan, Phil Whalen, Lew Welch, Gary Snyder, Kenneth Rexroth, Joanne Kyger, and Diane diPrima. Many of these poets identify with working people. Their poetry is often simple, accessible, and optimistic.

At its best, as seen in the work of Gary Snyder (1930-), San Francisco poetry evokes the delicate balance of the individual and the cosmos. In Snyder's "Above Pate Valley" (1955), the poet describes working on a trail crew in the mountains and finding obsidian arrowhead flakes from vanished Indian tribes:

On a hill snowed all but summer,
A land of fat summer deer,
They came to camp. On their
Own trails. I followed my own
Trail here. Picked up the
cold-drill,
Pick, singlejack, and sack
Of dynamite.
Ten thousand years.

Beat Poets

The San Franciso School blends into the next grouping — the Beat poets, who emerged in the 1950s. The term beat variously suggests musical downbeats, as in jazz; angelical beatitude or blessedness; and "beat up" — tired or hurt. The Beats (beatniks) were inspired by jazz, Eastern religion, and the wandering life. These were all depicted in the famous novel by Jack Kerouac *On the Road*, a sensation when it was published in 1957. An account of a 1947 cross-country car trip, the novel was written in three hectic weeks on a single roll of paper in what Kerouac called "spontaneous bop prose." The wild, improvisational style, hipster-mystic characters, and rejection of authority and convention fired the imaginations of young readers and helped usher in the freewheeling counterculture of the 1960s.

Most of the important Beats migrated to San Francisco from America's East Coast, gaining their initial national recognition in

ALLEN GINSBERG

Photo © The Bettmann Archive

California. The charismatic Allen Ginsberg (1926-1997) became the group's chief spokesperson. The son of a poet father and an eccentric mother committed to Communism, Ginsberg attended Columbia University, where he became fast friends with fellow students Kerouac (1922-1969) and William Burroughs (1914-1997), whose violent, nightmarish novels about the underworld of heroin addiction include *The Naked Lunch* (1959). These three were the nucleus of the Beat movement.

Other figures included publisher Lawrence Ferlinghetti (1919-), whose bookstore, City Lights, established in San Francisco's North Beach in 1951, became a gathering place. One of the best educated of the mid-20th century poets (he received a doctorate from the Sorbonne), Ferlinghetti's thoughtful, humorous, political poetry included *A Coney Island of the Mind* (1958); *Endless Life* (1981) is the title of his selected poems.

Gregory Corso (1930-2001), a petty criminal whose talent was nurtured by the Beats, is remembered for volumes of humorous poems, such as the often-anthologized "Marriage." A gifted poet, translator, and original critic, as seen in his insightful *American Poetry in the Twentieth Century* (1971), Kenneth Rexroth (1905-1982) played the role of elder statesman to the anti-tradition. A labor organizer from Indiana, he saw the Beats as a West Coast alternative to the East Coast literary establishment. He encouraged the Beats with his example and influence.

Beat poetry is oral, repetitive, and immensely effective in readings, largely because it developed out of poetry readings in underground clubs. Some might correctly see it as a great-grandparent of the rap music that became prevalent in the 1990s. Beat poetry was the most anti-establishment form of literature in the United States, but beneath its shocking words lies a love of country. The poetry is a cry of pain and rage at what the poets see as the loss of America's innocence and the tragic waste of its human and material resources.

Poems like Allen Ginsberg's *Howl* (1956) revolutionized traditional poetry.

> I saw the best minds of my
>   generation destroyed by
>   madness, starving hysterical
>   naked,
> dragging themselves through the
>   negro streets at dawn
>   looking for an angry fix,
> angelheaded hipsters burning
>   for the ancient heavenly
>   connection to the starry
>   dynamo in the
>   machinery of night...

The New York School

Unlike the Beat and San Franciso poets, the poets of the New York School were not interested in overtly moral questions, and, in general, they steered clear of political issues. They had the best formal educations of any group.

The major figures of the New York School — John Ashbery, Frank O'Hara,

JOHN ASHBERY

Photo © Nancy Crampton

and Kenneth Koch — met while they were undergraduates at Harvard University. They are quintessentially urban, cool, nonreligious, witty with a poignant, pastel sophistication. Their poems are fast moving, full of urban detail, incongruity, and an almost palpable sense of suspended belief.

New York City is the fine arts center of America and the birthplace of abstract expressionism, a major inspiration of this poetry. Most of the poets worked as art reviewers or museum curators, or collaborated with painters. Perhaps because of their feeling for abstract art, which distrusts figurative shapes and obvious meanings, their work is often difficult to comprehend, as in the later work of John Ashbery (1927-), perhaps the most critically esteemed poet of the late 20th century.

Ashbery's fluid poems record thoughts and emotions as they wash over the mind too swiftly for direct articulation. His profound, long poem, *Self-Portrait in a Convex Mirror* (1975), which won three major prizes, glides from thought to thought, often reflecting back on itself:

> A ship
> Flying unknown colors has
>   entered the harbor.
> You are allowing extraneous
>   matters
> To break up your day...

Surrealism and Existentialism

In his anthology defining the new

schools, Donald Allen includes a fifth group he cannot define because it has no clear geographical underpinning. This vague group includes recent movements and experiments. Chief among these are surrealism, which expresses the unconscious through vivid dreamlike imagery, and much poetry by women and ethnic minorities that has flourished in recent years. Though superficially distinct, surrealists, feminists, and minorities appear to share a sense of alienation from mainstream literature.

Although T.S. Eliot, Wallace Stevens, and Ezra Pound had introduced symbolist techniques into American poetry in the 1920s, surrealism, the major force in European poetry and thought in Europe during and after World War II, did not take root in the United States. Not until the 1960s did surrealism (along with existentialism) become domesticated in America under the stress of the Vietnam conflict.

During the 1960s, many American writers — W.S. Merwin, Robert Bly, Charles Simic, Charles Wright, and Mark Strand, among others — turned to French and especially Spanish surrealism for its pure emotion, its archetypal images, and its models of anti-rational, existential unrest.

Surrealists like Merwin tend to be epigrammatic, as in lines such as: "The gods are what has failed to become of us / If you find you no longer believe enlarge the temple." Bly's political surrealism criti-

AMY CLAMPITT

Photo © Nancy Crampton

cized values that he felt played a part in the Vietnam War in poems like "The Teeth Mother Naked at Last."

It's because we have new
    packaging for smoked
    oysters
that bomb holes appear in the
    rice paddies.

The more pervasive surrealist influence has been quieter and more contemplative, like the poem Charles Wright describes in "The New Poem" (1973):

It will not attend our sorrow.
It will not console our children.
It will not be able to help us.

Mark Strand's surrealism, like Merwin's, is often bleak; it speaks of an extreme deprivation. Now that traditions, values, and beliefs have failed him, the poet has nothing but his own cavelike soul:

I have a key
so I open the door and walk in.
It is dark and I walk in.
It is darker and I walk in.

WOMEN POETS AND FEMINISM

Literature in the United States, as in most other countries, was long evaluated on standards that often overlooked women's contributions. Yet there are many women poets of distinction in American writing. Not all are feminists, nor do their subjects invariably voice women's concerns. Also, regional, political, and racial differences have shaped their work. Among distinguished women poets are Amy Clampitt, Rita Dove, Louise Glück, Jorie Graham, Carolyn Kizer, Maxine Kumin, Denise Levertov, Audre Lorde, Gjertrud Schnackenberg, May Swenson, and Mona Van Duyn.

Before the 1960s, most women poets had adhered to an androgynous ideal, believing that gender made no difference in artistic excellence. This gender-blind position was, in effect, an early form of feminism that allowed women to argue for equal rights. By the late 1960s, American women — many active in the civil rights struggle and protests against the Vietnam conflict, or influenced by the counterculture — had begun to recognize their own marginalization. Betty Friedan's outspoken *The Feminine Mystique* (1963), published in the year Sylvia Plath committed suicide, decried women's low status. Another landmark book, Kate Millett's *Sexual Politics* (1969), made a case that male writings revealed a pervasive misogyny, or contempt for women.

In the 1970s, a second wave of feminist criticism emerged following the founding of the National Organization for Women (NOW) in 1966. Elaine Showalter's *A Literature of Their Own* (1977) identified a major tradition of British and American women authors. Sandra Gilbert and Susan Gubar's *The Madwoman in the Attic* (1979) traced misogyny in English classics, exploring its impact on works by women, such as Charlotte Brontë's

NIKKI GIOVANNI

Photo © Nancy Crampton

Jane Eyre. In that novel, a wife is driven mad by her husband's ill treatment and is imprisoned in the attic; Gilbert and Gubar compare women's muffled voices in literature to this suppressed female figure.

Feminist critics of the second wave challenged the accepted canon of great works on the basis that aesthetic standards were not timeless and universal but rather arbitrary, culture bound, and patriarchal. Feminism became in the 1970s a driving force for equal rights, not only in literature but in the larger culture as well. Gilbert and Gubar's *The Norton Anthology of Literature by Women* (1985) facilitated the study of women's literature, and a women's tradition came into focus.

Other influential woman poets before Sylvia Plath and Anne Sexton include Amy Lowell (1874-1925), whose works have great sensuous beauty. She edited influential Imagist anthologies and introduced modern French poetry and Chinese poetry in translation to the English-speaking literary world. Her work celebrated love, longing, and the spiritual aspect of human and natural beauty. H.D. (1886-1961), a friend of Ezra Pound and William Carlos Williams who had been psychoanalyzed by Sigmund Freud, wrote crystalline poems inspired by nature and by the Greek classics and experimental drama. Her mystical poetry celebrates goddesses. The contributions of Lowell and H.D., and those of other women poets of the early 20th century such as Edna St.

Vincent Millay, are only now being fully acknowledged.

MULTIETHNIC POETS

The second half of the 20th century witnessed a renaissance in multiethnic literature that has continued into the 21st century. In the 1960s, following the lead of African Americans, ethnic writers in the United States began to command public attention. The 1970s saw the founding of ethnic studies programs in universities.

In the 1980s, a number of academic journals, professional organizations, and literary magazines focusing on ethnic groups were initiated. Conferences devoted to the study of specific ethnic literatures had begun, and the canon of "classics" had been expanded to include ethnic writers in anthologies and course lists. Important issues included race and ethnicity, spiritual life, familial and gender roles, and language.

Minority poetry shares the variety and occasionally the anger of women's writing. It has flowered in works by Latino and Chicano Americans such as Gary Soto, Alberto Rios, and Lorna Dee Cervantes; in Native Americans such as Leslie Marmon Silko, Simon Ortiz, and Louise Erdrich; in African-American writers such as Amiri Baraka (LeRoi Jones), Michael S. Harper, Rita Dove, Maya Angelou, and Nikki Giovanni; and in Asian-American poets such as Cathy Song, Lawson Inada, and Janice Mirikitani.

A number of academic journals, professional organizations, and literary magazines focusing on ethnic groups were initiated. Conferences devoted to the study of specific ethnic literatures had begun, and the canon of "classics" had been expanded to include ethnic writers in anthologies and course lists.

Chicano/Latino Poetry

Spanish-influenced poetry encompasses works by many diverse groups. Among these are Mexican Americans, known since the 1950s as Chicanos, who have lived for many generations in the southwestern U.S. states annexed from Mexico in the Mexican-American War ending in 1848.

Among Spanish Caribbean populations, Cuban Americans and Puerto Ricans maintain vital and distinctive literary traditions. For example, the Cuban-American genius for comedy sets it apart from the elegiac lyricism of Chicano writers such as Rudolfo Anaya. New immigrants from Mexico, Central and South America, and Spain constantly replenish and enlarge this literary realm.

Chicano, or Mexican-American, poetry has a rich oral tradition in the *corrido*, or ballad, form. Seminal works stress traditional strengths of the Mexican community and the discrimination it has sometimes met with among whites. Sometimes the poets blend Spanish and English words in a poetic fusion, as in the poetry of Alurista and Gloria Anzaldúa. Their poetry is much influenced by oral tradition and is very powerful when read aloud.

Some poets have written largely in Spanish, in a tradition going back to the earliest epic written in the present-day United States — Gaspar Pérez de Villagrá's *Historia de la Nueva México*, commemorating the 1598 battle between invading Spaniards and the Pueblo Indians at

Acoma, New Mexico.

A central text in Chicano poetry, *I Am Joaquin* by Rodolfo Gonzales (1928-2005) evokes acculturation: the speaker is "Lost in a world of confusion/Caught up in a whirl of gringo society/Confused by the rules...."

Many Chicano writers have found sustenance in their ancient Mexican roots. Thinking of the grandeur of Mexico, Lorna Dee Cervantes (1954-) writes that "an epic corrido" chants through her veins, while Luis Omar Salinas (1937-) feels himself to be "an Aztec angel."

Much Chicano poetry is highly personal, dealing with feelings and family or members of the community. Gary Soto (1952-) writes out of the ancient tradition of honoring departed ancestors, but these words, written in 1981, describe the multicultural situation of Americans today:

> A candle is lit for the dead
> Two worlds ahead of us all

In the 1980s, Chicano poetry achieved a new prominence, and works by Cervantes, Soto, and Alberto Rios were widely anthologized.

Native-American Poetry

Native Americans have written fine poetry, most likely because a tradition of shamanistic song plays a vital role in their cultural heritage. Their work has excelled in vivid, living evocations of the natural world, which become almost mystical at

Photo © Nancy Crampton

GARY SOTO

LESLIE MARMON SILKO

Photo © Nancy Crampton

times. Indian poets have also voiced a tragic sense of irrevocable loss of their rich heritage.

Simon Ortiz (1941-), an Acoma Pueblo, bases many of his hard-hitting poems on history, exploring the contradictions of being an indigenous American in the United States today. His poetry challenges Anglo readers because it often reminds them of the injustice and violence at one time done to Native Americans. His poems envision racial harmony based on a deepened understanding.

In "Star Quilt," Roberta Hill Whiteman (1947-), a member of the Oneida tribe, imagines a multicultural future like a "star quilt, sewn from dawn light," while Leslie Marmon Silko (1948-), who is part Laguna Pueblo, uses colloquial language and traditional stories to fashion haunting, lyrical poems. In "In Cold Storm Light" (1981), Silko achieves a haiku-like resonance:

> out of the thick ice sky
>   running swiftly
> pounding
>   swirling above the treetops
> The snow elk come,
> Moving, moving
>   white song
> storm wind in the branches.

Louise Erdrich (1954-), like Silko also a novelist, creates powerful dramatic monologues that work like compressed dramas. They unsparingly depict families coping with alcoholism, unemployment, and poverty on the Chippewa reservation.

In Erdrich's "Family Reunion" (1984), a drunken, abusive uncle returns from years in the city. As he suffers from a heart disease, the abused niece, who is the speaker, remembers how this uncle had killed a large turtle years before by stuffing it with a firecracker. The end of the poem links Uncle Ray with the turtle he has victimized:

Somehow we find our way back, Uncle Ray
sings an old song to the body that pulls him
toward home. The gray fins that his hands have become
screw their bones in the dashboard. His face
has the odd, calm patience of a child who has always
let bad wounds alone, or a creature that has lived
for a long time underwater.
And the angels come
lowering their slings and litters.

African-American Poetry

Black Americans have produced many poems of great beauty with a considerable range of themes and tones. African-American literature is the most developed ethnic writing in America and is extremely diverse. Amiri Baraka (1934-), the best-known African-American poet of the 1960s and 1970s, has also written plays and taken an active role in politics. The writings of Maya Angelou (1928-) encompass various literary forms, including poetry, drama, and her well-known memoir, *I Know Why The Caged Bird Sings* (1969).

LOUISE ERDRICH

MAYA ANGELOU

Rita Dove (1952-) was named poet laureate of the United States for 1993-1995. Dove, a writer of fiction and drama as well, won the 1987 Pulitzer Prize for *Thomas and Beulah* (1986), in which she celebrates her grandparents through a series of lyric poems. She has said that she wrote the work to reveal the rich inner lives of poor people.

Michael S. Harper (1938-) has similarly written poems revealing the complex lives of African Americans faced with discrimination and violence. His dense, allusive poems often deal with crowded, dramatic scenes of war or urban life. They make use of surgical images in an attempt to heal. His "Clan Meeting: Births and Nations: A Blood Song" (1971), which likens cooking to surgery ("splicing the meats with fluids"), begins "we reconstruct lives in the intensive / care unit, pieced together in a buffet." The poem ends by splicing together images of the hospital, racism in the early American film *Birth of a Nation*, the Ku Klux Klan, film editing, and x-ray technology:

We reload our brains as the cameras,
the film overexposed
in the x-ray light,
locked with our double door
light meters: race and sex
spooled and rung in a hobby;
we take our bundle and go home.

History, jazz, and popular culture have inspired many African

Americans, from Harper (a college professor) to West Coast publisher and poet Ishmael Reed (1938-), known for spearheading multicultural writing through the Before Columbus Foundation and a series of magazines such as *Yardbird, Quilt,* and *Konch.*

Many African-American poets, such as Audre Lorde (1934-1992), have found nourishment in Afrocentrism, which sees Africa as a center of civilization since ancient times. In sensuous poems such as "The Women of Dan Dance With Swords in Their Hands To Mark the Time When They Were Warriors" (1978), she speaks as a woman warrior of ancient Dahomey, "arming whatever I touch" and "consuming" only "What is already dead."

Asian-American Poetry

Like poetry by Chicano and Latino writers, Asian-American poetry is exceedingly varied. Americans of Japanese, Chinese, and Filipino descent may often have lived in the United States for eight generations, while Americans of Korean, Thai, and Vietnamese heritage are likely to be fairly recent immigrants. Each group has grown out of a distinctive linguistic, historical, and cultural tradition.

Developments in Asian-American literature have included an emphasis on the Pacific Rim and women's writing. Asian Americans generally have resisted the common stereotypes as the "exotic" or "good" minority. Aestheticians have compared Asian and Western literary tra-

RITA DOVE

Photo © Christopher Felver / CORBIS

ditions — for example, comparing the concepts of *Tao* and *Logos.*

Asian-American poets have drawn on many sources, from Chinese opera to Zen Buddhism, and Asian literary traditions, particularly Zen, have inspired numerous non-Asian poets, as can be seen in the 1991 anthology *Beneath a Single Moon: Buddhism in Contemporary American Poetry.* Asian-American poets span a spectrum, from the iconoclastic posture taken by Frank Chin (1940-), co-editor of *Aiiieeeee!* (an early anthology of Asian-American literature), to the generous use of tradition by writers such as Maxine Hong Kingston (1940-). Janice Mirikitani (1942-), a sansei (third-generation Japanese American), evokes Japanese-American history and has edited several anthologies, such as *Third World Women* (1973); *Time To Greez! Incantations From the Third World* (1975); and *Ayumi: A Japanese American Anthology* (1980).

The lyrical *Picture Bride* (1983) of Chinese American Cathy Song (1955-) also dramatizes history through the lives of her family. Many Asian-American poets explore cultural diversity. In Song's "The Vegetable Air" (1988), a shabby town with cows in the plaza, a Chinese restaurant, and a Coca-Cola sign hung askew becomes an emblem of rootless multicultural contemporary life made bearable by art, in this case an opera on cassette:

then the familiar aria,
rising like the moon,

lifts you out of yourself, transporting you to another country where, for a moment, you travel light.

THE LANGUAGE SCHOOL, EXPERIMENTATION, AND NEW FORMALISM

At the end of the 20th century, directions in American poetry included the Language Poets loosely associated with *Temblor* magazine and Douglas Messerli, editor of *"Language" Poetries: An Anthology* (1987). Among them: Bruce Andrews, Lyn Hejinian, Bob Perelman, and Barrett Watten, author of *Total Syntax* (1985), a collection of essays. These poets stretch language to reveal its potential for ambiguity, fragmentation, and self-assertion within chaos. Ironic and postmodern, they reject "metanarratives" — ideologies, dogmas, conventions — and doubt the existence of transcendent reality. Michael Palmer writes:

This is Paradise, a mildewed book
Left too long in the house

Bob Perelman's "Chronic Meanings" (1993) begins:

The single fact is matter.
Five words can say only.
Black sky at night, reasonably.
I am, the irrational residue...

Viewing art and literary criticism as inherently ideological, they oppose modernism's closed forms, hierarchies, ideas of epiphany and

MAXINE HONG KINGSTON

Photo © Nancy Crampton

transcendence, categories of genre and canonical texts or accepted literary works. Instead they propose open forms and multicultural texts. They appropriate images from popular culture and the media, and refashion them. Like performance poetry, language poems often resist interpretation and invite participation.

Performance-oriented poetry — sets of chance operations such as those of composer John Cage, jazz improvisation, mixed media work, and European surrealism — have influenced many U.S. poets. Well-known figures include Laurie Anderson (1947-), author of the international hit *United States* (1984), which uses film, video, acoustics and music, choreography, and space-age technology. Sound poetry, emphasizing the voice and instruments, has been practiced by poets David Antin (who extemporizes his performances) and New Yorkers George Quasha (publisher of Station Hill Press), the late Armand Schwerner, and Jackson Mac Low. Mac Low has also written visual or concrete poetry, which makes a visual statement using placement and typography.

Ethnic performance poetry entered the mainstream with rap music, while across the United States over the last decade, poetry slams — open poetry reading contests that are held in alternative art galleries and literary bookstores — have become inexpensive, high-spirited, participatory entertainments.

At the opposite end of the theoretical spectrum are the self-styled New Formalists, who champion a return to form, rhyme, and meter. All groups are responding to the same problem — a perceived middle-brow complacency with the status quo, a careful and overly polished sound, often the product of poetry workshops, and an overemphasis on the personal lyric as opposed to the public gesture.

The Formal School is associated with Story Line Press; Dana Gioia, the poet who became chairman of the National Endowment for the Arts in 2003; Philip Dacey and David Jauss, poets and editors of *Strong Measures: Contemporary American Poetry in Traditional Forms* (1986); Brad Leithauser; and Gjertrud Schnackenberg. Robert Richman's *The Direction of Poetry: An Anthology of Rhymed and Metered Verse Written in the English Language Since 1975* is a 1988 anthology. Though these poets have been accused of retreating to 19th-century themes, they often draw on contemporary stances and images, along with musical languages and traditional, closed forms.

CHAPTER 8

AMERICAN PROSE, 1945-1990: REALISM AND EXPERIMENTATION

Narrative in the decades following World War II resists generalization: It was extremely various and multifaceted. It was vitalized by international currents such as European existentialism and Latin American magical realism, while the electronic era brought the global village. The spoken word on television gave new life to oral tradition. Oral genres, media, and popular culture increasingly influenced narrative.

In the past, elite culture influenced popular culture through its status and example; the reverse seems true in the United States in the postwar years. Serious novelists like Thomas Pynchon, Joyce Carol Oates, Kurt Vonnegut, Jr., Alice Walker, and E.L. Doctorow borrowed from and commented on comics, movies, fashions, songs, and oral history.

To say this is not to trivialize this literature: Writers in the United States were asking serious questions, many of them of a metaphysical nature. Writers became highly innovative and self-aware, or reflexive. Often they found traditional modes ineffective and sought vitality in more widely popular material. To put it another way, American writers in the postwar decades developed a postmodern sensibility. Modernist restructurings of point of view no longer sufficed for them; rather, the context of vision had to be made new.

THE REALIST LEGACY AND THE LATE 1940s

As in the first half of the 20th century, fiction in the second half reflected the character of each decade. The late 1940s saw the aftermath of World War II and the beginning of the Cold War.

World War II offered prime material: Norman Mailer (*The Naked and the Dead*, 1948) and James Jones (*From Here to Eternity*, 1951) were two writers who used it best. Both of them employed realism verging on grim naturalism; both took pains not to glorify combat. The same was true for Irwin Shaw's *The Young Lions* (1948). Herman Wouk, in *The Caine Mutiny* (1951), also showed that human foibles were as evident in wartime as in civilian life.

Later, Joseph Heller cast World War II in satirical and absurdist terms (*Catch-22*, 1961), arguing that war is laced with insanity. Thomas Pynchon presented an involuted, brilliant case parodying and displacing different versions of reality (*Gravity's Rainbow*, 1973). Kurt Vonnegut, Jr., became one of the shining lights of the counterculture during the early 1970s following publication of *Slaughterhouse-Five: or, The Children's Crusade* (1969), his antiwar novel about the firebombing of Dresden, Germany, by Allied forces during World War II (which Vonnegut witnessed on the ground as a prisoner of war).

The 1940s saw the flourishing of a new contingent of writers, including poet-novelist-essayist Robert Penn Warren, dramatists Arthur Miller, Lillian Hellman, and Tennessee Williams, and short story writers Katherine Anne Porter and Eudora Welty. All but Miller were from the South. All explored the fate of the individual within the family or community and focused on the balance between personal growth and responsibility to the group.

Robert Penn Warren
(1905-1989)

Robert Penn Warren, one of the southern Fugitives, enjoyed a fruitful career running through most of the 20th century. He showed a lifelong concern with democratic values as they appeared within historical context. The most enduring of his novels is *All the King's Men* (1946), focusing on the darker implications of the American dream as revealed in this thinly veiled account of the career of a flamboyant and sinister southern politician, Huey Long.

Arthur Miller (1915-2005)

New York-born dramatist Arthur Miller reached his personal pinnacle in 1949 with *Death of a Salesman*, a study of man's search for merit and worth in his life and the realization that failure invariably looms. Set within the family of the title character, Willy Loman, the play hinges on the uneven relationships of father and sons, husband and wife. It is a mirror of the literary attitudes of the 1940s, with its rich combination of realism tinged with naturalism; carefully drawn, rounded characters; and insistence on the value of the individual, despite failure and error. *Death of a Salesman* is a moving paean to the common man — to whom, as Willy Loman's widow eulogizes, "attention must be paid." Poignant and somber, it is also a story of dreams. As one character notes ironically, "a salesman has got to dream, boy. It comes

ROBERT PENN WARREN

Photo © Nancy Crampton

with the territory."

Death of a Salesman, a landmark work, still is only one of a number of dramas Miller wrote over several decades, including *All My Sons* (1947) and *The Crucible* (1953). Both are political — one contemporary and the other set in colonial times. The first deals with a manufacturer who knowingly allows defective parts to be shipped to airplane firms during World War II, resulting in the death of several American airmen. *The Crucible* depicts the Salem (Massachusetts) witchcraft trials of the 17th century in which Puritan settlers were wrongfully executed as supposed witches. Its message, though — that "witch hunts" directed at innocent people are anathema in a democracy — was relevant to the era in which the play was staged, the early 1950s, when an anti-Communist crusade led by U.S. Senator Joseph McCarthy and others ruined the lives of innocent people. Partly in response to *The Crucible*, Miller was called before the House (of Representatives) Un-American Activities Committee in 1956 and asked to provide the names of persons who might have Communist sympathies. Because of his refusal to do so, Miller was charged with contempt of Congress, a charge that was overturned on appeal.

A later Miller play, *Incident at Vichy* (1964), dealt with the Holocaust — the destruction of much of European Jewry at the hands of the Nazis and their collaborators. In *The Price* (1968), two brothers struggle to free themselves from the burdens of the past. Other of Miller's dramas include two one-act plays, *Fame* (1970) and *The Reason Why* (1970). His essays are collected in *Echoes Down the Corridor* (2000); his autobiography, *Timebends: A Life,* appeared in 1987.

Lillian Hellman (1906-1984)

Like Robert Penn Warren, Lillian Hellman's moral vision was shaped by the South. Her childhood was largely spent in New Orleans. Her compelling plays explore power's many guises and abuses. In *The Children's Hour* (1934), a manipulative girl destroys the lives of two women teachers by telling people they are lesbians. In *The Little Foxes* (1939), a rich old southern family fights over an inheritance. Hellman's anti-fascist *Watch on the Rhine* (1941) grew out of her trips to Europe in the 1930s. Her memoirs include *An Unfinished Woman* (1969) and *Pentimento* (1973).

For many years, Hellman had a close personal relationship with the remarkable scriptwriter Dashiell Hammett, whose streetwise detective character, Sam Spade, fascinated Depression-era Americans. Hammett invented the quintessentially American hardboiled detective novel: *The Maltese Falcon* (1930); *The Thin Man* (1934).

Hellman, like Arthur Miller, had refused to "name names" for the House Un-American Activities Committee, and she and Hammett

TENNESSEE WILLIAMS

were blacklisted (refused employment in the American entertainment industry) for a time. These events are recounted in Hellman's memoir, *Scoundrel Time* (1976).

Tennessee Williams (1911-1983)

Tennessee Williams, a native of Mississippi, was one of the more complex individuals on the American literary scene of the mid-20th century. His work focused on disturbed emotions within families — most of them southern. He was known for incantatory repetitions, a poetic southern diction, weird gothic settings, and Freudian exploration of human emotion. One of the first American writers to live openly as a homosexual, Williams explained that the longings of his tormented characters expressed their loneliness. His characters live and suffer intensely.

Williams wrote more than 20 full-length dramas, many of them autobiographical. He reached his peak relatively early in his career — in the 1940s — with *The Glass Menagerie* (1944) and *A Streetcar Named Desire* (1949). None of the works that followed over the next two decades and more reached the level of success and richness of those two pieces.

Katherine Anne Porter (1890-1980)

Katherine Anne Porter's long life and career encompassed several eras. Her first success, the short story "Flowering Judas" (1929), was set in Mexico during the revolution. The beautifully crafted short stories that gained her renown subtly unveil personal lives. "The Jilting of Granny Weatherall" (1930), for example, conveys large emotions with precision. Often she reveals women's inner experiences and their dependence on men.

Porter's nuances owe much to the stories of the New Zealand-born story writer Katherine Mansfield. Porter's story collections include *Flowering Judas* (1930), *Noon Wine* (1937), *Pale Horse, Pale Rider* (1939), *The Leaning Tower* (1944), and *Collected Stories* (1965). In the early 1960s, she produced a long, allegorical novel with a timeless theme — the responsibility of humans for each other. Titled *Ship of Fools* (1962), it was set in the late 1930s aboard a passenger liner carrying members of the German upper class and German refugees alike from the Nazi nation.

Not a prolific writer, Porter nonetheless influenced generations of authors, among them her southern colleagues Eudora Welty and Flannery O'Connor.

Eudora Welty (1909-2001)

Born in Mississippi to a well-to-do family of transplanted northerners, Eudora Welty was guided by Robert Penn Warren and Katherine Anne Porter. Porter, in fact, wrote an introduction to Welty's first collection of short stories, *A Curtain of Green* (1941). Welty modeled her

EUDORA WELTY

Photo © Nancy Crampton

nuanced work on Porter, but the younger woman was more interested in the comic and grotesque. Like fellow southerner Flannery O'Connor, Welty often took subnormal, eccentric, or exceptional characters for subjects.

Despite violence in her work, Welty's wit was essentially humane and affirmative, as, for example, in her frequently anthologized story "Why I Live at the P.O." (1941), in which a stubborn and independent daughter moves out of her house to live in a tiny post office. Her collections of stories include *The Wide Net* (1943), *The Golden Apples* (1949), *The Bride of the Innisfallen* (1955), and *Moon Lake* (1980). Welty also wrote novels such as *Delta Wedding* (1946), which is focused on a plantation family in modern times, and *The Optimist's Daughter* (1972).

THE 1950s

The 1950s saw the delayed impact of modernization and technology in everyday life. Not only did World War II defeat fascism, it brought the United States out of the Depression, and the 1950s provided most Americans with time to enjoy long-awaited material prosperity. Business, especially in the corporate world, seemed to offer the good life (usually in the suburbs), with its real and symbolic marks of success — house, car, television, and home appliances.

Yet loneliness at the top was a dominant theme for many writers; the faceless corporate man became a cultural stereotype in Sloan Wilson's best-selling novel *The Man in the Gray Flannel Suit* (1955). Generalized American alienation came under the scrutiny of sociologist David Riesman in *The Lonely Crowd* (1950).

Other popular, more or less scientific studies followed, ranging from Vance Packard's *The Hidden Persuaders* (1957) and *The Status Seekers* (1959) to William Whyte's *The Organization Man* (1956) and C. Wright Mills's more intellectual formulations — *White Collar* (1951) and *The Power Elite* (1956). Economist and academician John Kenneth Galbraith contributed *The Affluent Society* (1958). Most of these works supported the 1950s assumption that all Americans shared a common lifestyle. The studies spoke in general terms, criticizing citizens for losing frontier individualism and becoming too conformist (for example, Riesman and Mills) or advising people to become members of the "New Class" that technology and leisure time created (as seen in Galbraith's works).

The 1950s in literary terms actually was a decade of subtle and pervasive unease. Novels by John O'Hara, John Cheever, and John Updike explore the stress lurking in the shadows of seeming satisfaction. Some of the best work portrays men who fail in the struggle to succeed, as in Arthur Miller's *Death of a Salesman* and Saul Bellow's novella *Seize the*

The 1950s in literary terms actually was a decade of subtle and pervasive unease. Novels by John O'Hara, John Cheever, and John Updike explore the stress lurking in the shadows of seeming satisfaction.

Day. African-American Lorraine Hansberry (1930-1965) revealed racism as a continuing undercurrent in her moving 1959 play *A Raisin in the Sun*, in which a black family encounters a threatening "welcome committee" when it tries to move into a white neighborhood.

Some writers went further by focusing on characters who dropped out of mainstream society, as did J.D. Salinger in *The Catcher in the Rye*, Ralph Ellison in *Invisible Man*, and Jack Kerouac in *On the Road*. And in the waning days of the decade, Philip Roth arrived with a series of short stories reflecting a certain alienation from his Jewish heritage (*Goodbye, Columbus*). His psychological ruminations provided fodder for fiction, and later autobiography, into the new millennium.

The fiction of American-Jewish writers Bellow, Bernard Malamud, and Isaac Bashevis Singer — among others prominent in the 1950s and the years following — are also worthy, compelling additions to the compendium of American literature. The output of these three authors is most noted for its humor, ethical concern, and portraits of Jewish communities in the Old and New Worlds.

John O'Hara (1905-1970)

Trained as a journalist, John O'Hara was a prolific writer of plays, stories, and novels. He was a master of careful, telling detail and is best remembered for several realistic novels, mostly written in the 1950s, about outwardly successful people whose inner faults and dissatisfaction leave them vulnerable. These titles include *Appointment in Samarra* (1934), *Ten North Frederick* (1955), and *From the Terrace* (1959).

James Baldwin (1924-1987)

James Baldwin and Ralph Ellison mirror the African-American experience of the 1950s. Their characters suffer from a lack of identity, rather than from over-ambition.

Baldwin, the oldest of nine children born to a Harlem, New York, family, was the foster son of a minister. As a youth, Baldwin occasionally preached in the church. This experience helped shape the compelling, oral quality of his prose, most clearly seen in his excellent essays such as "Letter From a Region of My Mind," from the collection *The Fire Next Time* (1963). In this work, he argued movingly for an end to separation between the races.

Baldwin's first novel, the autobiographical *Go Tell It on the Mountain* (1953), is probably his best known. It is the story of a 14-year-old boy who seeks self-knowledge and religious faith as he wrestles with issues of Christian conversion in a storefront church. Other important Baldwin works include *Another Country* (1962) and *Nobody Knows My Name* (1961), a collection of passionate personal essays about racism, the role of the artist, and literature.

JAMES BALDWIN

Photo © Nancy Crampton

Ralph Ellison (1914-1994)

Ralph Ellison was a Midwesterner, born in Oklahoma, who studied at Tuskegee Institute in the southern United States. He had one of the strangest careers in American letters — consisting of one highly acclaimed book and little more.

The novel is *Invisible Man* (1952), the story of a black man who lives a subterranean existence in a cellar brightly illuminated by electricity stolen from a utility company. The book recounts his grotesque, disenchanting experiences. When he wins a scholarship to an all-black college, he is humiliated by whites; when he gets to the college, he witnesses the school's president spurning black American concerns. Life is corrupt outside college, too. For example, even religion is no consolation: A preacher turns out to be a criminal. The novel indicts society for failing to provide its citizens — black and white — with viable ideals and institutions for realizing them. It embodies a powerful racial theme because the "invisible man" is invisible not in himself but because others, blinded by prejudice, cannot see him for who he is.

Juneteenth (1999), Ellison's sprawling, unfinished novel, edited posthumously, reveals his continuing concern with race and identity.

Flannery O'Connor (1925-1964)

Flannery O'Connor, a native of Georgia, lived a life cut short by lupus, a blood disease. Still, she refused sentimentality, as is evident in her extremely humorous yet bleak and uncompromising stories.

Unlike Katherine Anne Porter, Eudora Welty, and Zora Neale Hurston, O'Connor most often held her characters at arm's length, revealing their inadequacy and silliness. The uneducated southern characters who people her novels often create violence through superstition or religion, as we see in her novel *Wise Blood* (1952), about a religious fanatic who establishes his own church.

Sometimes violence arises out of prejudice, as in "The Displaced Person" (1955), about an immigrant killed by ignorant country people who are threatened by his hard work and strange ways. Often, cruel events simply happen to the characters, as in "Good Country People" (1955), the story of a girl seduced by a man who steals her artificial leg.

The black humor of O'Connor links her with Nathanael West and Joseph Heller. Her works include short story collections *A Good Man Is Hard To Find* (1955), and *Everything That Rises Must Converge* (1965); the novel *The Violent Bear It Away* (1960); and a volume of letters, *The Habit of Being* (1979). *The Complete Stories* came out in 1971.

Saul Bellow (1915-2005)

Born in Canada and raised in Chicago, Saul Bellow was of Russian-Jewish background. In col-

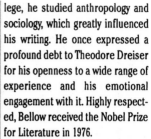

RALPH ELLISON

Photo © Nancy Crampton

lege, he studied anthropology and sociology, which greatly influenced his writing. He once expressed a profound debt to Theodore Dreiser for his openness to a wide range of experience and his emotional engagement with it. Highly respected, Bellow received the Nobel Prize for Literature in 1976.

Bellow's early, somewhat grim existentialist novels include *Dangling Man* (1944), a Kafkaesque study of a man waiting to be drafted into the army, and *The Victim* (1947), about relations between Jews and Gentiles. In the 1950s, his vision became more comic: He used a series of energetic and adventurous first-person narrators in *The Adventures of Augie March* (1953) — the study of a Huck Finn-like urban entrepreneur who becomes a black marketeer in Europe — and in *Henderson the Rain King* (1959), a brilliant and exuberant serio-comic novel about a middle-aged millionaire whose unsatisfied ambitions drive him to Africa.

Bellow's later works include *Herzog* (1964), about the troubled life of a neurotic English professor who specializes in the idea of the romantic self; *Mr. Sammler's Planet* (1970); *Humboldt's Gift* (1975); and the autobiographical *The Dean's December* (1982).

In the late 1980s, Bellow wrote two novellas in which elderly protagonists search for ultimate verities, *Something To Remember Me By* (1991) and *The Actual* (1997). His novel *Ravelstein* (2000) is a veiled account of the life of Bellow's friend Alan Bloom, the best-selling author of *The Closing of the American Mind* (1987), a conservative attack on the academy for a perceived erosion of standards in American cultural life.

Bellow's *Seize the Day* (1956) is a brilliant novella centered on a failed businessman, Tommy Wilhelm, who is so consumed by feelings of inadequacy that he becomes totally inadequate — a failure with women, jobs, machines, and the commodities market, where he loses all his money. Wilhelm is an example of the *schlemiel* of Jewish folklore — one to whom unlucky things inevitably happen.

Bernard Malamud (1914-1986)

Bernard Malamud was born in New York City to Russian-Jewish immigrant parents. In his second novel, *The Assistant* (1957), Malamud found his characteristic themes — man's struggle to survive against all odds, and the ethical underpinnings of recent Jewish immigrants.

Malamud's first published work was *The Natural* (1952), a combination of realism and fantasy set in the mythic world of professional baseball. Other novels include *A New Life* (1961), *The Fixer* (1966), *Pictures of Fidelman* (1969), and *The Tenants* (1971).

Malamud also was a prolific master of short fiction. Through his

BERNARD MALAMUD

Photo © Nancy Crampton

stories in collections such as *The Magic Barrel* (1958), *Idiots First* (1963), and *Rembrandt's Hat* (1973), he conveyed — more than any other American-born writer — a sense of the Jewish present and past, the real and the surreal, fact and legend.

Malamud's monumental work — for which he was awarded the Pulitzer Prize and National Book Award — is *The Fixer*. Set in Russia around the turn of the 20th century, it is a thinly veiled look at an actual case of blood libel — the infamous 1913 trial of Mendel Beiliss, a dark, anti-Semitic blotch on modern history. As in many of his writings, Malamud underscores the suffering of his hero, Yakob Bok, and the struggle against all odds to endure.

Isaac Bashevis Singer (1904-1991)

Nobel Prize-winning novelist and short story master Isaac Bashevis Singer — a native of Poland who immigrated to the United States in 1935 — was the son of the prominent head of a rabbinical court in Warsaw. Writing in Yiddish all his life, he dealt in mythic and realistic terms with two specific groups of Jews — the denizens of the Old World *shtetls* (small villages) and the ocean-tossed 20th-century emigrés of the pre-World War II and postwar eras.

Singer's writings served as bookends for the Holocaust. On the one hand, he described — in novels such as *The Manor* (1967) and *The Estate* (1969), set in 19th-century Russia, and *The Family Moskat* (1950), focused on a Polish-Jewish family between the world wars — the world of European Jewry that no longer exists. Complementing these works were his writings set after the war, such as *Enemies, A Love Story* (1972), whose protagonists were survivors of the Holocaust seeking to create new lives for themselves.

Vladimir Nabokov (1889-1977)

Like Singer, Vladimir Nabokov was an Eastern European immigrant. Born into an affluent family in Czarist Russia, he came to the United States in 1940 and gained U.S. citizenship five years later. From 1948 to 1959, he taught literature at Cornell University in upstate New York; in 1960 he moved permanently to Switzerland.

Nabokov is best known for his novels, which include the autobiographical *Pnin* (1957), about an ineffectual Russian emigré professor, and *Lolita* (U.S. edition, 1958), about an educated, middle-aged European who becomes infatuated with a 12-year-old American girl. Nabokov's pastiche novel, *Pale Fire* (1962), another successful venture, focuses on a long poem by an imaginary dead poet and the commentaries on it by a critic whose writings overwhelm the poem and take on unexpected lives of their own.

Nabokov is an important writer for his stylistic subtlety, deft satire, and ingenious innovations in form, which have inspired such novelists as John Barth. Nabokov was aware of his role as a mediator between the Russian and American literary worlds; he wrote a book on Gogol and translated Pushkin's *Eugene Onegin*. His daring, somewhat expressionist subjects helped introduce 20th-century European currents into the essentially realist American fictional tradition. Nabokov's tone, partly satirical and partly nostalgic, also suggested a new serio-comic emotional register made use of by writers such as Thomas Pynchon, who combines the opposing notes of wit and fear.

John Cheever (1912-1982)

John Cheever often has been called a "novelist of manners." He is also known for his elegant, suggestive short stories, which scrutinize the New York business world through its effects on the businessmen, their wives, children, and friends.

A wry melancholy and never quite quenched but seemingly hopeless desire for passion or metaphysical certainty lurks in the shadows of Cheever's finely drawn, Chekhovian tales, collected in *The Way Some People Live* (1943), *The Housebreaker of Shady Hill* (1958), *Some People, Places, and Things That Will Not Appear in My Next Novel* (1961), *The Brigadier and the Golf Widow* (1964), and *The World of Apples* (1973). His titles reveal his characteristic nonchalance, playfulness, and irreverence, and hint at his subject matter.

Cheever also published several novels — *The Wapshot Scandal*

(1964), *Bullet Park* (1969), and *Falconer* (1977) — the last of which was largely autobiographical.

John Updike (1932-)

John Updike, like Cheever, is also regarded as a writer of manners with his suburban settings, domestic themes, reflections of ennui and wistfulness, and, particularly, his fictional locales on the eastern seaboard of the United States, in Massachusetts and Pennsylvania.

Updike is best known for his five Rabbit books, depictions of the life of a man — Harry "Rabbit" Angstrom — through the ebbs and flows of his existence across four decades of American social and political history. *Rabbit, Run* (1960) is a mirror of the 1950s, with Angstrom an aimless, disaffected young husband. *Rabbit Redux* (1971) — spotlighting the counterculture of the 1960s — finds Angstrom still without a clear goal or purpose or viable escape route from the banal. In *Rabbit Is Rich* (1981), Harry has become a prosperous businessman during the 1970s, as the Vietnam era wanes. The final novel, *Rabbit at Rest* (1990), glimpses Angstrom's reconciliation with life, before his death from a heart attack, against the backdrop of the 1980s. In Updike's 1995 novella *Rabbit Remembered*, his adult children recall Rabbit.

Among Updike's other novels are *The Centaur* (1963), *Couples* (1968), *A Month of Sundays* (1975), *Roger's Version* (1986), and *S.*

JOHN UPDIKE

Photo © Nancy Crampton

(1988). Updike creates an alter ego — a writer whose fame ironically threatens to silence him — in another series of novels: *Bech: A Book* (1970), *Bech Is Back* (1982), and *Bech at Bay* (1998).

Updike possesses the most brilliant style of any writer today, and his short stories offer scintillating examples of its range and inventiveness. Collections include *The Same Door* (1959), *The Music School* (1966), *Museums and Women* (1972), *Too Far To Go* (1979), and *Problems* (1979). He has also written several volumes of poetry and essays.

J.D. Salinger (1919-)

A harbinger of things to come in the 1960s, J.D. Salinger has portrayed attempts to drop out of society. Born in New York City, he achieved huge literary success with the publication of his novel *The Catcher in the Rye* (1951), centered on a sensitive 16-year-old, Holden Caulfield, who flees his elite boarding school for the outside world of adulthood, only to become disillusioned by its materialism and phoniness.

When asked what he would like to be, Caulfield answers "the catcher in the rye," misquoting a poem by Robert Burns. In his vision, he is a modern version of a white knight, the sole preserver of innocence. He imagines a big field of rye so tall that a group of young children cannot see where they are running as they play their games. He is the only big person there. "I'm standing on the edge of some crazy cliff. What I have to do, I have to catch everybody if they start to go over the cliff." The fall over the cliff is equated with the loss of childhood innocence — a persistent theme of the era.

Other works by this reclusive, spare writer include *Nine Stories* (1953), *Franny and Zooey* (1961), and *Raise High the Roof Beam, Carpenters* (1963), a collection of stories from *The New Yorker* magazine. Since the appearance of one story in 1965, Salinger — who lives in New Hampshire — has been absent from the American literary scene.

Jack Kerouac (1922-1969)

The son of an impoverished French-Canadian family, Jack Kerouac also questioned the values of middle-class life. He met members of the Beat literary underground as an undergraduate at Columbia University in New York City. His fiction was much influenced by the loosely autobiographical work of southern novelist Thomas Wolfe.

Kerouac's best-known novel, *On the Road* (1957), describes beatniks wandering through America seeking an idealistic dream of communal life and beauty. *The Dharma Bums* (1958) also focuses on peripatetic counterculture intellectuals and their infatuation with Zen Buddhism. Kerouac also penned a book of poetry, *Mexico City Blues* (1959), and volumes about his life with such beatniks as experimental

The alienation and stress underlying the 1950s found outward expression in the 1960s in the United States in the civil rights movement, feminism, antiwar protests, minority activism, and the arrival of a counterculture whose effects are still being worked through American society.

novelist William Burroughs and poet Allen Ginsberg.

THE TURBULENT BUT CREATIVE 1960s

The alienation and stress underlying the 1950s found outward expression in the 1960s in the United States in the civil rights movement, feminism, antiwar protests, minority activism, and the arrival of a counterculture whose effects are still being worked through American society. Notable political and social works of the era include the speeches of civil rights leader Dr. Martin Luther King, Jr., the early writings of feminist leader Betty Friedan (*The Feminine Mystique*), and Norman Mailer's *The Armies of the Night* (1968), about a 1967 antiwar march.

The 1960s were marked by a blurring of the line between fiction and fact, novels and reportage that has carried through the present day. Novelist Truman Capote (1924-1984) — who had dazzled readers as an *enfant terrible* of the late 1940s and 1950s in such works as *Breakfast at Tiffany's* (1958) — stunned audiences with *In Cold Blood* (1965), a riveting analysis of a brutal mass murder in the American heartland that read like a work of detective fiction.

At the same time, the New Journalism emerged — volumes of nonfiction that combined journalism with techniques of fiction, or that frequently played with the facts, reshaping them to add to the drama and immediacy of the story being reported. In *The Electric Kool-Aid Acid Test* (1968), Tom Wolfe (1931-) celebrated the counterculture wanderlust of novelist Ken Kesey (1935-2001); *Radical Chic & Mau-Mauing the Flak Catchers* (1970) ridiculed many aspects of left-wing activism. Wolfe later wrote an exuberant and insightful history of the initial phase of the U.S. space program, *The Right Stuff* (1979), and a novel, *The Bonfire of the Vanities* (1987), a panoramic portrayal of American society in the 1980s.

As the 1960s evolved, literature flowed with the turbulence of the era. An ironic, comic vision also came into view, reflected in the fabulism of several writers. Examples include Ken Kesey's darkly comic *One Flew Over the Cuckoo's Nest* (1962), a novel about life in a mental hospital in which the wardens are more disturbed than the inmates, and the whimsical, fantastic *Trout Fishing in America* (1967) by Richard Brautigan (1935-1984).

The comical and fantastic yielded a new mode, half comic and half metaphysical, in Thomas Pynchon's paranoid, brilliant *V* and *The Crying of Lot 49*, John Barth's *Giles Goat-Boy*, and the grotesque short stories of Donald Barthelme (1931-1989), whose first collection, *Come Back, Dr. Caligari*, was published in 1964.

This new mode came to be called metafiction — self-conscious or reflexive fiction that calls attention to its own technique. Such "fiction about fiction" emphasizes language and style, and departs from the conventions of realism such as rounded characters, a believable plot enabling a character's development, and appropriate settings. In metafiction, the writer's style attracts the reader's attention. The true subject is not the characters, but rather the writer's own consciousness.

Critics of the time commonly grouped Pynchon, Barth, and Barthelme as metafictionists, along with William Gaddis (1922-1998), whose long novel *JR* (1975), about a young boy

who builds up a phony business empire from junk bonds, eerily forecasts Wall Street excesses to come. His shorter, more accessible *Carpenter's Gothic* (1985) combines romance with menace. Gaddis is often linked with midwestern philosopher/novelist William Gass (1924-), best known for his early, thoughtful novel *Omensetter's Luck* (1966), and for stories collected in *In the Heart of the Heart of the Country* (1968).

Robert Coover (1932-) is another metafiction writer. His collection of stories *Pricksongs & Descants* (1969) plays with plots familiar from folktales and popular culture, while his novel *The Public Burning* (1977) deconstructs the execution of Julius and Ethel Rosenberg, who were convicted of espionage.

Thomas Pynchon (1937-)

Thomas Pynchon, a mysterious, publicity-shunning author, was born in New York and graduated from Cornell University in 1958, where he may have come under the influence of Vladimir Nabokov. Certainly, his innovative fantasies use themes of translating clues, games, and codes that could derive from Nabokov. Pynchon's flexible tone can modulate paranoia into poetry.

All of Pynchon's fiction is similarly structured. A vast plot is unknown to at least one of the main characters, whose task it then becomes to render order out of chaos and decipher the world. This project, exactly the job of the traditional artist, devolves also upon the reader, who must follow along and watch for clues and meanings. This paranoid vision is extended across continents and time itself, for Pynchon employs the metaphor of entropy, the gradual running down of the universe. The masterful use of popular culture — particularly science fiction and detective fiction — is evident in his works.

Pynchon's work *V* (1963) is loosely structured around Benny Profane — a failure who engages in pointless wanderings and various weird enterprises — and his opposite, the educated Herbert Stencil, who seeks a mysterious female spy, V (alternatively Venus, Virgin, Void). *The Crying of Lot 49* (1966), a short work, deals with a secret system associated with the U.S. Postal Service. *Gravity's Rainbow* (1973) takes place during World War II in London, when rockets were falling on the city, and concerns a farcical yet symbolic search for Nazis and other disguised figures.

In Pynchon's comic novel *Vineland* (1990), set in northern California, shadowy forces within federal agencies endanger individuals. In the novel *Mason & Dixon* (1997), partly set in the wilderness of 1765, two English explorers survey the line that would come to divide the North and South in the United States. Again, Pynchon sees power wielded unjustly. Dixon asks: "No matter where...we go, shall we find all the World Tyrants and Slaves?" Despite its range, the violence, comedy, and flair for innovation in his work inexorably link Pynchon with the 1960s.

John Barth (1930-)

John Barth, a native of Maryland, is more interested in how a story is told than in the story itself, but where Pynchon deludes the reader by false trails and possible clues out of detective novels, Barth entices his audience into a carnival fun house full of distorting mirrors that exaggerate some features while minimizing others.

> "No matter where...we go, shall we find all the World Tyrants and Slaves?" Despite its range, the violence, comedy, and flair for innovation in his work inexorably link Pynchon with the 1960s.

Realism is the enemy for Barth, the author of *Lost in the Funhouse* (1968), 14 stories that constantly refer to the processes of writing and reading. Barth's intent is to alert the reader to the artificial nature of reading and writing and to prevent him or her from being drawn into the story as if it were real. To explode the illusion of realism, Barth uses a panoply of reflexive devices to remind his audience that they are reading.

Barth's earlier works, like Saul Bellow's, were questioning and existential, and took up the 1950s themes of escape and wandering. In *The Floating Opera* (1956), a man considers suicide. *The End of the Road* (1958) concerns a complex love affair. Works of the 1960s became more comical and less realistic. *The Sot-Weed Factor* (1960) parodies an 18th-century picaresque style, while *Giles Goat-Boy* (1966) is a parody of the world seen as a university.

Chimera (1972) retells tales from Greek mythology, and *Letters* (1979) uses Barth himself as a character, as Norman Mailer does in *The Armies of the Night*. In *Sabbatical: A Romance* (1982), Barth uses the popular fiction motif of the spy; this is the story of a woman college professor and her husband, a retired secret agent turned novelist. Later novels — *The Tidewater Tales* (1987), *The Last Voyage of Somebody the Sailor* (1991), and *Once Upon a Time: A Floating Opera* (1994) reveal Barth's "passionate virtuosity" (his own phrase) in negotiating the chaotic, oceanic world with the bright rigging of language.

Norman Mailer (1923-)

Norman Mailer made himself the most visible novelist of the 1960s and 1970s. Co-founder of the anti-establishment New York City weekly *The Village Voice*, Mailer publicized himself along with his political views. In his appetite for experience, vigorous style, and a dramatic public persona, Mailer follows in the tradition of Ernest Hemingway. To gain a vantage point on the assassination of President John F. Kennedy, Vietnam War protests, black liberation, and the women's movement, he constructed hip, existentialist, macho male personae (in her book *Sexual Politics*, Kate Millett identified Mailer as an archetypal male chauvinist). The irrepressible Mailer went on to marry six times and run for mayor of New York.

Mailer is the reverse of a writer like John Barth, for whom the subject is not as important as the way it is handled. Unlike the invisible Thomas Pynchon, Mailer constantly courts and demands attention.

A novelist, essayist, sometime politician, literary activist, and occasional actor, Mailer is always on the scene. From such New Journalism exercises as *Miami and the Siege of Chicago* (1968), an analysis of the 1968 U.S. presidential conventions, and his compelling study about the execution of a condemned murderer, *The*

NORMAN MAILER

Photo © Nancy Crampton

Executioner's Song (1979), Mailer has turned to writing such ambitious, if flawed, novels as *Ancient Evenings* (1983), set in the Egypt of antiquity, and *Harlot's Ghost* (1991), revolving around the U.S. Central Intelligence Agency.

Philip Roth (1933-)

Like Norman Mailer, Philip Roth has provoked controversy by mining his life for fiction. In Roth's case, his treatments of sexual themes and ironic analysis of Jewish life have drawn popular and critical attention, as well as criticism.

Roth's first book, *Goodbye, Columbus* (1959), satirized provincial Jewish suburbanites. In his best-known novel, the outrageous, best-selling *Portnoy's Complaint* (1969), a New York City administrator regales his taciturn psychoanalyst with off-color stories of his boyhood.

Although *The Great American Novel* (1973) delves into baseball lore, most of Roth's novels remain resolutely, even defiantly, autobiographical. In *My Life As a Man* (1974), under the stress of divorce, a man resorts to creating an alterego, Nathan Zuckerman, whose stories constitute one pole of the narrative, the other pole being the different kinds of readers' responses. Zuckerman seemingly takes over in a series of subsequent novels. The most successful is probably the first, *The Ghost Writer* (1979). It is told by Zuckerman as a young writer criticized by Jewish elders for fanning anti-Semitism. In *Zuckerman Bound* (1985), a novel has made Zuckerman rich but notorious. In *The Counterlife* (1986), the fifth Zuckerman novel, stories vie with stories, as Nathan's supposed life is contrasted with other imaginable lives. Roth's memoir *The Facts* (1988) twists the screw further; in it, Zuckerman criticizes Roth's own narrative style.

Roth continues wavering on the border between fact and fiction in *Patrimony: A True Story* (1991), a memoir about the death of his father. His recent novels include *American Pastoral* (1997), in which a daughter's 1960s radicalism wounds a father, and *The Human Stain* (2000), about a professor whose career is ruined by a racial misunderstanding based on language.

Roth is a profound analyst of Jewish strengths and weaknesses. His characterizations are nuanced; his protagonists are complex, individualized, and deeply human. Roth's series of autobiographical novels about a writer recalls John Updike's recent Bech series, and it is master-stylist Updike with whom Roth — widely admired for his supple, ingenious style — is most often compared.

Despite its brilliance and wit, some readers find Roth's work self-absorbed. Still, his vigorous accomplishment over almost 50 years has earned him a place among the most distinguished of American novelists.

PHILIP ROTH

Photo © Nancy Crampton

SOUTHERN WRITERS

Southern writing of the 1960s tended, like the then still largely agrarian southern region, to adhere to time-honored traditions. It remained rooted in realism and an ethical, if not religious, vision during this decade of radical change. Recurring southern themes include family, the family home, history, the land, religion, guilt, identity, death, and the search for redemptive meaning in life. Like William Faulkner and Thomas Wolfe (*Look Homeward, Angel*, 1929), who inspired the "southern renaissance" in literature, many southern writers of the 1960s were scholars and elaborate stylists, revering the written word as a link with traditions rooted in the classical world.

Many have been influential teachers. Kentucky-born Caroline Gordon (1895-1981), who married southern poet Allen Tate, was a respected professor of writing. She set her novels in her native Kentucky. Truman Capote was born in New Orleans and spent part of his childhood in small towns in Louisiana and Alabama, the settings for many of his early works in the elegant, decadent, southern gothic vein.

African-American writing professor Ernest Gaines (1933-), also born in New Orleans, set many of his moving, thoughtful works in the largely black rural bayou country of Louisiana. Perhaps his best known novel, *The Autobiography of Miss Jane Pittman* (1971), reflects on the sweep of time from the end of the Civil War in 1865 up to 1960. Concerned with human issues deeper than skin color, Gaines handles racial relations subtly.

Reynolds Price (1933-), a long-time professor at Duke University, was born in North Carolina, which furnishes the scenes for many of his works, such as *A Long and Happy Life* (1961). Like William Faulkner and Robert Penn Warren, he peoples his southern terrain with interlinked families close to their roots and broods on the passing of time and the imperative to expiate ancient wrongs. His meditative, poetic style recalls the classical literary tradition of the old South. Partially paralyzed due to cancer, Price has explored physical suffering in *The Promise of Rest* (1995), about a father tending his son who is dying of AIDS. His highly regarded novel *Kate Vaiden* (1986) reveals his ability to evoke a woman's life.

Walker Percy (1916-1990), a resident of Louisiana, was raised as a member of the southern aristocracy. His very readable novels — by turns comic, lyrical, moralizing, and satirical — reveal his awareness of social class and his conversion to Catholicism. His best novel is his first, *The Moviegoer* (1961). This story of a charming but aimless young New Orleans stockbroker shows the influence of French existentialism transplanted to the booming and often brash New South that burgeoned after World War II.

THE 1970s AND 1980s: CONSOLIDATION

By the mid-1970s, an era of consolidation had begun. The Vietnam conflict was over, followed soon afterward by U.S. recognition of the People's Republic of China and America's bicentennial celebration. Soon the 1980s — the "Me Decade" in Tom Wolfe's phrase — ensued, in which individuals tended to focus more on personal concerns than on larger social issues.

In literature, old currents remained, but the force behind pure experimentation dwindled.

New novelists like John Gardner, John Irving (*The World According to Garp*, 1978), Paul Theroux (*The Mosquito Coast*, 1981), William Kennedy (*Ironweed*, 1983), and Alice Walker (*The Color Purple*, 1982) surfaced with stylistically brilliant novels to portray moving human dramas. Concern with setting, character, and themes associated with realism returned, along with renewed interest in history, as in works by E.L. Doctorow.

Realism, abandoned by experimental writers in the 1960s, also crept back, often mingled with bold original elements — a daring structure like a novel within a novel, as in John Gardner's *October Light*, or black American dialect as in Alice Walker's *The Color Purple*. Minority literature began to flourish. Drama shifted from realism to more cinematic, kinetic techniques. At the same time, however, the Me Decade was reflected in such brash new talents as Jay McInerney (*Bright Lights, Big City*, 1984), Bret Easton Ellis (*Less Than Zero*, 1985), and Tama Janowitz (*Slaves of New York*, 1986).

E.L. Doctorow (1931-)

The novels of E.L. Doctorow demonstrate the transition from metafiction to a new and more human sensibility. His critically acclaimed novel about the high human cost of the Cold War, *The Book of Daniel* (1971), is based on the execution of Julius and Ethel Rosenberg for espionage, told in the voice of the bereaved son. Robert Coover's *The Public Burning* treats the same topic, but Doctorow's book conveys more warmth and emotion.

Doctorow's *Ragtime* (1975) is a rich, kaleidoscopic collage of the United States beginning in 1906. As John Dos Passos had done several decades earlier in his trilogy *U.S.A.*, Doctorow mingles fictional characters with real ones to capture the era's flavor and complexity. Doctorow's fictional history of the United States is continued in *Loon Lake* (1979), set in the 1930s, about a ruthless capitalist who dominates and destroys idealistic people.

Later Doctorow novels are the autobiographical *World's Fair* (1985), about an eight-year-old boy growing up in the Depression of the 1930s; *Billy Bathgate* (1989), about Dutch Schultz, a real New York gangster; and *The Waterworks* (1994), set in New York during the 1870s. *City of God* (2000) — the title referencing St. Augustine — turns to New York in the present. A Christian cleric's consciousness interweaves the city's generalized poverty, crime, and loneliness with stories of people whose lives touch his. The book hints at Doctorow's abiding belief that writing — a form of witnessing — is a mode of human survival.

Doctorow's techniques are eclectic. His stylistic exuberance and formal inventiveness link him with metafiction writers like Thomas Pynchon and John Barth, but his novels remain rooted in realism and history. His use of real people and events links him with the New Journalism of the 1960s and with Norman Mailer, Truman Capote, and Tom Wolfe, while his use of fictional memoir, as in *World's Fair*, looks forward to writers like Maxine Hong Kingston and the flowering of the memoir in the 1990s.

William Styron (1925-2006)

From the Tidewater area of Virginia, southerner William Styron wrote ambitious novels that set individuals in places and times that test the limits of their humanity. His early works include the acclaimed *Lie Down in Darkness* (1951), which begins with the suicide of a beautiful southern woman — who leaps from a New York skyscraper — and works backward in time to explore the dark forces within her family that drew her to her death.

The Faulknerian treatment, including dark southern gothic themes, flashbacks, and stream of consciousness monologues, brought Styron fame that turned to controversy when he published his Pulitzer Prize-winning *The Confessions of Nat Turner* (1967). This novel re-creates the most violent slave uprising in U.S. history, as seen through the eyes of its leader. The book came out at the height of the "black power" movement, and, unsurprisingly, the depiction of Nat Turner drew sharp criticism from many African-American observers, although some came to Styron's defense.

Styron's fascination with individual human acts set against backdrops of larger racial injustice continues in *Sophie's Choice* (1979), another tour de force about the doom of a lovely woman — the topic that Edgar Allan Poe, the presiding spirit of southern writers, found the most moving of all possible subjects. In this novel, a beautiful Polish woman who has survived Auschwitz is defeated by its remembered agonies, summed up in the moment she was made to choose which one of her children would live and which one would die. The book makes complex parallels between the racism of the South and the Holocaust.

More recently Styron, like many other writers, turned to the memoir form. His short account of his near-suicidal depression, *Darkness Visible: A Memoir of Madness* (1990), recalls the terrible undertow that his own doomed characters must have felt. In the autobiographical fictions in *A Tidewater Morning* (1993), the shimmering, oppressively hot Virginia coast where he grew up mirrors and extends the speaker's shifting consciousness.

John Gardner (1933-1982)

John Gardner, from a farming background in New York State, was his era's most important spokesperson for ethical values in literature until his death in a motorcycle accident. He was a professor of English specializing in the medieval period; his most popular novel, *Grendel* (1971), retells the Old English epic *Beowulf* from the monster's existentialist point of view. The short, vivid, and often comic novel is a subtle argument against the existentialism that fills its protagonist with self-destructive despair and cynicism.

A prolific and popular novelist, Gardner used a realistic approach but employed innovative techniques — such as flashbacks, stories within stories, retellings of myths, and contrasting stories — to bring out the truth of a human situation. His strengths are characterization (particularly his sympathetic portraits of ordinary people) and colorful style. Major works include *The Resurrection* (1966), *The Sunlight Dialogues* (1972), *Nickel Mountain* (1973), *October Light* (1976), and *Mickelsson's Ghosts* (1982).

Gardner's fictional patterns suggest the curative powers of fellowship, duty, and family obligations, and in this sense Gardner was a profoundly traditional and conservative author. He endeavored to demonstrate that certain values and acts lead to fulfilling lives. His book *On Moral Fiction* (1978) calls for novels that embody ethical values rather than dazzle with empty technical innovation. The book created a furor, largely because Gardner bluntly criticized important living authors — especially writers of metafiction — for failing to reflect ethical concerns. Gardner argued for a warm, human, ultimately more realistic and socially engaged fiction, such as that of Joyce Carol Oates and Toni Morrison.

Toni Morrison

Photo © Nancy Crampton

Joyce Carol Oates (1938-)

Joyce Carol Oates is the most prolific serious novelist of recent decades, having published novels, short stories, poetry, nonfiction, plays, critical studies, and essays. She uses what she has called "psychological realism" on a panoramic range of subjects and forms.

Oates has authored a Gothic trilogy consisting of *Bellefleur* (1980), *A Bloodsmoor Romance* (1982), and *Mysteries of Winterthurn* (1984); a nonfiction book, *On Boxing* (1987); and a study of Marilyn Monroe (*Blonde*, 2000). Her plots are dark and often hinge on violence, which she finds to be deeply rooted in the American psyche.

Toni Morrison (1931-)

African-American novelist Toni Morrison was born in Ohio to a spiritually oriented family. She attended Howard University in Washington, D.C., and has worked as a senior editor in a major Washington publishing house and as a distinguished professor at various universities.

Morrison's richly woven fiction has gained her international acclaim. In compelling, large-spirited novels, she treats the complex identities of black people in a universal manner. In her early work *The Bluest Eye* (1970), a strong-willed young black girl tells the story of Pecola Breedlove, who is driven mad by an abusive father. Pecola believes that her dark eyes have magically become blue and that they will make her lovable.

Morrison has said that she was creating her own sense of identity as a writer through this novel: "I was Pecola, Claudia, everybody." *Sula* (1973) describes the strong friendship of two women. Morrison paints African-American women as unique, fully individual characters rather than as stereotypes. Morrison's *Song of Solomon* (1977) has won several awards. It follows a black man, Milkman Dead, and his complex relations with his family and community. In *Tar Baby* (1981) Morrison deals with black and white relations. *Beloved* (1987) is the wrenching story of a woman who murders her children rather than allow them to live as slaves. It employs the dreamlike techniques of magical realism in depicting a mysterious figure, Beloved, who returns to live with the mother who has slit her throat.

Jazz (1992), set in 1920s Harlem, is a story of love and murder; in *Paradise* (1998), males of the all-black Oklahoma town of Ruby kill neighbors from an all-women's settlement. Morrison reveals that exclusion, whether by sex or race, however appealing it may seem, leads ultimately not to paradise but to a hell of human devising.

In her accessible nonfiction book *Playing in the Dark: Whiteness and the Literary Imagination* (1992), Morrison discerns a defining current of racial consciousness in American literature. Morrison has suggested that though her novels are consummate works of art, they contain political meanings: "I am

Morrison's richly woven fiction has gained her international acclaim. In compelling, large-spirited novels, she treats the complex identities of black people in a universal manner.

not interested in indulging myself in some private exercise of my imagination...yes, the work must be political." In 1993, Morrison won the Nobel Prize for Literature.

Alice Walker (1944-)

Alice Walker, an African-American and the child of a sharecropper family in rural Georgia, graduated from Sarah Lawrence College, where one of her teachers was the politically committed female poet Muriel Rukeyser. Other influences on her work have been Flannery O'Connor and Zora Neale Hurston.

A "womanist" writer, as Walker calls herself, she has long been associated with feminism, presenting black existence from the female perspective. Like Toni Morrison, Jamaica Kincaid, the late Toni Cade Bambara, and other accomplished contemporary black novelists, Walker uses heightened, lyrical realism to center on the dreams and failures of accessible, credible people. Her work underscores the quest for dignity in human life. A fine stylist, particularly in her epistolary dialect novel *The Color Purple*, her work seeks to educate. In this she resembles the black American novelist Ishmael Reed, whose satires expose social problems and racial issues.

Walker's *The Color Purple* is the story of the love between two poor black sisters that survives a separation over years, interwoven with the story of how, during that same period, the shy, ugly, and uneducated sister discovers her inner strength through the support of a female friend. The theme of the support women give each other recalls Maya Angelou's autobiography, *I Know Why the Caged Bird Sings*, which celebrates the mother-daughter connection, and the work of white feminists such as Adrienne Rich. *The Color Purple* portrays men as basically unaware of the needs and reality of women.

Although many critics find Walker's work too didactic or ideological, a large general readership appreciates her bold explorations of African-American womanhood. Her novels shed light on festering issues such as the harsh legacy of sharecropping (*The Third Life of Grange Copeland*, 1970) and female circumcision (*Possessing the Secret Joy*, 1992).

THE RISE OF MULTIETHNIC FICTION

Jewish-American writers like Saul Bellow, Bernard Malamud, Isaac Bashevis Singer, Arthur Miller, Philip Roth, and Norman Mailer were the first since the 19th-century abolitionists and African-American writers of slave narratives to address ethnic prejudice and the plight of the outsider. They explored new ways of projecting an awareness that was both American and specific to a subculture. In this, they opened the door for the flowering of multiethnic writing in the decades to come.

The close of the 1980s and the beginnings of the 1990s saw minority writing become a major fixture on the American literary landscape. This is true in drama as well as in prose. The late August Wilson (1945-2005) wrote an acclaimed cycle of plays about the 20th-century black experience that stands alongside the work of novelists Alice Walker, John Edgar Wideman, and Toni Morrison. Scholars such as Lawrence Levine (*The Opening of the American Mind: Canons, Culture and History*, 1996) and Ronald Takaki (*A Different Mirror: A History of Multicultural America*, 1993) provide invaluable context for understanding multiethnic literature and its meanings.

Asian Americans also took their place on the scene. Maxine Hong Kingston, author of *The Woman Warrior* (1976), carved out a place for her fellow Asian Americans. Among them is Amy Tan (1952-), whose luminous novels of Chinese life transposed to post-World War II America (*The Joy Luck Club*, 1989, and *The Kitchen God's Wife*, 1991) captivated readers. David Henry Hwang (1957-), a California-born son of Chinese immigrants, made his mark in drama, with plays such as *F.O.B.* (1981) and *M. Butterfly* (1986).

A relatively new group on the literary horizon were the Latino-American writers, including the Pulitzer Prize-winning novelist Oscar Hijuelos, the Cuban-born author of *The Mambo Kings Play Songs of Love* (1989). Leading writers of Mexican-American descent include Sandra Cisneros (*Woman Hollering Creek and Other Stories*, 1991); and Rudolfo Anaya, author of the poetic novel *Bless Me, Ultima* (1972).

Native-American fiction flowered. Most often the authors evoked the loss of traditional life based in nature, the stressful attempt to adapt to modern life, and their struggles with poverty, unemployment, and alcoholism. The Pulitzer Prize-winning *House Made of Dawn* (1968), by N. Scott Momaday (1934-), and his poetic *The Way to Rainy Mountain* (1969) evoke the beauty and despair of Kiowa Indian life. Of mixed Pueblo descent, Leslie Marmon Silko wrote the critically esteemed novel *Ceremony* (1977), which gained a large general audience. Like Momaday's works, hers is a "chant novel" structured on Native-American healing rituals.

Blackfoot poet and novelist James Welch (1940-2003) detailed the struggles of Native Americans in his slender, nearly flawless novels *Winter in the Blood* (1974), *The Death of Jim Loney* (1979), *Fools Crow* (1986), and *The Indian Lawyer* (1990). Louise Erdrich, part Chippewa, has written a powerful series of novels inaugurated by *Love Medicine* (1984) that capture the tangled lives of dysfunctional reservation families with a poignant blend of stoicism and humor.

AMERICAN DRAMA

After World War I, popular and lucrative musicals had increasingly dominated the Broadway theatrical scene. Serious theater retreated to smaller, less expensive theaters "off Broadway" or outside New York City.

This situation repeated itself after World War II. American drama had languished in the 1950s, constrained by the Cold War and McCarthyism. The energy of the 1960s revived it. The off-off-Broadway movement presented an innovative alternative to commercialized popular theater.

Many of the major dramatists after 1960 produced their work in small venues. Freed from the need to make enough money to pay for expensive playhouses, they were newly inspired by European existentialism and the so-called Theater of the Absurd associated with European playwrights Samuel Beckett, Jean Genet, and Eugene Ionesco, as well as by Harold Pinter. The best dramatists became innovative and even surreal, rejecting realistic theater to attack superficial social conventions.

Edward Albee (1928-)

The most influential dramatist of the early 1960s was Edward Albee, who was adopted into a well-off

EDWARD ALBEE

Photo: Scott Gries / Getty Images

family that had owned vaudeville theaters and counted actors among their friends. Helping produce European absurdist theater, Albee actively brought new European currents into U.S. drama. In *The American Dream* (1960), stick figures of Mommy, Daddy, and Grandma recite platitudes that caricature a loveless, conventional family.

Loss of identity and consequent struggles for power to fill the void propel Albee's plays, such as *Who's Afraid of Virginia Woolf?* (1962). In this controversial drama, made into a film starring Elizabeth Taylor and Richard Burton, an unhappily married couple's shared fantasy — that they have a child, that their lives have meaning — is violently exposed as an untruth.

Albee has continued to produce distinguished work over several decades, including *Tiny Alice* (1964); *A Delicate Balance* (1966); *Seascape* (1975); *Marriage Play* (1987); and *Three Tall Women* (1991), which follows the main character, who resembles Albee's overbearing adoptive mother, through three stages of life.

Amiri Baraka (1934-)

Poet Amiri Baraka, known for supple, speech-oriented poetry with an affinity to improvisational jazz, turned to drama in the 1960s. Always searching to find himself, Baraka has changed his name several times as he has sought to define his identity as a black American. Baraka explored various paths of life in his early years, flunking out of Howard University and becoming dishonorably discharged from the U.S. Air Force for alleged Communism. During these years, his true vocation of writing emerged.

During the 1960s, Baraka lived in New York City's Greenwich Village, where he knew many artists and writers including Frank O'Hara and Allen Ginsberg.

By 1965, Baraka had started the Black Arts Repertory Theater in Harlem, the black section of New York City. He portrayed black nationalist views of racism in disturbing plays such as *Dutchman* (1964), in which a white woman flirts with and eventually kills a younger black man on a New York City subway. The realistic first half of the play sparkles with witty dialogue and subtle characterization. The shocking ending risks melodrama to dramatize racial misunderstanding and the victimization of the black male protagonist.

Sam Shepard (1943-)

Actor/dramatist Sam Shepard spent his childhood moving with his family from army base to army base following his father, who had been a pilot in World War II. He spent his teen years on a ranch in the barren desert east of Los Angeles, California. In secondary school, Shepard found solace in the Beat poets; he learned jazz drumming and later played in a rock band. Shepard produced his first plays, *Cowboys* and *The Rock Garden*, in

AMIRI BARAKA

Photo © Nancy Crampton

1964. They prefigure his mature works in their western motifs and theme of male competition.

Of almost 50 works for stage and screen, Shepard's most esteemed are three interrelated plays evoking love and violence in the family: *Curse of the Starving Class* (1976), *Buried Child* (1978), and *True West* (1980), his best-known work. In *True West*, two middle-aged brothers, an educated screenwriter and a drifting thief, compete to write a true-to-life western play for a rich, urban movie producer. Each thinking he needs what the other has — success, freedom — the two brothers change places in an atmosphere of increasing violence fueled by alcohol. The play registers Shepard's concern with loss of freedom, authenticity, and autonomy in American life. It dramatizes the vanishing frontier (the drifter) and the American imagination (the writer), seduced by money, the media, and commercial forces, personified by the producer.

In his writing process, Shepard tries to re-create a zone of freedom by allowing his characters to act in unpredictable, spontaneous, sometimes illogical ways. The most famous example comes from *True West*. In a gesture meant to suggest lawless freedom, the distraught writer steals numerous toasters. Totally unrealistic yet oddly believable on an emotional level, the scene works as comedy, absurd drama, and irony.

Shepard lets his characters guide his writing, rather than beginning with a pre-planned plot, and his plays are fresh and lifelike. His surrealistic flair and experimentalism link him with Edward Albee, but his plays are earthier and funnier, and his characters are drawn more realistically. They convey a bold West Coast consciousness and make comments on America in their use of landscape motifs and specific settings and contexts.

David Mamet (1947-)

Equally important is David Mamet, raised in Chicago, whose writing was influenced by the Stanislavsky method of acting that revealed to him the way "the language we use...determines the way we behave, more than the other way around." His emphasis on language not as communication but as a weapon, evasion, and manipulation of reality give Mamet a contemporary, postmodern sensibility.

Mamet's hard-hitting plays include American Buffalo (1975), a two-act play of increasingly violent language involving a drug addict, a junk store, and an attempted theft; and Speed-the-Plow (1987). The acclaimed and frequently anthologized Glengarry Glen Ross (1982), about real estate salesmen, was made into an outstanding 1992 movie with an all-star cast. This play, like most of Mamet's work, reveals his intense engagement with some of America's unresolved issues — here, as if in an update of Arthur Miller's Death of a Salesman, one sees the need for dignity and job security, especially

Photo: Sara Krulwich / The New York Times

SAM SHEPARD

DAVID MAMET

Photo © Robin Holland / CORBIS OUTLINE

for older workers; competition between older and younger generations in the workplace; intense focus on profits at the expense of the welfare of workers; and — enveloping all — the corrosive atmosphere of competition carried to abusive lengths.

Mamet's Oleanna (1991) effectively dissects sexual harassment in a university setting. The Cryptogram (1994) imagines a child's horrific vision of family life. Recent plays include The Old Neighborhood (1991) and Boston Marriage (1999).

David Rabe (1940-)

Another noted dramatist is David Rabe, a Vietnam veteran who was one of the first to explore that war's upheaval and violence in The Basic Training of Pavlo Hummel (1971) and Sticks and Bones (1969). Subsequent plays include The Orphan (1973), based on Aeschylus's Oresteia; In the Boom Boom Room (1973), about the rape of a dancer; and Hurlyburly (1984) and Those the River Keeps (1990), both about Hollywood disillusionment. Rabe's recent works include The Crossing Guard (1994) and Corners (1998), about the concept of honor in the Mafia.

August Wilson (1945-2005)

The distinguished African-American dramatist August Wilson, born Frederick August Kittel, was the son of a German immigrant who did not concern himself with his family. Wilson endured poverty and racism and adopted the surname of his African-American mother as a teenager. Influenced by the black arts movement of the late 1960s, Wilson co-founded Pittsburgh's Black Horizons Theater.

Wilson's plays explore African-American experience, organized by decades. *Ma Rainey's Black Bottom* (1984), set in 1927 Chicago, depicts the famous blues singer. His acclaimed play *Fences* (1985), set in the 1950s, dramatizes the conflict between a father and a son, touching on the all-American themes of baseball and the American dream of success. *Joe Turner's Come and Gone* (1986) concerns boarding-house residents in 1911. *The Piano Lesson* (1987), set in the 1930s, crystallizes a family's dynamic by focusing on the heirloom piano. *Two Trains Running* (1990) takes place in a coffeehouse in the 1960s, while *Seven Guitars* (1995) explores the 1940s. ◼

AUGUST WILSON

CHAPTER 9

CONTEMPORARY AMERICAN POETRY

U.S. poetry since 1990 has been in the midst of a kaleidoscopic renaissance. In the latter half of the 20th century, there was, if not a consensus, at least a discernible shape to the poetic field, complete with well-defended positions. Well-defined schools dominated the scene, and critical discussions tended to the binary: formalism versus free verse, academic versus experimental.

Looking back, some have seen the post-World War II years as a heroic age in which American poetry broke free from constraints such as rhyme and meter and flung itself heart-first into new dimensions alongside the abstract expressionists in American painting. Others — experimentalists, multiethnic and global authors, and feminist writers among them — recall the era's blindness to issues of race and gender. These writers experience diversity as a present blessing and look forward to freedoms yet unimagined. Their contributions have made the poetry of the present a rich cornucopia with a genuinely popular base.

Among the general public, interest in poetry is at an all-time high. Poetry slams generate competitive camaraderie among beginning writers, informal writing groups provide support and critiques, and reading clubs proliferate. Writing programs flourish at all levels, brisk poetic exchanges zip over the Internet, and universities,

magazines, and enterprising authors mount Web sites. American poetry at present is a vast territory of free imagination, a pot on the boil, a dynamic work in progress.

The ferment of American poetry since 1990 makes the field decentralized and hard to define. Most anthologies showcase only one dimension of poetry, for example, women's writing — or groupings of ethnic writers, or poetry with a common inspiration — jazz poetry, cowboy poetry, Buddhist-influenced poems, hip-hop.

The few anthologists aspiring to represent the whole of contemporary American poetry begin with copious disclaimers and dwell on its disparate impulses: postmodernism, the expansion of the canon, ethnicities, immigration (with special mention of new voices out of South and Southeast Asia and the Middle East), the dawning of global literature, the elaboration of women's continuing contributions, the rise of Internet technology, the influence of specific teachers or writing programs or regional impulses, the ubiquitous media, and the role of the poet as the lone individual voice raised against the din of commercialism and conformity.

Poets themselves struggle to make sense of the flood of poetry. It is possible to envision a continuum, with poetry of the speaking, subjective self on one end, poetry of the world on the other, and a large middle range in which self and world merge.

Poetry of the speaking self tends to focus on vivid expression and exploration of deep, often buried, emotion. It is psychological and intense, and its settings are secondary. In the last half of the 20th century, the most influential poet of this sort was Robert Lowell, whose descents into his own psyche and his disturbed family background inspired confessional writing.

Poetry of the world, on the other hand, tends to build up meaning from narrative drive, detail, and context. It sets careful scenes. One of the most influential poets of the world was Elizabeth

Bishop, generally considered the finest American woman poet of later 20th century.

Robert Lowell and Elizabeth Bishop were life-long friends; both taught at Harvard University. Like Walt Whitman and Emily Dickinson in the 19th century, Lowell and Bishop are presiding generative spirits for later poets. And although they shared a kindred vision, their approaches were polar opposites. Lowell's knotty, subjective, rhetorical poetry wrests meaning from self-presentation and heightened language, while Bishop offers, instead, detailed landscapes in a deceptively simple prosaic style. Only on rereading does her precision and depth make itself felt.

Most poets hover somewhere between the two poles. Ultimately, great poetry — whether of the self or the world — overcomes such divisions; the self and the world becoming mirrors of each other. Nevertheless, for purposes of discussion, the two may be provisionally distinguished.

THE POETRY OF SELF

Poetry of self tends toward direct address or monologue. At its most intense, it states a condition of soul. The settings, though present, do not play definitive roles. This poetry may be psychological or spiritual, aspiring to a timeless realm. It may also, however, undercut spiritual certainty by referring all meaning back to language. Within this large grouping, therefore, one may find somewhat romantic, expressive poetry, but also language-based poems that question the very concepts of identity and meaning, seeing these as constructs.

Balancing these concerns, John Ashbery has said that he is interested in "the experience of experience," or what filters through his consciousness, rather than what actually happened. His "Soonest Mended" (1970) depicts a reality "out there" lying loose and seemingly simple, but lethal as a floor on which wheat and chaff (like human lives, or Walt Whitman's leaves of grass) are winnowed:

> ...underneath the talk lies
> The moving and not wanting to be moved, the loose
> Meaning, untidy and simple like a threshing floor.

The enigmatic, classically trained W.S. Merwin (1927-) continues to produce volumes of haunting subjective poetry. Merwin's poem "The River of Bees" (1967) ends:

> On the door it says what to do to survive
> But we were not born to survive
> Only to live

The word "only" ironically underscores how difficult it is to live fully as human beings, a nobler pursuit than mere survival. Both Ashbery and Merwin, precursors of the current generation of poets of self, characteristically write monologues detached from explicit contexts or narratives. Merwin's haunting existential lyrics plumb psychological depths, while Ashbery's unexpected use of words from many registers of human endeavor — psychology, farming, philosophy — looks forward to the Language School.

Recent poets of self have pushed more deeply into a phenomenological awareness of consciousness played out moment by moment. For Ann Lauterbach (1942-), the poem is an extension of the mind in action; she has said that her poetry is "an act of self-construction, the voice its threshold." Language poet Lyn Hejinian (1941-) expresses the movement of consciousness in her autobiographical prose poem *My Life* (1987), which employs disjunction, surprising leaps, and chance intersections: "I picture an idea at the moment I come to it, our collision." Rae Armantrout (1947-) uses silences and subtle, oblique associative clusters; the title poem of her volume *Necromance* (1991) warns that "emphatic / precision / is revealed as / hostility." Another experimental poet, Leslie Scalapino (1947-), writes poems as an "examination of the mind in the process of whatever it's creating."

Much experimental poetry of self is elliptical, nonlinear, nonnarrative, and nonobjective; at its best, it is, however, not solipsistic but rather circles around an "absent center." Poetry of self often involves a public performance. In the case of women poets, the erasures, notions of silence, and disjunctions are often associated with Julia Kristeva and other French feminist theoreticians. Poet Susan Howe (1937-), who has developed a complex visual poetics to interweave the historical and personal, has noted the difficulty of tracing back female lines in archives and genealogies and the erasure of women in cultural history. For her, as a woman, "the gaps and silences are where you find yourself."

Jorie Graham (1950-)

One of the most accomplished poets of the subjective self is Jorie Graham. Born in New York, she grew up in Italy and studied at the Sorbonne in France, at New York University (specializing in film, which continues to influence her work), and at the Iowa Writers' Workshop, where she later taught. Since then, she has been a professor at Harvard University.

Graham's work is suffused with cosmopolitan references, and she sees the history of the United States as a part of a larger international engagement over time. The title poem in her Pulitzer Prize-winning collection *The Dream of the Unified Field: Selected Poems, 1974-1994* (1995) addresses this complex

JORIE GRAHAM

Photo: Estate of
Thomas Victor

and changing history. The poem brings together disparate elements in large-gestured free association — the poet's walk through the white flecks of a snowstorm to return a friend's black dance leotard, a flock of black starlings (birds that drive out native species), a single black crow (a protagonist of Native-American oral tradition) evoked as "one ink-streak on the early evening snowlit scene."

These sense impressions summon up the poet's childhood memories of Europe and her black-garbed dance teacher, and broaden out into the history of the New World. Christopher Columbus's contact with Native Americans on a white sandy beach is likened to the poet's white snowstorm: "He thought he saw Indians fleeing through the white before the ship," and "In the white swirl, he placed a large cross."

All these elements are subordinated to the moving mind that contains them and that constantly questions itself. This mind, or "unified field" (a set of theories in physics that attempt to relate all forces in the universe), is likened to the snowstorm of the beginning:

Nothing true or false in itself. Just
motion. Many strips of
motion. Filaments of falling marked
by the tiny certainties of flakes.

Graham focuses on the mind as a portal of meaning and distortion, both a part of the world and a separate vantage point. As in a film's montage, her voice threads together disparate visions and experiences. *Swarm* (2000) deepens Graham's metaphysical bent, emotional depth, and urgency.

THE POETRY OF VOICE

At its furthest extreme, poetry of self obliterates the self if it lacks a counterbalancing sensibility. The next stage may be a poetry of various voices or fictive selves, breaking the monolithic idea of self into fragments and characters. The dramatic monologues of Robert Browning are 19th-century antecedents. The fictive "I" feels solid but does not involve the actual author, whose self remains offstage.

This strain of poetry often takes subjects from myth and popular culture, typically seeing modern relationships as redefinitions or versions of older patterns. Among contemporary poets of voice or monologue are Brigit Pegeen Kelly, Alberto Rios, and the Canadian poet Margaret Atwood.

Usually, the poetry of voice is written in the first person, but the third person can make a similar impact if the viewpoint is clearly that of the characters, as in Rita Dove's *Thomas and Beulah*. In this volume, Dove intertwines biography and history to dramatize her grandparents' lives. Like many African Americans in the early 20th century, they fled poverty and racism in the rural South for work in the urban North. Dove endows

Louise Glück

their humble lives with dignity. Thomas's first job, as a laborer on the third shift, requires him to live in a barracks and share a mattress with two men he never meets. His work is "a narrow grief," but music lifts his spirits like a beautiful woman (forecasting Beulah, whom he has not yet met). When Thomas sings

> he closes his eyes.
> He never knows when she'll
>   be coming
> but when she leaves, he always
> tips his hat.

Louise Glück (1943-)

One of the most impressive poets of voice is Louise Glück. Born in New York City, Glück, the U.S. poet laureate for 2003-2004, grew up with an abiding sense of guilt due to the death of a sister born before her. At Sarah Lawrence College and Columbia University, she studied with poets Leonie Adams and Stanley Kunitz, and she has attributed her psychic survival to psychoanalysis and her studies in poetry. Much of her poetry deals with tragic loss.

Each of Glück's books attempts new techniques, making it difficult to summarize her work. Her early volumes, such as *The House on Marshland* (1975) and *The Triumph of Achilles* (1985), handle autobiographical material at a psychic distance, while in later books she is more direct. *Meadowlands* (1996) employs comic wit and references to the *Odyssey* to depict a failing marriage.

In Glück's memorable *The Wild Iris* (1992), different kinds of flowers utter short metaphysical monologues. The book's title poem, an exploration of resurrection, could be an epigraph for Glück's work as a whole. The wild iris, a gorgeous deep blue flower growing from a bulb that lies dormant all winter, says: "It is terrible to survive / as consciousness / buried in the dark earth." Like Jorie Graham's vision of the self merged in the snowstorm, Glück's poem ends with a vision of world and self merged — this time in the water of life, blue on blue:

You who do not remember
passage from the other world
I tell you I could speak again:
   whatever
returns from oblivion returns
to find a voice;

from the center of my life came
a great fountain, deep blue
shadows on azure seawater.

Like Graham, Glück merges the self into the world through a fluid imagery of water. While Graham's frozen water — snow — resembles sand, the earth ground up at the sea's edge, Glück's blue fresh water — signifying her heart — merges with the salt sea of the world.

CHARLES WRIGHT

Photo © Nancy Crampton

THE POETRY OF PLACE

A number of poets — these are not groups, but nationwide tendencies — find deep inspiration in specific landscapes. Instances are Robert Hass's lyrical evocations of Northern California, Mark Jarman's Southern California coastlines and memories of surfing, Tess Gallagher's poems set in the Pacific Northwest, and Simon Ortiz's and Jimmy Santiago Baca's poems emanating from southwestern landscapes. Each subregion has inspired poetry: C.D. (Carolyn) Wright's hardscrabble upper South is far from Yusef Komunyakaa's humid Louisiana Gulf.

Poetry of place is not based on landscape description; rather, the land, and its history, is a generative force implicated in the way its people, including the poet, live and think. The land is felt as what D.H. Lawrence called a "spirit of place."

Charles Wright (1935-)

One of the most moving poets of place is Charles Wright. Raised in Tennessee, Wright is a cosmopolitan southerner. He draws on Italian and ancient Chinese poetry, and infuses his work with southern themes such as the burden of a tragic past, seen in his poetic series "Appalachian Book of the Dead," which is based on the ancient *Egyptian Book of the Dead.* His works include *Country Music: Selected Early Poems* (1982); *Chickamauga* (1995); and *Negative Blue: Selected Later Poems* (2000). Wright's intense poetry offers moments of spiritual insight rescued, or rather constructed, from the ravages of time and circumstance. A purposeful awkwardness — seen in his unexpected turns of colloquial phrase and preference for long, broken lines with odd numbers of syllables — endows his poems with a burnished grace, like that of gnarled old farm tools polished with the wear of hands. This handmade, earned, sometimes wry quality makes Wright's poems feel contemporary and prevents them from seeming pretentious.

The disparity between transcendent vision and human frailty lies at the heart of Wright's vision. He is drawn to grand themes — stars, constellations, history — on the one hand, and to tiny tactile elements — fingers, hairs — on the other. His title poem "Chickamauga" relies on the reader's knowledge: Chickamauga, Georgia, on September 19 and 20, 1862, was the scene of a decisive battle in the U.S. Civil War between the North and the South. The South failed to destroy the Union (northern) army and opened a way for the North's scorched-earth invasion of the South via Atlanta, Georgia.

"Chickamauga" can be read as a meditation on landscape, but it is also an elegiac lament and the poet's *ars poetica.* It begins with a simple observation: "Dove-twirl in the tall grass." This seeming idyll is the moment just before a hunter shoots; the slain soldiers, never mentioned in the poem, have been forgotten, mowed down like doves or grass. The "conked magnolia tree" undercuts the romantic "midnight and magnolia" stereotype of the antebellum-plantation South. The poem merges present and past in a powerful epitaph for lost worlds and ideals.

Dove-twirl in the tall grass.
End-of-summer glaze next door
On the gloves and split ends of the conked magnolia tree.
Work sounds: truck back-up-beep, wood tin-hammer, cicada, fire horn.

History handles our past like spoiled fruit.
Mid-morning, late-century light
calicoed under the peach trees.
Fingers us here. Fingers us here and here.

The poem is a code with no message:
The point of the mask is not the mask but the face underneath,
Absolute, incommunicado,
unhoused and peregrine.

The gill net of history will pluck us soon enough
From the cold waters of self-contentment we drift in
One by one
into its suffocating light and air.

Structure becomes an element of belief, syntax
And grammar a catechist,
Their words what the beads say,
words thumbed to our discontent.

The poem sees history as a construct, a "code with no message." Each individual exists in itself, unknowable outside its own terms and time, "not the mask but the face underneath." Death is inevitable for us as for the fallen soldiers, the Old South, and the caught fish. Nevertheless, poetry offers a partial consolation: Our articulated discontent may yield a measure of immortality.

THE POETRY OF FAMILY

An even more grounded strain of poetry locates the poetic subject in a matrix of belonging — to family, community, and changing traditions. Often the traditions called into play are ethnic or international.

A few poets, such as Sharon Olds (1942-), expose their own unhealed wounds, resorting to the confessional mode, but most contemporary poets write with an affection that, however rueful, is nonetheless genuine. Stephen Dunn

(1939-) is an example: In his poems, relationships are a means of knowing. In some poets, respect for family and community carries with it a sense of affirmation, if not an explicitly devotional sensibility. This is not a conservative poetry; often it confronts change, loss, and struggle with the powers of ethnic or non-Western literary tradition.

Lucille Clifton (1936-) finds solace in the black community. Her colloquial language and strong faith are a potent combination. The moving elegies to his mother of Agha Shahid Ali (1949-2001) draw on a dazzling array of classical Middle Eastern poetic forms, intertwining his mother's life with the suffering of his family's native Kashmir.

Malaysian-Chinese American Shirley Geok-lin Lim (1944-) powerfully contrasts her difficult family in Malaysia with her new family in California. Chicana poet Lorna Dee Cervantes memorializes her harsh, impoverished family life in California; Louise Erdrich brings her unpredictable, tragicomic Native-American family members to vital life.

Li-Young Lee (1957-)

Tragic history arches over Li-Young Lee, whose Chinese-born father, at one time a physician to Mao Tse-tung, was later imprisoned in Indonesia. Born in Jakarta, Indonesia, Lee lived the life of a refugee, moving with his family to Hong Kong, Macao, and Japan before finding refuge in the United States, where his father became a

LI-YOUNG LEE

Photo © Dorothy Alexander

Protestant minister in Pennsylvania. Lee won acclaim for his books *Rose* (1986) and *The City in Which I Love You* (1990).

Lee is sensuous, filial — he movingly depicts his family and his father's decline — and outspoken in his commitment to the spiritual dimensions of poetry. His most influential poem, "Persimmons" (1986), from his book *Rose*, evokes his Asian background through the persimmon, a fruit little known in the United States. Fruits and flowers are traditional subjects of Chinese art and poetry, but unusual in the West. The poem contains a pointed yet humorous critique of a provincial schoolteacher Lee encountered in the United States who presumes to understand persimmons and language.

Lee's poem "Irises" (1986), from the same volume, suggests that we drift through a "dream of life" but, like the iris, "waken dying — violet becoming blue, growing / black, black." The poem and its handling of color resonate with Glück's wild iris.

The title poem of *The City in Which I Love You* announces Lee's affirmative entrance into a larger community of poetry. It ends:

my birthplace vanished, my
    citizenship earned,
in league with stones of the earth, I
enter, without retreat or help
    from history,
the days of no day, my earth
of no earth, I re-enter

the city in which I love you.
And I never believed that the
   multitude
of dreams and many words were
   vain.

THE POETRY OF THE BEAUTIFUL

Yet another strain of intensely lyrical, image-driven poetry celebrates beauty despite, or in the midst of, modern life in all its suffering and confusion. Many poets could be included here — Joy Harjo (1951-), Sandra McPherson (1943-), Henri Cole (1965-) — as the strains of poetry are overlapping, not mutually exclusive.

Some of the finest contemporary poets use imagery not as decoration, but to explore new subjects and terrain. Harjo imagines horses as a way of retrieving her Native-American heritage, while McPherson and Cole create images that seem to come alive.

Mark Doty (1953-)

Since the late 1980s, Mark Doty has been publishing supple, beautiful poetic meditations on art and relationships — with lovers, friends, and a host of communities. His vivid, exact, sensory imagery is often a mode of knowing, feeling, and reaching out. Through images, Doty makes us feel a kinship with animals, strangers, and the work of artistic creation, which for him involves a way of seeing.

It is possible to enjoy Doty by following his evolving ideas of community. In "A Little Rabbit Dead in

MARK DOTY

Photo © Miriam Berkley

the Grass" from *Source* (2001), a dead rabbit provokes a philosophical meditation. This particular rabbit, like a poem, is important in itself and as a text, an "artfully crafted thing" on whose brow "some trace / of thought seems written." The next poem in *Source*, "Fish R Us," likens the human community to a bag of fish in a pet store tank, "each fry / about the size of this line." Like people, or ideas, the fish want freedom: They "want to swim forward," but for now they "pulse in their golden ball." The sense of a shared organic connection with others is carried throughout the volume. The third poem, "At the Gym," envisions the imprint of sweaty heads on exercise equipment as "some halo / the living made together."

Doty finds in Walt Whitman a personal and poetic guide. Doty has also written memorably of the tragic AIDS epidemic. His works include *My Alexandria* (1993), *Atlantis* (1995), and his vivid memoir *Firebird* (1999). *Still Life With Oysters and Lemon* (2001) is a recent collection.

Doty's poems are both reflexive (referencing themselves as art) and responsive to the outer world. He sees the imperfect yet vital body, especially the skin, as the margin — a kind of text — where internal and external meet, as in his short poem, also from *Source*, about getting a tattoo, "To the Engraver of My Skin."

I understand the pact is mortal,
agree to bear this permanence.

I contract with limitation; I say
no and no then yes to you, and sign

— here, on the dotted line —
for whatever comes, I do: our time,

our outline, the filling-in of our
    details
(it's density that hurts, always,

not the original scheme). I'm here
for revision, discoloration; here to
    fade

and last, ineradicable, blue. Write
    me!
This ink lasts longer than I do.

THE POETRY OF SPIRIT

A spiritual focus permeates another strand of contemporary American poetry. In this work, the deepest relationship is that between the individual and a timeless essence beyond — though linked with — artistic beauty. Older poets who heralded a spiritual consciousness include Gary Snyder, who helped introduce Zen to American poetry, and poet-translator Robert Bly, who brought an awareness of Latin American surrealism to U.S. poetry. In recent times, Coleman Barks has translated many books of the 13th-century mystic poet Rumi.

Spiritually attuned contemporary U.S. poets include Arthur Sze (1950-), who is said to have a Zen-like sensibility. His poems offer lit-

JANE HIRSHFIELD

Photo © Jerry Bauer

eral and seemingly simple observations that are also meditations, such as these lines from "Throwing Salt on a Path" (1987): "Shrimp smoking over a fire. Ah, / the light of a star never stops, but travels." Shoveling snow, he notes: "The salt now clears a path in the snow, expands the edges of the universe."

Jane Hirshfield (1953-)

Jane Hirshfield makes almost no explicit references to Buddhism in her poems, yet they breathe the spirit of her many years of Zen meditation and her translations from the ancient court poetry of two Japanese women, Ono no Komachi and Izumi Shikibu. Hirshfield has edited an anthology, *Women in Praise of the Sacred: 43 Centuries of Spiritual Poetry by Women* (1994).

Hirshfield's poetry manifests what she calls the "mind of indirection" in her book about writing poetry, *Nine Gates: Entering the Mind of Poetry* (1997). This orientation draws on a reverence for nature, an economy of language, and a Buddhist sense of impermanence. Her own "poetry of indirection" works by nuance, association (often to seasons and weathers, evocative of world views and moods), and natural imagery.

Hirshfield's poem "Mule Heart," from her poetry collection *The Lives of the Heart* (1997), vividly evokes a mule without ever mentioning it. Hirshfield drew on her memory of a mule used to carry loads up steep hills on the Greek island of Santorini to write this poem, which she has called a kind of recipe for getting through a difficult time. The poem conjures the reader to take heart. This humble mule has its own beauty (bridle bells) and strength.

On the days when the rest
have failed you,
let this much be yours —
flies, dust, an unnameable odor,
the two waiting baskets:
one for the lemons and passion,
the other for all you have lost.
Both empty,
it will come to your shoulder,
breathe slowly against your bare
arm.
If you offer it hay, it will eat.
Offered nothing,
it will stand as long as you ask.
The little bells of the bridle will
hang
beside you quietly,
in the heat and the tree's thin
shade.
Do not let its sparse mane
deceive you,
or the way the left ear swivels
into dream.
This too is a gift of the gods,
calm and complete.

THE POETRY OF NATURE

The New World riveted the attention of Americans during the revolutionary era of the late 1700s, when Philip Freneau made a point of celebrating flora and fauna native to the Americas as a way of forging an American iden-

MARY OLIVER

Photo © Nancy Crampton

tity. Transcendentalism and agrarianism focused on America's relation to nature in the 19th and early 20th centuries.

Today environmental concerns inform a powerful strain of ecologically oriented U.S. poetry. The late A.R. Ammons was one recent progenitor, and Native-American poets, such as the late James Welch and Leslie Marmon Silko, never lost a reverence for nature. Contemporary poets rooted in a natural vision include Pattiann Rogers (1940-) and Maxine Kumin (1925-). Rogers brings natural history into focus, while Kumin writes feelingly of her personal life on a farm and her raising of horses.

Mary Oliver (1935-)

One of the most celebrated poets of nature is Mary Oliver. A stunning, accessible poet, Oliver evokes plants and animals with visionary intensity. Oliver was born in Ohio but has lived in New England for years, and her poems, like those of Robert Frost, draw on its varied landscape and changing seasons. Oliver finds meaning in encounters with nature, continuing in the Transcendental tradition of Henry David Thoreau and Ralph Waldo Emerson, and her work has a strong ethical dimension. Oliver's works include *American Primitive* (1983), *New and Selected Poems* (1992), *White Pine* (1994), *Blue Pastures* (1995), and the essays in *The Leaf and the Cloud* (2000).

For Oliver, no natural fact is too humble to afford insights, or what

Emerson called "spiritual facts," as in her poem "The Black Snake" (1979). Though the speaker, as a driver of an automobile, is implicated in the snake's demise, she stops and removes the snake's body from the road — an act of respect. She recognizes the often vilified snake, with its negative associations with the biblical book of Genesis and death, as a "dead brother," and she appreciates his gleaming beauty. The snake teaches her death, but also a new genesis and delight in life, and she drives on, thinking about the "light at the center of every cell" that entices all created life "forward / happily all spring" — always unaware of where we will meet our end. This *carpe diem* is an invitation to a more rooted, celebratory awareness.

When the black snake
flashed onto the morning road,
and the truck could not swerve —
death, that is how it happens.

Now he lies looped and useless
as an old bicycle tire.
I stop the car
and carry him into the bushes.

He is as cool and gleaming
as a braided whip, he is as beautiful and quiet
as a dead brother.
I leave him under the leaves

and drive on, thinking
about *death*: its suddenness,
its terrible weight,
its certain coming. Yet under

reason burns a brighter fire, which the bones
have always preferred.
It is the story of endless good fortune.
It says to oblivion: not me!

It is the light at the center of every cell.
It is what sent the snake coiling and flowing forward
happily all spring through the green leaves before
he came to the road.

Oliver's poems find countless ways to celebrate the simple yet transcendent fact of being alive. In "Hummingbird Pauses at the Trumpet Vine" (1992), she reminds us that most of existence is "waiting or remembering," since most of the world's time we are "not here, / not born yet, or died." An intensity reminiscent of the late poet James Wright burns through many of Oliver's poems, such as "Poppies" (1991-1992). This poem begins with a description of the "orange flares; swaying / in the wind, their congregations are a levitation." It ends with a taunt at death: "what can you do / about it — deep, blue night?"

THE POETRY OF WIT

On the spectrum from poetry of self to poetry of the world, wit — including humor, a sense of the incongruous, and flights of fancy — lies close to world. Wit depends on the intersection of two or more frames of reference and on acute discrimination; this is a worldly poetry.

Poetry of wit locates the poetic occasion in everyday life raised to a humorous, surrealistic, or allegorical pitch. Usually the language is colloquial so that the fantastic situations have the heft of reality. Older masters of this vein are Charles Simic and Mark Strand; among younger poets, its practitioners include Stephen Dobyns and Mark Halliday.

The everyday language, humor, surprising action, and exaggeration of this poetry makes it unusually accessible, though the best of this work only gives up its secrets on repeated rereading.

Billy Collins (1941-)

The most influential of the poets of wit today is Billy Collins. Collins, who was the U.S. poet laureate for 2001-2003, is refreshing and exhilarating, as was Frank O'Hara a generation earlier. Like O'Hara, Collins uses everyday language to record the myriad details of everyday life, freely mixing quotidian events (eating, doing chores, writing) with cultural references. His humor and originality have brought him a wide audience. Though some have faulted Collins for being too accessible, his unpredictable flights of fancy open out into mystery.

Collins's is a domesticated form of surrealism. His best poems, too long to reproduce here, quickly propel the imagination up a stairway of increasingly surrealistic situations, at the end offering an emotional landing, a mood one can rest on, if temporarily, like a final modulation in music. The short poem "The Dead," from *Sailing Alone Around the Room: New and Selected Poems* (2001), gives some sense of Collins's fanciful flight and gentle settling down, as if a bird had come to rest.

The dead are always looking down on us, they say,
while we are putting on our shoes or making a sandwich,
they are looking down through the glass-bottom boats of heaven
as they row themselves slowly through eternity.

They watch the tops of our heads

BILLY COLLINS

ROBERT PINSKY

moving below on earth,
and when we lie down in a field or on a couch,
drugged perhaps by the hum of a warm afternoon,
they think we are looking back at them,

which makes them lift their oars and fall silent
and wait, like parents, for us to close our eyes.

THE POETRY OF HISTORY

Poetry inspired by history is in some ways the most difficult and ambitious of all. In this vein, poets venture into the world with a lower-case "i," open to all that has shaped them. The faith of these poets is in experience.

An older poet working in this vein is Michael S. Harper, who interweaves African-American history with his family's experiences in a form of montage. Frank Bidart has similarly merged political events such as the assassination of U.S. President John F. Kennedy with personal life. Ed Hirsch, Gjertrud Schnackenberg, and Rita Dove imbue some of their finest poems with similarly irreducible memories of their personal pasts, centering on touchstone moments.

Robert Pinsky (1940-)

Among the most accomplished of the poets of history is Robert Pinsky. U.S. poet laureate from 1997 to 2000, Pinsky links colloquial speech to technical virtuosity. He is insistently local and personal, but his poems extend into historical and national contexts. Like the works of Elizabeth Bishop, his conversational poetry wields seeming artlessness with subtle art.

Pinsky's influential book of criticism, *The Situation of Poetry* (1976), recommended a poetry with the virtues of prose, and he carried out that mandate in his book-length poem *An Explanation of America* (1979) and in *History of My Heart* (1984), though later books, including *The Want Bone* (1990), unleash a lyricism also seen in his impressive collected poems entitled *The Figured Wheel* (1996).

The title poem from *The Figured Wheel* is among Pinsky's finest works, but it is difficult to excerpt. The brief poem "The Want Bone," suggested by the jaw of a shark seen on a friend's mantel, displays Pinsky's technical brilliance (internal rhymes like "limber grin," slant rhymes as in "together" and "pleasure," and polysyllables pattering lightly against a drum-firm iambic line). The poem begins by describing the shark as the "tongue of the waves" and ends with its singing — from the realm of the dead — a paean of endless desire. The ego or self may be critiqued here: It is a pointless hunger, an O or zero, and its satisfaction a hopeless illusion.

The tongue of the waves tolled in the earth's bell.
Blue rippled and soaked in the fire of blue.
The dried mouthbones of a shark in the hot swale
Gaped on nothing but sand on either side.

The bone tasted of nothing and smelled of nothing,
A scalded toothless harp, uncrushed, unstrung.
The joined arcs made the shape of birth and
      craving
And the welded-open shape kept mouthing O.

Ossified cords held the corners together
In groined spirals pleated like a summer dress.
But where was the limber grin, the gash of
      pleasure?

Infinitesimal mouths bore it away,

The beach scrubbed and etched and pickled it clean.
But O I love you it sings, my little my country
My food my parent my child I want you my own
My flower my fin my life my lightness my O.

THE POETRY OF THE WORLD

On the furthest extreme of the poetic spectrum lies poetry of the world, presided over by the spirit of Elizabeth Bishop. This is a downbeat, or outcast, poetry that at first reading seems anti-poetical. It may seem too prosaic, too caught up with mere incidentals, to count for anything lasting. The hesitant delivery is the opposite of oracular, and the subject at first seems lost or merely descriptive. Nevertheless, the best of this poetry cuts through multiple perspectives, questions the very notion of personal identity, and understands suffering from an ethical perspective.

Older poets writing in this manner are Richard Hugo, Gwendolyn Brooks, and Phil Levine. Contemporary voices such as Ellen Bryant Voigt and Yusef Komunyakaa have been influenced by their almost naturalistic vision, and they are drawn to violence and its far-reaching shadow.

Yusef Komunyakaa (1947-)

Louisiana-raised Yusef Komunyakaa, born James Willie Brown, Jr., served in Vietnam directly after graduation from secondary school, winning a Bronze Star. He was a reporter for the military newspaper *Southern Cross*, and has written vivid poems set in the war. Often, as in "Camouflaging the Chimera" (1988), there is an element of suspense, danger, and ambush. Komunyakaa has spoken of the need for poetry to afford a "series of surprises." Like the poet Michael S. Harper, he often uses jazz methods, and he has written of the poetry's need for free improvisation and openness to other voices, as in a musicians' "jam session." He has co-edited *The Jazz Poetry Anthology* (1991, 1996) and published a volume of essays entitled *Blue Notes* (2000), while he first gained recognition with *Neon Vernacular* (1993).

One of Komunyakaa's enduring themes concerns identity. His poem "Facing It" (1988), set at the Vietnam Veterans Memorial in Washington, D.C., begins with a riff that merges his own face with memories and reflected faces:

My black face fades,
hiding inside the black granite.
I said I wouldn't,
dammit: No tears.
I'm stone. I'm flesh.
My clouded reflection eyes me
like a bird of prey, the profile of night
slanted against morning. I turn
this way — the stone lets me go.
I turn that way — I'm inside
the Vietnam Veterans Memorial
again, depending on the light
to make a difference.
I go down the 58,022 names,
half-expecting to find
my own in letters like smoke.
I touch the name Andrew Johnson;
I see the booby trap's white flash.
Names shimmer on a woman's
  blouse
but when she walks away
the names stay on the wall.
Brushstrokes flash, a red bird's
wings cutting across my stare.
The sky. A plane in the sky.
A white vet's image floats
closer to me, then his pale eyes
look through mine. I'm a window.

YUSEF KOMUNYAKAA

Photo: Jamer Keyser / Time Life Pictures / Getty Images

He's lost his right arm
inside the stone. In the black mirror
a woman's trying to erase names:
No, she's brushing a boy's hair.

CYBER-POETRY

At the extreme end of the poetic spectrum, cyber-poetry is a new worldly poetry. For many young American adults, the book is secondary to the computer monitor, and reading a spoken human language comes after exposure to binary codes.

Computer-based literature has taken shape since the early 1990s; with the advent of the World Wide Web, some experimental poetry has shifted its focus to a paperless, virtual, global realm.

Recurring motifs in cyber-poetry include self-reflexive critiques of technologically driven work; computer icons, graphics, and hypertext links festoon vast webs of relationships, while dimensional layers — animation, sonics, hyperlinked texts — proliferate in multiple directions, sometimes created by multiple and unknown authors.

Outlets for this work come and go; they have included the CD-ROM poetry magazines *The Little Magazine*, *Cyberpoetry*, *Java Poetry*, *New River*, *Parallel*, and many others. *Writing From the New Coast: Technique* (1993), an influential gathering of poetic statements accompanied by a collection of poems edited by Juliana Spahr and Peter Gizzi, helped catalyze experimental poetry in the electronic age. It celebrates irreducible multiplicity and the primacy of historical context, attacking the very notions of identity and universality as repressive bourgeois constructs.

Jorie Graham and other experimental poets of self have arrived at similar viewpoints, coming from opposite directions. Ultimate or contingent, poems exist at the intersection of word and world.

CHAPTER 10

CONTEMPORARY AMERICAN LITERATURE

The United States is one of the most diverse nations in the world. Its dynamic population of about 300 million boasts more than 30 million foreign-born individuals who speak numerous languages and dialects. Some one million new immigrants arrive each year, many from Asia and Latin America.

Literature in the United States today is likewise dazzlingly diverse, exciting, and evolving. New voices have arisen from many quarters, challenging old ideas and adapting literary traditions to suit changing conditions of the national life. Social and economic advances have enabled previously underrepresented groups to express themselves more fully, while technological innovations have created a fast-moving public forum. Reading clubs proliferate, and book fairs, literary festivals, and "poetry slams" (events where youthful poets compete in performing their poetry) attract enthusiastic audiences. Selection of a new work for a book club can launch an unknown writer into the limelight overnight.

On a typical Sunday the list of best-selling books in the *New York Times Book Review* testifies to the extraordinary diversity of the current American literary scene. In January, 2006, for example, the list of paperback best-sellers included "genre" fiction — steamy romances by Nora Roberts, a new thriller by John Grisham, murder mysteries — alongside nonfiction science books by the anthropologist Jared Diamond, popular sociology by *The New Yorker* magazine writer Malcolm Gladwell, and accounts of drug rehabilitation and crime. In the last category was a reprint of Truman Capote's groundbreaking *In Cold Blood*, a 1965 "nonfiction novel" that blurs the distinction between high literature and journalism and had recently been made into a film.

Books by non-American authors and books on international themes were also prominent on the list. Afghan-American Khaled Hosseini's searing novel, *The Kite Runner*, tells of childhood friends in Kabul separated by the rule of the Taliban, while Azar Nafisi's memoir, *Reading Lolita in Teheran*, poignantly recalls teaching great works of western literature to young women in Iran. A third novel, Arthur Golden's *Memoirs of a Geisha* (made into a movie), recounts a Japanese woman's life during World War II.

In addition, the best-seller list reveals the popularity of religious themes. According to *Publishers Weekly*, 2001 was the first year that Christian-themed books topped the sales lists in both fiction and nonfiction. Among the hardcover best-sellers of that exemplary Sunday in 2006, we find Dan Brown's novel *The DaVinci Code* and Anne Rice's tale *Christ the Lord: Out of Egypt*.

Beyond the *Times*' best-seller list, chain bookstores offer separate sections for major religions including Christianity, Islam, Judaism, Buddhism, and sometimes Hinduism.

In the Women's Literature section of bookstores one finds works by a "Third Wave" of feminists, a movement that usually refers to young women in their 20s and 30s who have grown up in an era of widely accepted social equality in the United States. Third Wave feminists feel sufficiently empowered to emphasize the individuality of choices women make. Often associated in the popular mind with a return to tradition and child-rearing, lipstick, and "feminine" styles, these young women have reclaimed the word "girl" — some decline to call themselves feminist. What is often called "chick lit" is a flourishing offshoot. *Bridget Jones's Diary* by the British writer Helen Fielding and Candace Bushnell's *Sex and the City* featuring urban single women with romance in mind have spawned a popular genre among young women.

Nonfiction writers also examine the phenomenon of post-feminism. *The Mommy Myth* (2004) by Susan Douglas and Meredith Michaels analyzes the role of the media in the "mommy wars," while Jennifer Baumgardner and Amy Richards' lively *ManifestA: Young Women, Feminism, and the Future* (2000) discusses women's activism in the age of the Internet. Caitlin Flanagan, a magazine writer who calls herself an "anti-feminist," explores conflicts between domestic life and professional life for women. Her 2004 essay in *The Atlantic*, "How Serfdom Saved the Women's Movement," an account of how professional women depend on immigrant women of a lower class for their childcare, triggered an enormous debate.

It is clear that American literature at the turn of the 21st century has become democratic and heterogeneous. Regionalism has flowered, and international, or "global," writers refract U.S. culture through foreign perspectives. Multiethnic writing continues to mine rich veins, and as each ethnic literature matures, it creates its own traditions. Creative nonfiction and memoir have flourished. The short story genre has gained luster, and the "short" short story has taken root. A new generation of playwrights continues the American tradition of exploring current social issues on stage. There is not space here in this brief survey to do justice to the glittering diversity of American literature today. Instead, one must consider general developments and representative figures.

POSTMODERNISM, CULTURE AND IDENTITY

Postmodernism suggests fragmentation: collage, hybridity, and the use of various voices, scenes, and identities. Postmodern authors question external structures, whether political, philosophical, or artistic. They tend to distrust the master-narratives of modernist thought, which they see as politically suspect. Instead, they mine popular culture genres, especially science fiction, spy, and detective stories, becoming, in effect, archaeologists of pop culture.

Don DeLillo's *White Noise*, structured in 40 sections like video clips, highlights the dilemmas of representation: "Were people this dumb before television?" one character wonders. David Foster Wallace's gargantuan (1,000 pages, 900 footnotes) *Infinite Jest* mixes up wheelchair-bound terrorists, drug addicts, and futuristic descriptions of a country like the United States. In *Galatea 2.2*, Richard Powers interweaves sophisticated technology with private lives.

Influenced by Thomas Pynchon, postmodern authors fabricate complex plots that demand imaginative leaps. Often they flatten historical depth into one dimension; William Vollmann's novels slide between vastly different times and places as easily as a computer mouse moves between texts.

Creative Nonfiction: Memoir and Autobiography

Many writers hunger for open, less canonical genres as vehicles for their postmodern visions. The rise of global, multiethnic, and women's literature — works in which writers reflect on experiences shaped by culture, color, and gender — has endowed autobiography and memoir with special allure. While the boundaries of the terms are debated, a memoir is typically shorter or more limited in scope, while an autobiography makes some attempt at a comprehensive overview of the writer's life.

Postmodern fragmentation has rendered problematic for many writers the idea of a finished self that can be articulated successfully in one sweep. Many turn to the memoir in their struggles to ground an authentic self. What constitutes authenticity, and to what extent the writer is allowed to embroider upon his or her memories of experience in works of nonfiction, are hotly contested subjects of writers' conferences.

Writers themselves have contributed penetrating observations on such questions in books about writing, such as *The Writing Life* (1989) by Annie Dillard. Noteworthy memoirs include *The Stolen Light* (1989) by Ved Mehta. Born in India, Mehta was blinded at the age of three. His account of flying alone as a young blind person to study in the United States is unforgettable. Irish American Frank McCourt's mesmerizing *Angela's Ashes* (1996) recalls his childhood of poverty, family alcoholism, and intolerance in Ireland with a surprising warmth and humor. Paul Auster's *Hand to Mouth* (1997) tells of poverty that blocked his writing and poisoned his soul.

The Short Story: New Directions

The story genre had to a degree lost its luster by the late 1970s. Experimental metafiction stories had been penned by Donald Barthelme, Robert Coover, John Barth, and William Gass and were no longer on the cutting edge. Large-circulation weekly magazines that had showcased short fiction, such as the *Saturday Evening Post*, had collapsed.

It took an outsider from the Pacific Northwest — a gritty realist in the tradition of Ernest Hemingway — to revitalize the genre. Raymond Carver (1938-1988) had studied under the late novelist John Gardner, absorbing Gardner's passion for accessible artistry fused with moral vision. Carver rose above alcoholism and harsh poverty to become the most influential story writer in the United States. In his collections *Will You Please Be Quiet, Please?* (1976), *What We Talk About When We Talk About Love* (1981), *Cathedral* (1983), and *Where I'm Calling From* (1988), Carver follows confused working people through dead-end jobs, alcoholic binges, and rented rooms with an understated, minimalist style of writing that carries tremendous impact.

Linked with Carver is novelist and story writer Ann Beattie (1947-), whose middle-class characters often lead aimless lives. Her stories reference political events and popular songs, and offer distilled glimpses of life decade by decade in the changing United States. Recent collections are *Park City* (1998) and *Perfect Recall* (2001).

Inspired by Carver and Beattie, writers crafted impressive neorealist story collections in the mid-1980s, including Amy Hempel's *Reasons to*

Live (1985), David Leavitt's *Family Dancing* (1984), Richard Ford's *Rock Springs* (1987), Bobbie Ann Mason's *Shiloh and Other Stories* (1982), and Lorrie Moore's *Self-Help* (1985). Other noteworthy figures include the late Andre Dubus, author of *Dancing After Hours* (1996), and the prolific John Updike, whose recent story collections include *The Afterlife and Other Stories* (1994).

Today, as is discussed later in this chapter, writers with ethnic and global roots are informing the story genre with non-Western and tribal approaches, and storytelling has commanded critical and popular attention. The versatile, primal tale is the basis of several hybridized forms: novels that are constructed of interlinking short stories or vignettes, and creative nonfictions that interweave history and personal history with fiction.

The Short Short Story: Sudden or Flash Fiction

The short short is a very brief story, often only one or two pages long. It is sometimes called "flash fiction" or "sudden fiction" after the 1986 anthology *Sudden Fiction*, edited by Robert Shapard and James Thomas.

In short short stories, there is little space to develop a character. Rather, the element of plot is central: A crisis occurs, and a sketched-in character simply has to react. Authors deploy clever narrative or linguistic patterns; in some cases, the short short resembles a

RAYMOND CARVER

Photo © Marion Ettlinger / CORBIS OUTLINE

prose poem.

Supporters claim that short shorts' "reduced geographies" mirror postmodern conditions in which borders seem closer together. They find elegant simplicity in these brief fictions. Detractors see short shorts as a symptom of cultural decay, a general loss of reading ability, and a limited attention span. In any event, short shorts have found a certain niche: They are easy to forward in an e-mail, and they lend themselves to electronic distribution. They make manageable in-class readings and models for writing assignments.

Drama

Contemporary drama mingles realism with fantasy in postmodern works that fuse the personal and the political. The exuberant Tony Kushner (1956-) has won acclaim for his prize-winning *Angels in America* plays, which vividly render the AIDS epidemic and the psychic cost of closeted homosexuality in the 1980s and 1990s. *Part One: Millennium Approaches* (1991) and its companion piece, *Part Two: Perestroika* (1992), together last seven hours. Combining comedy, melodrama, political commentary, and special effects, they interweave various plots and marginalized characters.

Women dramatists have attained particular success in recent years. Prominent among them is Beth Henley (1952-), from Mississippi, known for her portraits of southern women. Henley gained national recognition for her *Crimes of the Heart* (1978), which was made into a film in 1986, a warm play about three eccentric sisters whose affection helps them survive disappointment and despair. Later plays, including *The Miss Firecracker Contest* (1980), *The Wake of Jamey Foster* (1982), *The Debutante Ball* (1985), and *The Lucky Spot* (1986), explore southern forms of socializing — beauty contests, funerals, coming-out parties, and dance halls.

Wendy Wasserstein (1950-2006), from New York, wrote early comedies including *When Dinah Shore Ruled the Earth* (1975), a parody of beauty contests. She is best known for *The Heidi Chronicles* (1988), about a successful woman professor who confesses to deep unhappiness and adopts a baby. Wasserstein continued exploring women's aspirations in *The Sisters Rosensweig* (1991), *An American Daughter* (1997), and *Old Money* (2000).

Younger dramatists such as African American Suzan-Lori Parks (1964-) build on the successes of earlier women. Parks, who grew up on various army bases in the United States and Germany, deals with political issues in experimental works whose timelessness and ritualism recall Irish-born writer Samuel Beckett. Her best-known work, *The America Play* (1991), revolves around the assassination of President Abraham Lincoln by John Wilkes Booth. She returns to this theme in *Topdog/Underdog* (2001), which tells the story of two African-American brothers named Lincoln and Booth and their lifetime of sibling rivalry.

REGIONALISM

A pervasive regionalist sensibility has gained strength in American literature in the past two decades. Decentralization expresses the postmodern U.S. condition, a trend most evident in fiction writing; no longer does any one viewpoint or code successfully express the nation. No one city defines artistic movements, as New York City once did. Vital arts communities have arisen in many cities, and electronic technology has de-centered literary life.

As economic shifts and social change redefine America, a yearning for tradition has set in. The most sustaining and distinctively American myths partake of the land, and writers are turning to the Civil War South, the Wild West of the rancher, the rooted life of the midwestern farmer, the southwestern tribal homeland, and other localized realms where the real and the mythic mingle. Of course, more than one region has inspired many writers; they are included here in regions formative to their vision or characteristic of their mature work.

The Northeast

The scenic Northeast, region of lengthy winters, dense deciduous forests, and low rugged mountain chains, was the first English-speaking colonial area, and it retains the feel of England. Boston, Massachusetts, is the cultural powerhouse, boasting research institutions and scores of universities. Many New England writers depict characters that continue the Puritan legacy, embodying the middle-class Protestant work ethic and progressive commitment to social reform. In the rural areas, small, independent farmers struggle to survive in the world of global marketing.

Novelist Joyce Carol Oates sets many of her gothic works in upstate New York. Richard Russo (1949-), in his appealing *Empire Falls* (2001), evokes life in a dying mill town in Maine, the state where Stephen King (1947-) locates his popular horror novels.

The bittersweet fictions of Massachusetts-based Sue Miller (1943-), such as *The Good Mother* (1986), examine counterculture lifestyles in Cambridge, a city known for cultural and social diversity, intellectual vitality, and technological innovation. Another writer from Massachusetts, Anita Diamant (1951-), earned popular acclaim with *The Red Tent* (1997), a feminist historical novel based on the biblical story of Dinah.

Russell Banks (1940-), from poor, rural New Hampshire, has turned from experimental writing to more realistic works, such as *Affliction* (1989), his novel about working-class New Hampshire characters. For Banks, acknowledging one's roots is a fundamental part of one's identity. In *Affliction*, the narrator scorns people who have "gone to Florida, Arizona, and California, bought a trailer or a condo, turned their skin to leather playing shuffleboard all day and waited to die." Banks's recent works include *Cloudsplitter* (1998), a historical novel about the 19th-century abolitionist John Brown.

The striking stylist Annie Proulx (1935-) crafts stories of struggling northern New Englanders in *Heart Songs* (1988). Her best novel, *The Shipping News* (1993), is set even further north, in Newfoundland, Canada. Proulx has also spent years in the West, and one of her short stories inspired the 2006 movie "Brokeback Mountain."

William Kennedy (1928-) has written a dense and entwined cycle of novels set in Albany, in northern New York State, including his acclaimed *Ironweed*. The title of his insider's history of Albany gives some idea of his gritty, colloquial style and teeming cast of often unsavory characters: *O Albany! Improbable City of Political Wizards, Fearless Ethnics, Spectacular Aristocrats, Splendid Nobodies, and Underrated Scoundrels* (1983). Kennedy has been hailed as an elder statesman of a small Irish-American literary movement that includes the late Mary McCarthy, Mary Gordon, Alice McDermott, and Frank McCourt.

Three writers who studied at Brown University in Rhode Island around the same time and took classes with British writer Angela Carter are often mentioned as the nucleus of a "next generation." Donald Antrim (1959-) satirizes academic life in *The Hundred Brothers* (1997), set in an enormous library from which one can see home-less people. Rick Moody (1961-) is best known for his novel *The Ice Storm* (1994). The novels of Jeffrey Eugenides (1960-) include *Middlesex* (2002), which narrates the experience of a hermaphrodite. Impressive stylists with off-center visions bordering on the absurd, Antrim, Moody, and Eugenides carry further the opposite traditions of John Updike and Thomas Pynchon. Often linked with these three younger novelists is the exuberant postmodernist David Foster Wallace (1962-). Wallace, who was born in Ithaca, New York, gained acclaim for his complex serio-comic novel *The Broom of the System* (1987) and the pop culture-saturated stories in *Girl With Curious Hair* (1989).

The Mid-Atlantic

The fertile Mid-Atlantic states, dominated by New York City with its great harbor, remain a gateway for waves of immigrants. Today the region's varied economy encompasses finance, commerce, and shipping, as well as advertising and fashion. New York City is the home of the publishing industry, as well as prestigious art galleries and museums.

Don DeLillo (1936-), from New York City, began as an advertising writer, and his novels explore consumerism among their many themes. *Americana* (1971) concludes: "To consume in America is not to buy, it is to dream." DeLillo's protagonists seek identities based on images. *White Noise* (1985) concerns Jack Gladney and his family, whose experience is mediated by various texts, especially advertisements. One passage suggests DeLillo's style: "...the emptiness, the sense of cosmic darkness. Mastercard, Visa, American Express." Fragments of advertisements that drift unattached through the book emerge from Gladney's media-parroting subconscious, generating the subliminal white noise of the title. DeLillo's later novels include politics and historical figures: *Libra* (1988) envisions the assassination of President John F.

Kennedy as an explosion of frustrated consumerism; *Underworld* (1997) spins a web of interconnections between a baseball game and a nuclear bomb in Kazakhstan.

In multidimensional, polyglot New York, fictions featuring a shadowy postmodern city abound. An example is the labyrinthine New York trilogy *City of Glass* (1985), *Ghosts* (1986), and *The Locked Room* (1986) by Paul Auster (1947-). In this work, inspired by Samuel Beckett and the detective novel, an isolated writer at work on a detective story addresses Paul Auster, who is writing about Cervantes. The trilogy suggests that "reality" is but a text constructed via fiction, thus erasing the traditional border between reality and illusion. Auster's trilogy, in effect, self-deconstructs. Similarly, Kathy Acker (1948-1997) juxtaposed passages from works by Cervantes and Charles Dickens with science fiction in postmodern pastiches such as *Empire of the Senseless* (1988), a quest through time and space for an individual voice.

New York City hosts many groups of writers with shared interests. Jewish women include noted essayist Cynthia Ozick (1928-), who hails from the Bronx, the setting of her novel *The Puttermesser Papers* (1997). Her haunting novel *The Shawl* (1989) gives a young mother's viewpoint on the Holocaust. The droll, conversational *Collected Stories* (1994) of Grace Paley (1922-) capture the syncopated rhythms of the city.

Don DeLillo

Younger writers associated with life in the fast lane are Jay McInerney (1955-), whose *Story of My Life* (1988) is set in the drug-driven youth culture of the boom-time 1980s, and satirist Tama Janowitz (1957-). Their portraits of loneliness and addiction in the anonymous hard-driving city recall the works of John Cheever.

Nearby suburbs claim the imaginations of still other writers. Mary Gordon (1949-) sets many of her female-centered works in her birthplace, Long Island, as does Alice McDermott (1953-), whose novel *Charming Billy* (1998) dissects the failed promise of an alcoholic.

Mid-Atlantic domestic realists include Richard Bausch (1945-), from Baltimore, author of *In the Night Season* (1998) and the stories in *Someone to Watch Over Me* (1999). Bausch writes of fragmented families, as does Anne Tyler (1941-), also from Baltimore, whose eccentric characters negotiate disorganized, isolated lives. A master of detail and understated wit, Tyler writes in spare, quiet language. Her best-known novels include *Dinner at the Homesick Restaurant* (1982) and *The Accidental Tourist* (1985), which was made into a film in 1988. *The Amateur Marriage* (2004) sets a divorce against a panorama of American life over 60 years.

African Americans have made distinctive contributions. Feminist essayist and poet Audre Lorde's autobiographical *Zami: A New*

Spelling of My Name (1982) is an earthy account of a black woman's experience in the United States. Bebe Moore Campbell (1950-), from Philadelphia, writes feisty domestic novels including *Your Blues Ain't Like Mine* (1992). Gloria Naylor (1950-), from New York City, explores different women's lives in *The Women of Brewster Place* (1982), the novel that made her name.

Critically acclaimed John Edgar Wideman (1941-) grew up in Homewood, a black section of Pittsburgh, Pennsylvania. His Faulknerian Homewood Trilogy — *Hiding Place* (1981), *Damballah* (1981), and *Sent for You Yesterday* (1983) — uses shifting viewpoints and linguistic play to render black experience. His best-known short piece, "Brothers and Keepers" (1984), concerns his relationship with his imprisoned brother. In *The Cattle Killing* (1996), Wideman returns to the subject of his famous early story "Fever" (1989). His novel *Two Cities* (1998) takes place in Pittsburgh and Philadelphia.

David Bradley (1950-), also from Pennsylvania, set his historical novel *The Chaneysville Incident* (1981) on the "underground railroad," a network of citizens who provided opportunity and assistance for southern black slaves to find freedom in the North at the time of the U.S. Civil War.

Trey Ellis (1962 -) has written the novels *Platitudes* (1988), *Home Repairs* (1993), and *Right Here,*

Anne Tyler

Photo: Diana Walker / Getty Images

Right Now (1999), screenplays including "The Tuskegee Airmen" (1995), and a 1989 essay "The New Black Aesthetic" discerning a new multiethnic sensibility among the younger generation.

Writers from Washington, D.C., four hours' drive south from New York City, include Ann Beattie (1947-), whose short stories were mentioned earlier. Her slice-of-life novels include *Picturing Will* (1989), *Another You* (1995), and *My Life, Starring Dara Falcon* (1997).

America's capital city is home to many political novelists. Ward Just (1935-) sets his novels in Washington's swirling military, political, and intellectual circles. Christopher Buckley (1952-) spikes his humorous political satire with local details; his *Little Green Men* (1999) is a spoof about official responses to aliens from outer space. Michael Chabon (1963-), who grew up in the Washington suburbs but later moved to California, depicts youths on the dazzling brink of adulthood in *The Mysteries of Pittsburgh* (1988); his novel inspired by a comic book, *The Amazing Adventures of Kavalier and Clay* (2000), mixes glamour and craft in the manner of F. Scott Fitzgerald.

The South

The South comprises disparate regions in the southeastern United States, from the cool Appalachian Mountain chain and the broad Mississippi River valley to the steamy cypress bayous of the Gulf

Coast. Cotton and the plantation culture of slavery made the South the richest section in the country before the U.S. Civil War (1860-1865). But after the war, the region sank into poverty and isolation that lasted a century. Today, the South is part of what is called the Sun Belt, the fastest growing part of the United States.

The most traditional of the regions, the South is proud of its distinctive heritage. Enduring themes include family, land, history, religion, and race. Much southern writing has a depth and humanity arising from the devastating losses of the Civil War and soul searching over the region's legacy of slavery.

The South, with its rich oral tradition, has nourished many women storytellers. In the upper South, Bobbie Ann Mason (1940-) from Kentucky, writes of the changes wrought by mass culture. In her most famous story, "Shiloh" (1982), a couple must change their relationship or separate as housing subdivisions spread "across western Kentucky like an oil slick." Mason's acclaimed short novel *In Country* (1985) depicts the effects of the Vietnam War by focusing on an innocent young girl whose father died in the conflict.

Lee Smith (1944-) brings the people of the Appalachian Mountains into poignant focus, drawing on the well of American folk music in her novel *The Devil's Dream* (1992). Jayne Anne Phillips

Bobbie Ann Mason

Photo: Jymi Bolden / CityBeat

(1952-) writes stories of misfits — *Black Tickets* (1979) — and a novel, *Machine Dreams* (1984), set in the hardscrabble mountains of West Virginia.

The novels of Jill McCorkle (1958-) capture her North Carolina background. Her mystery-enshrouded love story *Carolina Moon* (1996) explores a years-old suicide in a coastal village where relentless waves erode the foundations from derelict beach houses. The lush native South Carolina of Dorothy Allison (1949-) features in her tough autobiographical novel *Bastard Out of Carolina* (1992), seen through the eyes of a dirt-poor, illegitimate 12-year-old tomboy nicknamed Bone. Mississippian Ellen Gilchrist (1935-) sets most of her colloquial *Collected Stories* (2000) in small hamlets along the Mississippi River and in New Orleans, Louisiana.

Southern novelists mining male experience include the acclaimed Cormac McCarthy (1933-), whose early novels such as *Suttree* (1979) are archetypically southern tales of dark emotional depths, ignorance, and poverty, set against the green hills and valleys of eastern Tennessee. In 1974, McCarthy moved to El Paso, Texas, and began to plumb western landscapes and traditions. *Blood Meridian: Or the Evening of Redness in the West* (1985) is an unsparing vision of The Kid, a 14-year-old from Tennessee who becomes a cold-hearted killer in Mexico in the 1840s. McCarthy's best-selling epic Border Trilogy —

All the Pretty Horses (1992), *The Crossing* (1994), and *Cities of the Plain* (1998) — invests the desert between Texas and Mexico with mythic grandeur.

Other noted authors are North Carolinian Charles Frazier (1950-), author of the Civil War novel *Cold Mountain* (1997); Georgia-born Pat Conroy (1945-), author of *The Great Santini* (1976) and *Beach Music* (1995); and Mississippi novelist Barry Hannah (1942-), known for his violent plots and risk-taking style.

A very different Mississippi-born writer is Richard Ford (1944-), who began writing in a Faulknerian vein but is best known for his subtle novel set in New Jersey, *The Sportswriter* (1986), and its sequel, *Independence Day* (1995). The latter is about Frank Bascombe, a dreamy, evasive drifter who loses all the things that give his life meaning – a son, his dream of writing fiction, his marriage, lovers and friends, and his job. Bascombe is sensitive and intelligent — his choices, he says, are made "to deflect the pain of terrible regret" — and his emptiness, along with the anonymous malls and bald new housing developments that he endlessly cruises through, mutely testify to Ford's vision of a national malaise.

Many African-American writers hail from the South, including Ernest Gaines from Louisiana, Alice Walker from Georgia, and Florida-born Zora Neale Hurston, whose 1937 novel, *Their Eyes Were*

RICHARD FORD

Photo © Don MacLellan / CORBIS SYGMA

Watching God, is considered to be the first feminist novel by an African American. Hurston, who died in the 1960s, underwent a critical revival in the 1990s. Ishmael Reed, born in Tennessee, set *Mumbo Jumbo* (1972) in New Orleans. Margaret Walker (1915-1998), from Alabama, authored the novel *Jubilee* (1966) and essays *On Being Female, Black, and Free* (1997).

Story writer James Alan McPherson (1943-), from Georgia, depicts working-class people in *Elbow Room* (1977); *A Region Not Home: Reflections From Exile* (2000), whose title reflects his move to Iowa, is a memoir. Chicago-born ZZ Packer (1973-), McPherson's student at the Iowa Writers' Workshop, was raised in the South, studied in the mid-Atlantic, and now lives in California. Her first work, a volume of stories titled *Drinking Coffee Elsewhere* (2003), has made her a rising star. Prolific feminist writer bell hooks (born Gloria Watkins in Kentucky in 1952) gained fame for cultural critiques including *Black Looks: Race and Representation* (1992) and autobiographies beginning with *Bone Black: Memories of Girlhood* (1996).

Experimental poet and scholar of slave narratives (*Freeing the Soul*, 1999), Harryette Mullen (1953-) writes multivocal poetry collections such as *Muse & Drudge* (1995). Novelist and story writer Percival Everett (1956-), who was originally from Georgia, writes subtle, open-ended fiction; recent volumes are *Frenzy* (1997) and *Glyph* (1999).

Many African-American writers whose families followed patterns of internal migration were born outside the South but return to it for inspiration. Famed science-fiction novelist Octavia Butler (1947-), from California, draws on the theme of bondage and the slave narrative tradition in *Wild Seed* (1980); her *Parable of the Sower* (1993) treats addiction. Sherley Anne Williams (1944-), also from California, writes of interracial friendship between southern women in slave times in her fact-based historical novel *Dessa Rose* (1986). New York-born Randall Kenan (1963-) was raised in North Carolina, the setting of his novel *A Visitation of Spirits* (1989) and his stories *Let the Dead Bury Their Dead* (1992). His *Walking on Water: Black American Lives at the Turn of the Twenty-First Century* (1999) is nonfiction.

The Midwest

The vast plains of America's midsection — much of it between the Rocky Mountains and the Mississippi River — scorch in summer and freeze in scouring winter storms. The area was opened up with the completion of the Erie Canal in 1825, attracting Northern European settlers eager for land. Early 20th-century writers with roots in the Midwest include Ernest Hemingway, F. Scott Fitzgerald, Sinclair Lewis, and Theodore Dreiser.

Midwestern fiction is grounded in realism. The domestic novel has flourished in recent years, portraying webs of relationships between kin, the local community, and the environment. Agribusiness and development threaten family farms in some parts of the region, and some novels sound the death knell of farming as a way of life.

Domestic novelists include Jane Smiley (1949-), whose *A Thousand Acres* (1991) is a contemporary, feminist version of the *King Lear* story. The lost kingdom is a large family farm held for four generations, and the forces that undermine it

are a concatenation of the personal and the political. Kent Haruf (1943-) creates stronger characters in his sweeping novel of the prairie, *Plainsong* (1999).

Michael Cunningham (1952-), from Ohio, began as a domestic novelist in *A Home at the End of the World* (1990). *The Hours* (1998), made into a movie, brilliantly interweaves Virginia Woolf's *Mrs. Dalloway* with two women's lives in different eras. Stuart Dybek (1942-) has written sparkling story collections including *I Sailed With Magellan* (2003), about his childhood on the South Side of Chicago.

Younger urban novelists include Jonathan Franzen (1959-), who was born in Missouri and raised in Illinois. Franzen's best-selling panoramic novel *The Corrections* (2001) — titled for a downturn in the stock market — evokes midwestern family life over several generations. The novel chronicles the physical and mental deterioration of a patriarch suffering from Parkinson's disease; as in Smiley's *A Thousand Acres*, the entire family is affected. Franzen pits individuals against large conspiracies in *The Twenty-Seventh City* (1988) and *Strong Motion* (1992). Some critics link Franzen with Don DeLillo, Thomas Pynchon, and David Foster Wallace as a writer of conspiracy novels.

The Midwest has produced a wide variety of writing, much of it informed by international influences. Richard Powers (1957-), from Illinois, has lived in Thailand and The Netherlands. His challenging postmodern novels interweave personal lives with technology. *Galatea 2.2* (1995) updates the mad scientist theme; the scientists in this case are computer programmers.

African-American novelist Charles Johnson (1948-), an ex-cartoonist who was born in Illinois and moved to Seattle, Washington, draws on disparate traditions such as Zen and the slave narrative in novels such as *Oxherding Tale* (1982). Johnson's accomplished, picaresque novel *Middle Passage* (1990) blends the international history of slavery with a sea tale echoing *Moby-Dick*. *Dreamer* (1998) re-imagines the assassination of Dr. Martin Luther King, Jr.

Robert Olen Butler (1945-), born in Illinois and a veteran of the Vietnam War, writes about Vietnamese refugees in Louisiana in their own voices in *A Good Scent From a Strange Mountain* (1992). His stories in *Tabloid Dreams* (1996) — inspired by zany news headlines — were enlarged into the humorous novel *Mr. Spaceman* (2000), in which a space alien learns English from watching television and abducts a bus full of tourists in order to interview them on his spaceship.

Native-American authors from the region include part-Chippewa Louise Erdrich, who has set a series of novels in her native North Dakota. Gerald Vizenor (1935-) gives a comic, postmodern portrait of contemporary Native-American life in *Darkness at Saint Louis Bearheart* (1978) and *Griever: An American Monkey King in China* (1987). Vizenor's *Chancers* (2000) deals with skeletons buried outside of their homelands.

Popular Syrian-American novelist Mona Simpson (1957-), who was born in Wisconsin, is the author of *Anywhere But Here* (1986), a look at mother-daughter relationships.

The Mountain West

The western interior of the United States is a largely wild area that stretches along the majestic Rocky Mountains running slantwise from Montana at the Canadian border to the hills of Texas on the U.S. border with Mexico. Ranching and mining have long provided the region's economic backbone, and the Anglo tradition in the region emphasizes an independent frontier spirit.

Western literature often incorporates conflict. Traditional enemies in the 19th-century West are the cowboy versus the Indian, the farmer/settler versus the outlaw, the rancher versus the cattle rustler. Recent antagonists include the oilman versus the ecologist, the developer versus the archaeologist, and the citizen activist versus the representative of nuclear and military facilities, many of which are housed in the sparsely populated West.

One writer has cast a long shadow over western writing, much as William Faulkner did in the South. Wallace Stegner (1909-1993) records the passing of the western wilderness. In his masterpiece *Angle of Repose* (1971), a historian imagines his educated grandparents' move to the "wild" West. His last book surveys his life in the West as a writer: *Where the Bluebird Sings to the Lemonade Springs* (1992). For a quarter century, Stegner directed Stanford University's writing program; his list of students reads like a "who's who" of western writing: Raymond Carver, Ken Kesey, Thomas McGuane, Larry McMurtry, N. Scott Momaday, Tillie Olsen, and Robert Stone. Stegner also influenced the contemporary Montana school of writers associated with McGuane, Jim Harrison, and some works of Richard Ford, as well as Texas writers like McMurtry.

Novelist Thomas McGuane (1939-) typically depicts one man going alone into a wild area, where he engages in an escalating conflict. His works include *The Sporting Club* (1968) and *The Bushwacked Piano* (1971), in which the hero travels from Michigan to Montana on a demented mission of courtship. McGuane's enthusiasm for hunting and fishing has led critics to compare him with Ernest Hemingway. Michigan-born Jim Harrison (1937-), like McGuane, spent many years living on a ranch. In his first novel, *Wolf: A False Memoir* (1971), a man seeks to view a wolf in the wild in hopes of changing his life. His later, more pessimistic fiction includes *Legends of the Fall* (1979) and *The Road Home* (1998).

In Richard Ford's Montana novel *Wildlife* (1990), the desolate landscape counterpoints a family's breakup. Story writer, eco-critic, and nature essayist Rick Bass (1958-), born in Texas and educated as a petroleum geologist, writes of elemental confrontations between outdoorsmen and nature in his story collection *In the Loyal Mountains* (1995) and the novel *Where the Sea Used To Be* (1998).

Texan Larry McMurtry (1936-) draws on his ranch childhood in *Horseman, Pass By* (1961), made into the movie *Hud* in 1963, an unsentimental portrait of the rancher's world. *Leaving Cheyenne* (1963) and its successor, *The Last Picture Show* (1966), which was also made into a film, evoke the fading of a way of life in Texas small towns. McMurtry's best-known work is *Lonesome Dove* (1985), an archetypal western epic novel about a cattle drive in the 1870s that became a successful television miniseries. His recent works include *Comanche Moon* (1997).

The West of multiethnic writers is less heroic and often more forward looking. One of the best-known Chicana writers is Sandra Cisneros (1954-). Born in Chicago, Cisneros has lived in Mexico and Texas; she focuses on the large cultural border between Mexico and the United States as a creative, contradictory zone in which Mexican-American women must reinvent themselves. Her best-selling *The House on Mango Street* (1984), a series of interlocking vignettes told from a young girl's viewpoint, blazed the trail for other Latina writers and introduced readers to the vital Chicago barrio.

LARRY McMURTRY

Photo © Richard Robinson

Cisneros extended her vignettes of Chicana women's lives in *Woman Hollering Creek* (1991). Pat Mora (1942-) offers a Chicana view in *Nepantla: Essays From the Land in the Middle* (1993), which addresses issues of cultural conservation.

Native Americans from the region include the late James Welch, whose *The Heartsong of Charging Elk* (2000) imagines a young Sioux who survives the Battle of Little Bighorn and makes a life in France. Linda Hogan (1947-), from Colorado and of Chickasaw heritage, reflects on Native-American women and nature in novels including *Mean Spirit* (1990), about the oil rush on Indian lands in the 1920s, and *Power* (1998), in which an Indian woman discovers her own inner natural resources.

The Southwest

For centuries, the desert Southwest developed under Spanish rule, and much of the population continues to speak Spanish, while some Native-American tribes reside on ancestral lands. Rainfall is unreliable, and agriculture has always been precarious in the region. Today, massive irrigation projects have boosted agricultural production, and air conditioning attracts more and more people to sprawling cities like Salt Lake City in Utah and Phoenix in Arizona.

In a region where the desert ecology is so fragile, it is not surprising that there are many environmentally oriented writers. The activist Edward Abbey (1927-1989) celebrated the desert wilderness of Utah in *Desert Solitaire: A Season in the Wilderness* (1968).

Trained as a biologist, Barbara Kingsolver (1955-) offers a woman's viewpoint on the Southwest in her popular trilogy set in Arizona: *The Bean Trees* (1988), featuring Taylor Greer, a tomboyish young woman who takes in a Cherokee child; *Animal Dreams* (1990); and *Pigs in Heaven* (1993). *The Poisonwood Bible* (1998) concerns a missionary family in Africa. Kingsolver addresses political themes unapologetically, admitting, "I want to change the world."

The Southwest is home to the greatest number of Native-American writers, whose works reveal rich mythical storytelling, a spiritual treatment of nature, and deep respect for the spoken word. The most important fictional theme is healing, understood as restoration of harmony. Other topics include poverty, unemployment, alcoholism, and white crimes against Indians.

Native-American writing is more philosophical than angry, however, and it projects a strong ecological vision. Major authors include the distinguished N. Scott Momaday, who inaugurated the contemporary Native-American novel with *House Made of Dawn*; his recent works include *The Man Made of Words* (1997). Part-Laguna novelist Leslie Marmon Silko, the author of *Ceremony*, has also published *Gardens in the Dunes* (1999), evoking Indigo, an orphan cared for by a white woman at the turn of the 20th century.

Numerous Mexican-American writers reside in the Southwest, as they have for centuries. Distinctive concerns include the Spanish language, the Catholic tradition, folkloric forms, and, in recent years, race and gender inequality, generational conflict, and political activism. The culture is strongly patriarchal, but new female Chicana voices have arisen.

The poetic nonfiction book *Borderlands/La Frontera: The New Mestiza* (1987), by Gloria Anzaldúa (1942-), passionately imagines a hybrid feminine consciousness of the borderlands made up of strands from Mexican, Native-American, and Anglo cultures. Also noteworthy is New Mexican writer Denise Chavez (1948-), author of the story collection *The Last of the Menu Girls* (1986). Her *Face of an Angel* (1994), about a waitress who has been working on a manual for waitresses for 30 years, has been called an authentically Latino novel in English.

California Literature

California could be a country all its own with its enormous multiethnic population and huge economy. The state is known for spawning social experiments, youth movements (the Beats, hippies, techies), and new technologies (the "dot-coms" of Silicon Valley) that can have unexpected consequences.

Northern California, centered on

SANDRA CISNEROS

San Francisco, enjoys a liberal, even utopian literary tradition seen in Jack London and John Steinbeck. It is home to hundreds of writers, including Native American Gerald Vizenor, Chicana Lorna Dee Cervantes, African Americans Alice Walker and Ishmael Reed, and internationally minded writers like Norman Rush (1933-), whose novel *Mating* (1991) draws on his years in Africa.

Northern California houses a rich tradition of Asian-American writing, whose characteristic themes include family and gender roles, the conflict between generations, and the search for identity. Maxine Hong Kingston helped kindle the renaissance of Asian-American writing, at the same time popularizing the fictionalized memoir genre.

Another Asian-American writer from California is novelist Amy Tan, whose best-selling *The Joy Luck Club* became a hit film in 1993. Its interlinked story-like chapters delineate the different fates of four mother-and-daughter pairs. Tan's novels spanning historical China and today's United States include *The Hundred Secret Senses* (1995), about half-sisters, and *The Bonesetter's Daughter* (2001), about a daughter's care for her mother. The refreshing, witty *Gish Jen* (1955-), whose parents emigrated from Shanghai, authored the lively novels *Typical American* (1991) and *Mona in the Promised Land* (1996).

Japanese-American writers in-

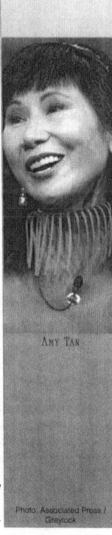

Amy Tan

Photo: Associated Press / Greylock

clude Karen Tei Yamashita (1951-), born and raised in California, whose nine-year stay in Brazil inspired *Through the Arc of the Rain Forest* (1990) and *Brazil-Maru* (1992). Her *Tropic of Orange* (1997) evokes polyglot Los Angeles. Japanese-American fiction writers build on the early work of Toshio Mori, Hisaye Yamamoto, and Janice Mirikitani.

Southern California literature has a very different tradition associated with the newer city of Los Angeles, built by boosters and land developers despite the obvious problem of lack of water resources. Los Angeles was from the start a commercial enterprise; it is not surprising that Hollywood and Disneyland are some of its best-known legacies to the world. As if to counterbalance its shiny facade, a dystopian strain of Southern California writing has flourished, inaugurated by Nathanael West's Hollywood novel, *The Day of the Locust* (1939).

Loneliness and alienation stalk the creations of Gina Berriault (1926–1999), whose characters eke out stunted lives lived in rented rooms in *Women in Their Beds* (1996). Joan Didion (1934-) evokes the free-floating anxiety of California in her brilliant essays *Slouching Towards Bethlehem* (1968). In 2003, Didion penned *Where I Was From*, a narrative account of how her family moved west with the frontier and settled in California. Another Angelino, Dennis Cooper (1953-), writes cool novels about an underworld of numb, alienated men.

Thomas Pynchon best captured the strange combination of ease and unease that is Los Angeles in his novel about a vast conspiracy of outcasts, *The Crying of Lot 49*. Pynchon inspired the prolific postmodernist William Vollmann (1959-), who has gained popularity with youthful, counterculture readers for his long, surrealistic meta-narratives such as the multivolume *Seven Dreams: A Book of North American Landscapes*, inaugurated with *The Ice-Shirt* (1990), about Vikings, and fantasies like *You Bright and Risen Angels: A Cartoon* (1987), about a war between virtual humans and insects.

Another ambitious novelist living in Southern California is the flamboyant T. Coraghessan Boyle (1948-), known for his many exuberant novels including *World's End* (1987) and *The Road to Wellville* (1993), about John Harvey Kellogg, American inventor of breakfast cereal.

Mexican-American writers in Los Angeles sometimes focus on low-grade racial tension. Richard Rodriguez (1944-), author of *Hunger of Memory: The Education of Richard Rodriguez* (1982), argues against bilingual education and affirmative action in *Days of Obligation: An Argument With My Mexican Father* (1992). Luis Rodriguez's (1954-) memoir of macho Chicano gang life in Los Angeles, *Always Running* (1993), testifies to the city's dark underside.

The Latin-American diaspora has influenced Helena Maria Viramontes (1954-), born and raised in the barrio of East Los Angeles. Her works portray that city as a magnet for a vast and growing number of Spanish-speaking immigrants, particularly Mexicans and Central Americans fleeing poverty and warfare. In powerful stories such as "The Cariboo Café" (1984), she interweaves Anglos, refugees from death squads, and illegal immigrants who come to the United States in search of work.

The Northwest

In recent decades, the mountainous, densely forested Northwest, centered around Seattle in the state of Washington, has emerged as a cultural center known for liberal views and a passionate appreciation of nature. Its most influential recent writer was Raymond Carver.

David Guterson (1956-), born in Seattle, gained a wide readership when his novel *Snow Falling on Cedars* (1994) was made into a movie. Set in Washington's remote, misty San Juan Islands after World War II, it concerns a Japanese American accused of a murder. In Guterson's moving novel *East of the Mountains* (1999), a heart surgeon dying of cancer goes back to the land of his youth to commit suicide, but discovers reasons to live. The penetrating novel *Housekeeping* (1980) by Marilynne Robinson (1944-) sees this wild, difficult territory through female eyes. In her luminous, long-awaited second novel, *Gilead* (2004), an upright elderly preacher facing death writes a family history for his young son that looks back as far as the Civil War.

Although she has lived in many regions, Annie Dillard (1945-) has made the Northwest her own in her crystalline works such as the brilliant poetic essay entitled "Holy the Firm" (1994), prompted by the burning of a neighbor child. Her description of the Pacific Northwest evokes both a real and spiritual landscape: "I came here to study hard things — rock mountain and salt sea — and to temper my spirit on their edges." Akin to Henry David Thoreau and Ralph Waldo Emerson, Dillard seeks enlightenment in nature. Dillard's striking essay collection is *Pilgrim at Tinker Creek* (1974). Her one novel, *The Living* (1992), celebrates early pioneer families beset by disease, drowning, poisonous fumes, gigantic falling trees, and burning wood houses as they imperceptibly assimilate with indigenous tribes, Chinese immigrants, and newcomers from the East.

Sherman Alexie (1966-), a Spokane/Coeur d'Alene Indian, is the youngest Native-American novelist to achieve national fame. Alexie gives unsentimental and humorous accounts of Indian life with an eye for incongruous mixtures of tradition and pop culture. His story cycles include *Reservation Blues* (1995) and *The Lone Ranger and Tonto Fistfight in Heaven* (1993), which inspired the effective film of reservation life *Smoke Signals* (1998), for which Alexie wrote the screenplay. *Smoke Signals* is one of the very few movies made by Native Americans rather than about them. Alexie's recent story collection is *The Toughest Indian in the World* (2000), while his harrowing novel *Indian Killer* (1996) recalls Richard Wright's *Native Son*.

GLOBAL AUTHORS: VOICES FROM THE CARIBBEAN AND LATIN AMERICA

Writers from the English-speaking Caribbean islands have been shaped by the British literary curriculum and colonial rule, but in recent years their focus has shifted from London to New York and Toronto. Themes include the beauty of the islands, the innate wisdom of their people, and aspects of immigration and exile — the breakup of family, culture shock, changed gender roles, and assimilation.

Two forerunners merit mention. Paule Marshall (1929-), born in Brooklyn, is not technically a global

SHERMAN ALEXIE

writer, but she vividly recalls her experiences as the child of Barbadian immigrants in Brooklyn in *Brown Girl, Brownstones* (1959). Dominican novelist Jean Rhys (1894-1979) penned *Wide Sargasso Sea* (1966), a haunting and poetic refiguring of Charlotte Brontë's *Jane Eyre*. Rhys lived most of her life in Europe, but her book was championed by American feminists for whom the "madwoman in the attic" had become an iconic figure of repressed female selfhood.

Rhys's work opened the way for the angrier voice of Jamaica Kincaid (1949-), from Antigua, whose unsparing autobiographical works include the novels *Annie John* (1985), *Lucy* (1990), and *The Autobiography of My Mother* (1996). Born in Haiti but educated in the United States, Edwidge Danticat (1969-) came to attention with her stories *Krik? Krak!* (1995), entitled for a phrase used by storytellers from the Haitian oral tradition. Danticat evokes her nation's tragic past in her historical novel *The Farming of the Bones* (1998).

Many Latin American writers diverge from the views common among Chicano writers with roots in Mexico, who have tended to be romantic, nativist, and left wing in their politics. In contrast, Cuban-American writing tends to be cosmopolitan, comic, and politically conservative. Gustavo Pérez Firmat's memoir, *Next Year in Cuba: A Chronicle of Coming of Age in America* (1995), celebrates baseball as much as Havana. The title is ironic: "Next year in Cuba" is a phrase of Cuban exiles clinging to their vision of a triumphant return. *The Pérez Family* (1990), by Christine Bell (1951-), warmly portrays confused Cuban families — at least half of them named Pérez — in exile in Miami. Recent works of novelist Oscar Hijuelos (1951-) include *The Fourteen Sisters of Emilio Montez O'Brien* (1993), about Cuban Irish Americans, and *Mr. Ives' Christmas* (1995), the story of a man whose son has died.

Writers with Puerto Rican roots include Nicholasa Mohr (1938-), whose *Rituals of Survival: A Woman's Portfolio* (1985) presents the lives of six Puerto Rican women, and Rosario Ferré (1938-), author of *The Youngest Doll* (1991). Among the younger writers is Judith Ortiz Cofer (1952-), author of *Silent Dancing: A Partial Remembrance of a Puerto Rican Childhood* (1990) and *The Latin Deli* (1993), which combines poetry with stories. Poet and essayist Aurora Levins Morales (1954-) writes of Puerto Rico from a cosmopolitan Jewish viewpoint.

The best-known writer with roots in the Dominican Republic is Julia Alvarez (1950-). In *How the García Girls Lost Their Accents* (1991), upper-class Dominican women struggle to adapt to New York City. *¡Yo!* (1997) returns to the García sisters, exploring identity through the stories of 16 characters. Junot Diaz (1948-) offers a much harsher vision in the story collection *Drown* (1996), about

JAMAICA KINCAID

Photo © Nancy Crampton

young men in the slums of New Jersey and the Dominican Republic.

Major Latin American writers who first became prominent in the United States in the 1960s — Argentina's Jorge Luis Borges, Colombia's Gabriel García Márquez, Chile's Pablo Neruda, and Brazil's Jorge Amado — introduced U.S. authors to magical realism, surrealism, a hemispheric sensibility, and an appreciation of indigenous cultures. Since that first wave of popularity, women and writers of color have found audiences, among them Chilean-born novelist Isabel Allende (1942-). The niece of Chilean president Salvador Allende, who was assassinated in 1973, Isabel Allende memorialized her country's bloody history in *La casa de los espíritus* (1982), translated as *The House of the Spirits* (1985). Later novels (written and published first in Spanish) include *Eva Luna* (1987) and *Daughter of Fortune* (1999), set in the California gold rush of 1849. Allende's evocative style and woman-centered vision have gained her a wide readership in the United States.

GLOBAL AUTHORS: VOICES FROM ASIA AND THE MIDDLE EAST

Many writers from the Indian subcontinent have made their home in the United States in recent years. Bharati Mukherjee (1940-) has written an acclaimed story collection, *The Middleman and Other Stories* (1988); her novel *Jasmine* (1989) tells the story of an illegal immigrant woman. Mukherjee was raised in Calcutta; her novel *The Holder of the World* (1993) imagines passionate adventures in 17th-century India for characters in Nathaniel Hawthorne's *The Scarlet Letter*. *Leave It to Me* (1997) follows the nomadic struggles of a girl abandoned in India who seeks her roots. Mukherjee's haunting story "The Management of Grief" (1988), about the aftermath of a terrorist bombing of a plane, has taken on new resonance since September 11, 2001.

Indian-born Meena Alexander (1951-), of Syrian heritage, was raised in North Africa; she reflects on her experience in her memoir *Fault Lines* (1993). Poet and story writer Chitra Banerjee Divakaruni (1956-), born in India, has written the sensuous, women-centered novels *The Mistress of Spices* (1997) and *Sister of My Heart* (1999), as well as story collections including *The Unknown Errors of Our Lives* (2001).

Jhumpa Lahiri (1967-) focuses on the younger generation's conflicts and assimilation in *Interpreter of Maladies: Stories of Bengal, Boston, and Beyond* (1999) and her novel *The Namesake* (2003). Lahiri draws on her experience: Her Bengali parents were raised in India, and she was born in London but raised in the United States.

Southeast Asian-American authors, especially those from Korea and the Philippines, have found strong voices in the last decade.

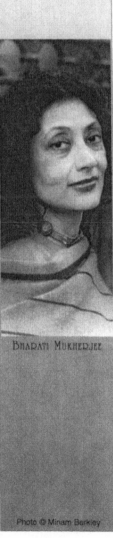

BHARATI MUKHERJEE

Photo © Miriam Berkley

Among recent Korean-American writers, pre-eminent is Chang-rae Lee (1965-). Born in Seoul, Korea, Lee's remarkable novel *Native Speaker* (1995) interweaves public ideals, betrayal, and private despair. His moving second novel, *A Gesture Life* (1999), explores the long shadow of a wartime atrocity — the Japanese use of Korean "comfort women."

Theresa Hak Kyung Cha (1951-1982), born in Korea, blends photographs, videos, and historical documents in her experimental *Dictee* (1982) to memorialize the suffering of Koreans under Japanese occupying forces. Malaysian-American poet Shirley Geok-lin Lim, of ethnic Chinese descent, has written a challenging memoir, *Among the White Moon Faces* (1996). Her autobiographical novel is *Joss and Gold* (2001), while her stories are collected in *Two Dreams* (1997).

Philippine-born writers include Bienvenido Santos (1911-1996), author of the poetic novel *Scent of Apples* (1979), and Jessica Hagedorn (1949-), whose surrealistic pop culture novels are *Dogeaters* (1990) and *The Gangster of Love* (1996). In very different ways, they both are responding to the poignant autobiographical novel of Filipino-American migrant laborer Carlos Bulosan (1913–1956), *America Is in the Heart* (1946).

Noted Vietnamese-American filmmaker and social theorist Trinh Minh-Ha (1952-) combines storytelling and theory in her feminist work *Woman, Native, Other* (1989). From China, Ha Jin (1956-) has authored the novel *Waiting* (1999), a sad tale of an 18-year separation whose realistic style, typical of Chinese fiction, strikes American ears as fresh and original.

The newest voices come from the Arab-American community. Lebanese-born Joseph Geha (1944-) has set his stories in *Through and Through* (1990) in Toledo, Ohio; Jordanian-American Diana Abu-Jaber (1959-), born in New York, has written the novel *Arabian Jazz* (1993).

Poet and playwright Elmaz Abinader (1954-), is author of a memoir, *Children of the Roojme: A*

CHANG-RAE LEE

Family's Journey From Lebanon (1991). In "Just Off Main Street" (2002), Abinader has written of her bicultural childhood in 1960s small-town Pennsylvania: "...my family scenes filled me with joy and belonging, but I knew none of it could be shared on the other side of that door."

American literature has traversed an extended, winding path from pre-colonial days to contemporary times. Society, history, technology all have had a telling impact on it. Ultimately, though, there is a constant — humanity, with all its radiance and its malevolence, its tradition and its promise. ∎

GLOSSARY

Abolitionism: An active movement to end slavery in the U.S. North before the Civil War in the 1860s.

Allusion: An implied or indirect reference in a literary text to another text.

Beatnik: The artistic and literary rebellion against established society of the 1950s and early 1960s, associated with Jack Kerouac, Allen Ginsberg, and others. "Beat" suggests holiness ("beatification") and suffering ("beaten down").

Boston Brahmins: Influential and respected 19th-century New England writers who maintained the genteel tradition of upper-class values.

Calvinism: A strict theological doctrine of the French Protestant church reformer John Calvin (1509-1564) and the basis of Puritan society. Calvin held that all humans were born sinful and only God's grace (not the church) could save a person from hell.

Canon: An accepted or sanctioned body of literary works considered to be permanently established and of high quality.

Captivity narrative: An account of capture by Native-American tribes, such as those created by writers Mary Rowlandson and John Williams in colonial times.

Character writing: A popular 17th- and 18th-century literary sketch of a character who represents a group or type.

Chekhovian: Similar in style to the works of the Russian author Anton Pavlovitch Chekhov. Chekhov (1860-1904), one of the major short story writers and dramatists of modern times, is known for both his humorous one-act plays and his full-length tragedies.

Civil War: The war (1861-1865) between the northern U.S. states, which remained in the Union, and the southern states, which seceded and formed the Confederacy. The victory of the North ended slavery and preserved the Union.

Conceit: An extended metaphor. The term is used to characterize aspects of Renaissance metaphysical poetry in England and colonial poetry, such as that of Anne Bradstreet, in colonial America.

Cowboy poetry: Verse based on oral tradition, and often rhymed or metered, that celebrates the traditions of the western U.S. cattle culture. Its subjects include nature, history, folklore, family, friends, and work. Cowboy poetry has its antecedents in the ballad style of England and the Appalachian South.

Domestic novel: A novel about home life and family that often emphasizes the personalities and attributes of its characters over the plot. Many domestic novels of the 19th and early 20th centuries employed a certain amount of sentimentality — usually a blend of pathos and humor.

Enlightenment: An 18th-century movement that focused on the ideals of good sense, benevolence, and a belief in liberty, justice, and equality as the natural rights of man.

Existentialism: A philosophical movement embracing the view that the suffering individual must create meaning in an unknowable, chaotic, and seemingly empty universe.

Expressionism: A post-World War I artistic movement, of German origin, that distorted appearances to communicate inner emotional states.

Fabulist: A creator or writer of fables (short narratives with a moral, typically featuring animals as characters) or of supernatural stories incorporating elements of myth and legend.

Faulknerian: In a style reminiscent of William Faulkner (1897-1962), one of America's major 20th-century novelists, who chronicled the decline and decay of the aristocratic South. Unlike earlier regionalists who wrote about local color, Faulkner created literary works that are complex in form and often violent and tragic in content.

GLOSSARY

Faust: A literary character who sold his soul to the devil in order to become all-knowing, or godlike; protagonist of plays by English Renaissance dramatist Christopher Marlowe (1564-1593) and German Romantic writer Johann Wolfgang von Goethe (1749-1832).

Feminism: The view, articulated in the 19th century, that women are inherently equal to men and deserve equal rights and opportunities. More recently, feminism is a social and political movement that took hold in the United States in the late 1960s and soon spread globally.

Fugitives: Poets who collaborated in *The Fugitive*, a magazine published between 1922 and 1928 in Nashville, Tennessee. The collaborators, including such luminaries as John Crowe Ransom, Robert Penn Warren, and Allen Tate, rejected "northern" urban, commercial values, which they felt had taken over America, and called for a return to the land and to American traditions that could be found in the South.

Genre: A category of literary forms (novel, lyric poem, epic, for example).

Global literature: Contemporary writing from the many cultures of the world. Selections include literature ascribed to various religious, ideological, and ethnic groups within and across geographic boundaries.

Hartford Wits: A conservative late 18th-century literary circle centered at Yale College in Connecticut (also known as the Connecticut Wits).

Hip-hop poetry: Poetry that is written on a page but performed for an audience. Hip-hop poetry, with its roots in African-American rhetorical tradition, stresses rhythm, improvisation, free association, rhymes, and the use of hybrid language.

Hudibras: A mock-heroic satire by English writer Samuel Butler (1612-1680). Hudibras was imitated by early American revolutionary-era satirists.

Iambic: A metrical foot consisting of one short syllable followed by one long syllable, or of one unstressed syllable followed by one stressed syllable.

Image: Concrete representation of an object, or something seen.

Imagists: A group of mainly American poets, including Ezra Pound and Amy Lowell, who used sharp visual images and colloquial speech; active from 1912 to 1914.

Iowa Writers' Workshop: A graduate program in creative writing at the University of Iowa in which talented, generally young writers work on manuscripts and exchange ideas about writing with each other and with established poets and prose writers.

Irony: A meaning, often contradictory, concealed behind the apparent meaning of a word or phrase.

Kafkaesque: Reminiscent of the style of Czech-born novelist and short story writer Franz Kafka (1883-1924). Kafka's works portray the oppressiveness of modern life, and his characters frequently find themselves in threatening situations for which there is no explanation and from which there is no escape.

Knickerbocker School: New York City-based writers of the early 1800s who imitated English and European literary fashions.

Language poetry: Poetry that stretches language to reveal its potential for ambiguity, fragmentation, and self-assertion within chaos. Language poets favor open forms and multicultural texts; they appropriate images from popular culture and the media, and refashion them.

GLOSSARY

McCarthy era: The period of the Cold War (late 1940s and early 1950s) during which U.S. Senator Joseph McCarthy pursued American citizens whom he and his followers suspected of being members or former members of, or sympathizers with, the Communist party. His efforts included the creation of "blacklists" in various professions — rosters of people who were excluded from working in those fields. McCarthy ultimately was denounced by his Senate colleagues.

Metafiction: Fiction that emphasizes the nature of fiction, the techniques and conventions used to write it, and the role of the author.

Metaphysical poetry: Intricate type of 17th-century English poetry employing wit and unexpected images.

Middle Colonies: The present-day U.S. mid-Atlantic states — New York, New Jersey, Maryland, Pennsylvania, and Delaware — known originally for commercial activities centered around New York City and Philadelphia.

Midwest: The central area of the United States, from the Ohio River to the Rocky Mountains, including the Prairie and Great Plains regions (also known as the Middle West).

Minimalism: A writing style, exemplified in the works of Raymond Carver, that is characterized by spareness and simplicity.

Mock-epic: A parody using epic form (also known as mock-heroic).

Modernism: An international cultural movement after World War I expressing disillusionment with tradition and interest in new technologies and visions.

Motif: A recurring element, such as an image, theme, or type of incident.

Muckrakers: American journalists and novelists (1900-1912) whose spotlight on corruption in business and government led to social reform.

Multicultural: The creative interchange of numerous ethnic and racial subcultures.

Myth: A legendary narrative, usually of gods and heroes, or a theme that expresses the ideology of a culture.

Naturalism: A late 19th- and early 20th-century literary approach of French origin that vividly depicted social problems and viewed human beings as helpless victims of larger social and economic forces.

Neoclassicism: An 18th-century artistic movement, associated with the Enlightenment, drawing on classical models and emphasizing reason, harmony, and restraint.

New England: The region of the United States comprising the present-day northeastern states of Maine, Vermont, New Hampshire, Massachusetts, Rhode Island, and Connecticut and noted for its early industrialization and intellectual life. Traditionally, New England is the home of the shrewd, independent, thrifty "Yankee" trader.

New Journalism: A style of writing made popular in the United States in the 1960s by Tom Wolfe, Truman Capote, and Norman Mailer, who used the techniques of story-telling and characterization of fiction writers in creating nonfiction works.

Objectivist: A mid-20th-century poetic movement, associated with William Carlos Williams, stressing images and colloquial speech.

Old Norse: The ancient Norwegian language of the sagas, virtually identical to modern Icelandic.

Oral Tradition: Transmission by word of mouth; tradition passed down through generations; verbal folk tradition.

Plains Region: The middle region of the United States that slopes eastward from the Rocky Mountains to the Prairie.

Poet Laureate: An individual appointed as a consultant in poetry to the U.S. Library of Congress for a term of generally one year. During his or her term, the Poet Laureate seeks to raise the national consciousness to a greater appreciation of poetry.

Poetry slam: A spoken-word poetry competition.

Postmodernism: A media-influenced aesthetic sensibility of the late 20th century characterized by open-endedness and collage. Postmodernism questions the foundations of cultural and artistic form through self-referential irony and the juxtaposition of elements from popular culture and electronic technology.

Prairie: The level, unforested farm region of the midwestern United States.

Primitivism: A belief that nature provides truer and more healthful models than does culture. An example is the myth of the "noble savage."

Puritans: English religious and political reformers who fled their native land in search of religious freedom, and who settled and colonized New England in the 17th century.

Reformation: A northern European political and religious movement of the 15th through 17th centuries that attempted to reform Catholicism; eventually gave rise to Protestantism.

Reflexive: Self-referential. A literary work is reflexive when it refers to itself.

Regional writing: Writing that explores the customs and landscape of a region of the United States.

Revolutionary War: The War of Independence, 1775-1783, fought by the American colonies against Great Britain.

Romance: Emotionally heightened, symbolic American novels associated with the Romantic period.

Romanticism: An early 19th-century movement that elevated the individual, the passions, and the inner life. Romanticism, a reaction against neoclassicism, stressed strong emotion, imagination, freedom from classical correctness in art forms, and rebellion against social conventions.

Saga: An ancient Scandinavian narrative of historical or mythical events.

Salem Witch Trials: Proceedings for alleged witchcraft held in Salem, Massachusetts, in 1692. Nineteen persons were hanged and numerous others were intimidated into confessing or accusing others of witchcraft.

Self-help book: A book telling readers how to improve their lives through their own efforts. The self-help book has been a popular American genre from the mid-19th century to the present.

Separatists: A strict Puritan sect of the 16th and 17th centuries that preferred to separate from the Church of England rather than reform. Many of those who first settled America were Separatists.

Slave narrative: The first black literary prose genre in the United States, featuring accounts of the lives of African Americans under slavery.

South: A region of the United States comprising the states of Alabama, Arkansas, Florida, Georgia, Kentucky, Louisiana, Mississippi, Missouri, North Carolina, South Carolina, Tennessee, Virginia, and West Virginia, as well as eastern Texas.

Surrealism: A European literary and artistic movement that uses illogical, dreamlike images and events to suggest the unconscious.

Syllabic versification: Poetic meter based on the number of syllables in a line.

Synthesis: A blending of two senses; used by Edgar Allan Poe and others to suggest hidden correspondences and create exotic effects.

GLOSSARY

Tall tale: A humorous, exaggerated story common on the American frontier, often focusing on cases of superhuman strength.

Theme: An abstract idea embodied in a literary work.

Tory: A wealthy pro-English faction in America at the time of the Revolutionary War in the late 1700s.

Transcendentalism: A broad, philosophical movement in New England during the Romantic era (peaking between 1835 and 1845). It stressed the role of divinity in nature and the individual's intuition, and exalted feeling over reason.

Trickster: A cunning character of tribal folk narratives (for example those of African Americans and Native Americans) who breaks cultural codes of behavior; often a culture hero.

Vision song: A poetic song that members of some Native-American tribes created when purifying themselves through solitary fasting and meditation.

INDEX

INDEX

INDEX

INDEX

INDEX

INDEX

INDEX

INDEX

INDEX

INDEX

INDEX

INDEX

INDEX

Printed at RPC EAP Manila 06-0823

INDEX